ADVANCES IN
LIBRARY ADMINISTRATION
AND ORGANIZATION


*Volume 13* • 1995

# ADVANCES IN LIBRARY ADMINISTRATION AND ORGANIZATION

*Editors:* DELMUS E. WILLIAMS
Dean, University Libraries
University of Akron

EDWARD D. GARTEN
Dean of Libraries and Information Technologies
University of Dayton

VOLUME 13 • 1995

 JAI PRESS INC.

Greenwich, Connecticut                    London, England

Copyright © 1995 JAI PRESS INC.
55 Old Post Road No. 2
Greenwich, Connecticut 06836

JAI PRESS LTD.
The Courtyard
28 High Street
Hampton Hill
Middlesex TW12 1PD
England

All rights reserved. No part of this publication may be reproduced, stored on a retrieval
system, or transmitted in any form or by any means, electronic, mechanical, photocopying,
filming, recording or otherwise without prior permission in writing from the publisher.

ISBN: 1-55938-931-1

Manufactured in the United States of America

025.105
A244
v. 13

# CONTENTS

# INTRODUCTION

The first volume of *Advances in Library Administration and Organization*, published in 1982, began with an introduction by Carl Jackson that provided the author's overview of the problems facing library managers and a rationale for the development of this series. Jackson talked about the need for careful study of new management paradigms, professionalism, collection development, budgeting, and technology. He also offered readers a glimpse of the topics that would be covered with distinction from that time until this. Unfortunately, Jackson died shortly after writing that introduction, but Jerry McCabe and Bernie Kreissman have worked hard to implement Jackson's vision.

Over the last twelve years McCabe and Kreissman have produced twelve volumes of papers that have made an important contribution to the literature of librarianship. Their aim has been to provide a forum for research articles of interest to library managers that are longer than most journal articles but shorter than most books. The idea has been to relieve authors of the kinds of constraints that are most often found in other genre to encourage the production of thoughtful pieces covering all areas of library administration. The results have been commendable both in allowing more experienced managers to discuss fully topics that interest them and in identifying new scholars who are talking about things that are important to us all.

Now the time has come for a changing of the guard. Last year, Jerry and Bernie honored Ed Garten of the University of Dayton and myself by asking if we would be interested in continuing their work, and we accepted. Both of us are experienced library administrators. Ed directed libraries at Northern State University in South Dakota and Tennessee Technological University before assuming responsibility for the libraries at the University of Dayton in 1985. In 1994, he also assumed responsibility for academic computing on that campus. Ed was also the founding editor for the LAMA magazine *Library Administration and Management*, and he recently has edited books on consulting in libraries and accreditation. My career has taken a similar path. I spent over six years as library director at the University of Alabama in Huntsville before assuming the position of Dean of University Libraries at the University of Akron in 1991. I have written extensively over the last two decades about the impact of change on library organizations and on a variety of topics relating to ways in which libraries can shape themselves in the face of a changing climate. Together, Ed and I hope to carry forward the tradition that has been developed in this series and to maintain the standard for quality that has made the series worth noting.

What are the issues that we need to address? Just as Jackson noted in 1982, library managers must still concern themselves with the collections we are building, the technologies that we are using, the funds we are allotted, and the skills that must be developed within the staffs that we employ. But much has changed since 1982 in the way libraries operate and in the environment in which they must work. These changes add new dimensions to how they do business and how they must be led. Technology and networks have become linchpins of library services, and, while we are still being asked to stretch scarce funds to build library collections, more and more energy is being spent defining resources that are needed by our clients but not held locally and then retrieving those resources on demand.

At the same time, the emergence of varying technologies, the way in which those technologies can be used to meet the needs of library users, and the relationship of library technology and other technologies on campus are changing the way in which library managers group services. Library managers are reconsidering how services must be grouped and developing new paradigms for service that are different both in form and content than those offered in a traditional library. They are also beginning to assign appropriate priorities to both traditional library services and to services like computing, media production, and telecommunications that have traditionally been administered by offices outside of the library. Library managers are being asked to integrate library activities with those of other information resources on campus, provide the kinds of space and furnishings that will accommodate emerging technologies, and organizing and allocating that space to accommodate a changing service program in a rational way, all add to the complexity of library operations.

Coping with this kind of complexity presents a challenge for the library manager. Library organizations are changing by any measure, and the rate at which those changes are occurring is increasing exponentially. The library that I entered as a professional twenty years ago seemed to be the last constant in society; the one that I lead now seems almost to a model for the kind of transformational change that is occurring throughout our society.

What does all of this mean to *Advances in Library Administration and Organization* and to those who read it? As a new editor, it seems to me that it means that the need for thoughtful, in depth consideration of all of the problems that confront managers striving to shepherd organizations through a period of transformational change is more critical than ever before. It is not enough to focus on the problems and concerns of the new century we are about to enter. Managers are responsible for taking the legacies that we have been given, extracting those elements of traditional library programs that are still important to our users, and helping our organizations migrate into a new information environment as vital components of an information society. The sharing of ideas among managers as to the what and how of this migration has gained new importance in this effort. The ground is new and the ideas that will be most used must be gleaned by casting a wide net among both practitioners and scholars working in our profession.

Ed Garten and I both feel that *Advances in Library Administration and Organization* has a vital role to play in this information exchange. Over the next few years, we hope to offer you an array of articles, many of them longer, but all of them well reasoned, that offer the ideas gleaned from dissertations, conference presentations, scholarly articles based on ideas current in the literature of management both within and outside of librarianship, and other things that will make the manager consider what is best in library management and develop theory and practice that will overcome the weaknesses that exist. We offer a forum both for leaders in the profession and for new authors. With your help, we can succeed. We offer this volume as our first effort, and we look forward to the many that will follow.

Delmus E. Williams
Edward D. Garten
*Editors*

# THE TRUSTEE/DIRECTOR ROLE IN A LIBRARY NETWORK

Ralph E. Russell

Librarianship as a cooperative resource sharing venture began with the good Abbot of Swinford who first unchained a book in the library and let someone take it from the monastery. It has been a phenomenon of the past three decades, however, that cooperative efforts have burgeoned and, in doing so, have acquired some of the characteristics of big business—large capitol investment, complicated and multitudinous contracts, significant numbers of staff, sophisticated software, hardware, and telecommunications, and an impressive revenue stream. For instance, SOLINET (Southeastern Library Network) had FY94 revenues of $19.4 million; OCLC had FY94 annual revenues of $132.4 million. As networks and cooperative efforts have become pivotal to the functioning of our libraries and to the satisfying of our users, the role of librarians on governing boards for those networks has grown dramatically in importance. The library community may no longer be indifferent to the effectiveness or reliability of our networks or our bibliographic

Advances in Library Administration and Organization, Volume 13, pages 1-9.
Copyright © 1995 by JAI Press Inc.
All rights of reproduction in any form reserved.
ISBN: 1-55938-931-1

utility. Its ability to satisfy the information/document needs of its own constituencies is integrally tied to the effectiveness of these organizations.

This paper will examine the role of the trustee/director on a bibliographic utility or library network governing board. Such an examination will help create more effective members of those organizations, generate better understanding of the role of governing boards, and may encourage individuals to seek a role in these organizations and their boards. For the purposes of the paper, both kinds of entities will be referred to as networks.

The context of the paper is the two governing boards on which the author served: SOLINET and OCLC. The author's term on the SOLINET Board of Directors was 1978-1982; his term on the OCLC Board of Trustees was from 1988-1994. These comments are his own; he speaks for neither board.

SOLINET and OCLC are chartered in Georgia and Ohio, respectively, to provide an important public benefit and to serve a significant social purpose. Because their stated purposes include the delivery of automated information and products to libraries, they are technology intensive. That is one reason for the cash flow required for the functioning of the organizations. Library networks share a number of characteristics. They:

1.  are nonprofit, membership organizations;
2.  pull together resources from many libraries to accomplish what a single library could not accomplish alone;
3.  are technology intensive, functioning on computers, software, and telecommunications systems;
4.  require large revenue streams, which is due in great part to their technology-intensive nature;
5.  are the linchpins for resource sharing and cost effective delivery of information (In other words, they are crucial to library services, and we have few alternatives.); and,
6.  possess a formalized structure.

The nonprofit designation of SOLINET and OCLC is important because it opens up opportunities for creative bond financing, exempts the organizations from paying federal tax on income related to their exempt purpose, may give the organizations a break on local taxes, and can broaden access to foundation and government support. The federal tax code provides guidelines as to what portion of a nonprofit organization's income may come from sources unrelated to the corporate mission. Nonprofit status is jealously guarded and the loss of it is a trustee's recurrent nightmare.

Individual state law contains the job description for trustees/directors with appropriate caveats for shortcomings. The Ohio Code calls upon a trustee to perform his or her duties in good faith "and with the care that an ordinarily prudent person in a like position would use under similar circumstances."[1] He or she is expected not to act in personal interest, and may not use the position for the gain of him or herself, friends, or relatives. The language in the Georgia Code is similar.[2]

In addition to the responsibilities defined by state law, trustees/directors are expected to insure that the organization fulfills its mission as defined in its charter or articles of incorporation which state the purpose of the organization. The language may be echoed in the organization's bylaws and other internal governance documents which provide important guidance for governing boards and staff.

SOLINET's purpose, as stated in its Articles of Incorporation, is:

> to provide cost-effective services and information and to support cooperative activities which will strengthen resource sharing among, and improve the effectiveness of, member institutions. To achieve these ends, Solinet may maintain and operate a computerized network and service center which, by means of electronic data processing and telecommunications may increase the availability of the data and resources of the member institutions.[3]

OCLC's purposes as stated in the Articles of Incorporation are:

> To establish, maintain, and operate a computerized library network and to promote the evolution of library use, of libraries themselves, and of librarianship, and to provide processes and products for the benefit of library users and libraries, including such objectives as increasing availability of library resources to individual library patrons and reducing rate-of-rise of library per-unit costs, all for the fundamental public purpose of furthering ease of access to and use of the ever expanding body of worldwide scientific, literary and educational knowledge and information.[4]

The trustee/director is concerned with the overarching public purpose, financial health, setting organizational direction, hiring and evaluating the CEO, evaluating organizational performance, strategic planning, setting policy, and communication.

The single most important item on the trustee/director's agenda is to view the world through the filter of those stated public purposes. The organization strays from its purposes at its peril. It is essential that the public purposes provide the context for considering new services, products, and ventures, enhancements of existing products and services, acquisitions, joint ventures, and anything else toward which the organization seems to be advancing. The organizational purposes must be the guiding principle; if there is a possibility of a perceived variation away from it, the action should be conscious, planned, and acknowledged publicly with justification. OCLC's judicious acquisition of Information Dimensions Inc. (IDI) and MAPS (Micrographic Preservation Services) is clearly complementary and supportive of its public purpose. IDI's customer base in special libraries and its development of premier computer software products for managing electronic documents and text on mainframe computers, microcomputers, workstations, and PC's contributes to OCLC's strength in serving all kinds of libraries. It is a strategic "fit" for OCLC. The mission of MAPS, preservation through micrographics, provides continuing access to documents which are vulnerable to the ravages of time, chemicals, and light on paper materials. SOLINET's preservation services offer expertise and leadership in preserving library collections in the Southeast and is viewed by the SOLINET board as highly supportive of SOLINET'S mission. It is through the leadership of SOLINET staff, working with member librarians, that several major grants have been procured—both for preserving library materials and for training library preservation staff.

Another major responsibility of a trustee/director is fiduciary. The ongoing financial health of the organization is essential if it is to continue to provide public benefit and to fund research and development efforts, without which the products and services for members quickly become dated or worse, obsolete. The issuance of industrial revenue bonds for the financing of the OCLC headquarter building and, in the early nineties, for financing the new modular computer system and the new packet-switched telecommunications network were prudent and appropriate actions for OCLC to pursue. And, going beyond the issue of solvency, it is the board's responsibility to see that the members' money and resources are used appropriately and prudently. OCLC's refunding a nine percent (average) telecommunications credit totalling $3 million to the membership over 18 months in 1993-1994, and changing that into a permanent price reduction for telecommunications costs to members, is both sound management and even better psychology in a time when libraries are beset with spiraling prices and increased demand for information and documents.

Once elected, the trustee/director is concerned with all the members and their needs, not just a single type of library, because the board is responsible for organizational direction and thrust. We are all influenced by our environments. At the point of election to a network board, however, the individual director becomes an advocate for all of the members—not just the segment of the professional community within which he or she works. Propounding a parochial or limited view is failing to abide by the basic tenets of trusteeship—care and nurture of the whole organization. Responsible board members must be ever watchful of the organization's total program. The United Way scandal in 1992 was a riveting experience to behold for any nonprofit director/trustee. The United Way Board was astonished and embarrassed to discover that United Way and its subsidiaries were enmeshed in ventures of both questionable relationship to the organization's purpose and questionable financing.[5] Kenneth L. Albrecht (1992), President of the National Charities Information Bureau said:

> One of the impacts of the United Way situation will be that not-for-profit boards will look more closely at facts and will probably be even more attentive than many of them have been in the past (p. 8).

Sound financial planning and budget development are crucial to any organization's health and longevity. In developing financial plans, board members' reactions to management's assumptions and plans are key development components. Projected budgets are built on assumptions about revenues and expenditures, which are tied to programs. Those assumptions need to be examined in the light of day and discussed. The trustee/director who is also managing a library budget has valuable insight from the grassroots level to share with network management as they review budgets and plans. The evolving price structure for OCLC's reference services is a result of staff seeking and hearing input from board members, Users' Council delegates, and member librarians.

Trustees/directors also play a crucial role in assessing and refining the leadership of the organization. The ongoing evaluation of the CEO by the governing board and feedback to him or her are essential. But it must be done with respect and sensitivity. Since the chief executive officer sets the tone and the management style for the organization, organizational effectiveness is the rationale for ongoing feedback to the CEO. This process is facilitated by mutually developing (with boards, network management, and staff) goals and objectives for the next evaluation against which the CEO is to be measured. The goals and objectives are echoed from the strategic plan and other planning documents the board generates or is privy to. And, one of the most difficult jobs of any board of trustees/directors is to fire a CEO. Again, if there are clearly stated objectives against which his or her performance is measured (and found lacking), the process is rational. The norm is the annual evaluation of the CEO with continuing feedback in formal and informal means between those annual benchmarks.

Closely tied to evaluation of the CEO is evaluation of the organization's performance. With the advent of strategic planning, there is usually a consensus in writing about where the organization is going and how it intends to get there. In broad terms, the evaluation is simple: either we did or we didn't achieve a goal. In evaluating the organization as well as the CEO, there is continuing need to seek more than answers to the evident questions; if we achieve part of an objective, what is the reason for partial fulfillment? Are there extraordinary costs associated with the achievement of some of our objectives? Are they worth the cost? Has the environment changed? Should we reevaluate the validity of those objectives? Or, should we recast the objectives? The reports from staff may indicate that the objectives are achieved but the membership is not happy for any number of reasons. And lack of interest as manifested in declining revenues is sure to get a governing board's attention.

Effective strategic planning is the road map that enables an organization to attain its goals. As a composite statement, it articulates where the organization is headed. If management insures that things are done right, the plan identifies the right things to do. OCLC President Wayne Smith has given inspired leadership in formulating coherent and visionary plans. He has done so using effectively a complicated organization with a large international constituency. OCLC's planning documents are produced after thorough discussions by board members and senior staff before going to Users Council and other interested parties. As with all good plans, the essence is usually brief enough that it can be easily remembered. For instance, in the early nineties, the goals were installing a new network, installing a new online system for cataloging and resource sharing, and launching a new core business in reference services. Those were achieved. By mid-1993, new goals were focus on reference services, enhancements to PRISM, and international expansion (Smith, 1993). The umbrella plan under which these more short-term goals are subsumed is "Journey to the 21st Century," a summary of OCLC's strategic plan from 1990 to 2000.

The board sets policy; management executes those policies. In a presentation to OCLC Users Council on pricing, OCLC Trustee Ann Wolpert said:

> The Board looks at pricing in the context of the mix of products and services OCLC offers, and the relationship between revenues and costs. The trustees are concerned with pricing as it affects the forest, rather than individual trees. However, their interest in the forest covers the environment of the forest, the ecological stresses in the forest, the health of the major stands of trees, and the effect of pricing strategy on forest management practices. While they may not debate the price of a FTU, they are concerned with pricing as it affects OCLC's stated public purpose, OCLC's ability to attract and retain a satisfied membership base, and OCLC's financial health.[5]

The last important function for a trustee/director is communication. He or she can certainly receive, as well as explain and relay, information in various ways to the membership. Probably the most effective means of communicating is within home groups: city, state, region. It is important that network members have the opportunity to hear, react, and provide input to their network's plans. And the most critical of the trustee/director's communication is the advice to the network or bibliographic utility's management and staff. Since the governing board is elected from the membership (the majority of the trustees are librarians in the case of both OCLC and SOLINET), their input/advice/reaction to (and occasional challenging of) important aspects of the organization's management and planning is essential. Libraries expect their networks to anticipate their needs; if planning for a new service/product is not begun until the need is articulated by a significant portion of the membership, it is already too late to benefit libraries and their users in a timely fashion. In the early 1980s, SOLINET embarked on an ambitious purchase of mainframe hardware to build a regional automated bibliographic system; because of poor communication to and from the Board of Directors and an overwhelming lack of support from the membership (which probably was caused, in part, by the poor communication from the board about the proposed bibliographic system and its purposes), the program was aborted. Subsequent SOLINET boards and management exercised prudent management to recoup losses and pay the debts, but it was tight times financially for several years. For another example, OCLC's decision to abandon exclusive marketing of CD-ROM versions of databases such as ERIC and leave them to joint ventures with successful vendors such as Silverplatter was based on input from various constituencies, some of which came through board members. The decision process included much information gathering, analysis, and discussion.

The communication between trustees and members is important because it sustains the network's credibility in both directions. A good example was the issue of copyright of the OCLC database. There was much dissension among the membership; many members spoke passionately against the decision to copyright the database. OCLC trustees spent much time clarifying the issues and providing rationale to the membership and public for the board's decision to copyright the database. And it was done in various groups at local, state, regional, and national levels.

This paper has reviewed the roles of trustees/directors on the boards of a library network, Solinet, and a bibliographic utility, OCLC; how is this relevant? An organization is as good as its management and governing board. A forward-thinking membership organization that anticipates members' needs, provides reliable, relevant, and timely products and services, and does all of this at a reasonable price requires both management and governing boards who are bright, knowledgeable, committed to the organization's mission, ethical, industrious, and sensitive leaders.

Most of the governing boards come from the membership. There are areas of service opportunity that match an individual's expertise and interest, and some which do not involve board membership. For instance, both SOLINET and OCLC support and use advisory committees and task forces. Those are wide-ranging groups who are selected for their expertise. SOLINET's Board of Directors, for another example, is elected at the annual membership meeting in May; there is a call for nominations each winter.

SOLINET currently sends ten delegates to OCLC's Users Council for three meetings each year; this is the primary membership advisory body to OCLC. Delegates are elected from the regional and state networks, have a voice in advising OCLC, and receive a relevant continuing education in what is happening in American libraries. OCLC's Board of Trustees has nine librarian trustees out of fifteen. Every two years, two Users Council delegates are elected for six-year terms on the Board.

These organizations will play a larger role in our future. What better platform is there from which to influence our professional future than the governance structure of networks and bibliographic utilities?

Librarians have accomplished much since the abbot unchained the book and let someone take it from its resting place. We know that the future is longer than the past, and that technology will continue to expand our options and improve our services. A proactive stance and informed, insightful leadership are required to nurture high quality organizations. Effective library services and access to information demand network and bibliographic utility governing boards who are competent and knowledgeable leaders. The boards will be as good—and effective—as we make them.

## NOTES

1. *Ohio Code [Revised]* 1702.30 b.
2. *Official Code of Georgia Annotated*, 14-3-113.1(a)1.
3. Restatement of Articles of Incorporation of Southeastern Library Network, Inc. (1987), Article III, para. (a) 10.
4. Amended Articles of Incorporation of OCLC, Article Third, January 29, 1981.
5. Ann Wolpert, Presentation to OCLC Users Council, Pricing Panel Discussion, Columbus, Ohio, June 1, 1992.

## REFERENCES

Albrecht, K.L. 1992. *New York Times*, April 19, 1992, p. 8.
Smith, K.W. 1993. *OCLC Newsletter*, 205 (September/October), p. 3.

# LIBRARY AUTOMATION'S EFFECT ON THE INTERIOR DESIGN OF CALIFORNIA PUBLIC LIBRARIES

E. Ruth Harder

Technologies for public service have affected the assignable interior public service areas of libraries. Prime concerns for library design are function and aesthetics, specifically in the areas of space utilization, furnishings, and lighting. The best library interiors are those in which there is no obvious disparity between all the elements that create the whole. The basic Latin terms relating to architecture are *firmitas* or structural stability, *utilitas* or function, and *venustas* or aesthetic appearance (*Encyclopedia Britannica*, 1988). These terms are also relatable to interiors.

Libraries are often the focal point of a community, campus, or business complex and should be designed to last. The interior appointments and furnishings should be solid and able to withstand frequent usage. The basic component of library design is function. How well a library building functions is important. When a building

Advances in Library Administration and Organization, Volume 13, pages 11-55.
Copyright © 1995 by JAI Press Inc.
All rights of reproduction in any form reserved.
ISBN: 1-55938-931-1

interior is functional, it is probably arranged well and lighted properly. A library becomes beautiful to both the staff and the users whenever it works efficiently. And the physical appearance, the ambiance, may determine whether or not people find the library an inviting and comfortable place to research information. Aesthetic design does not necessarily bring function along with it, but when serious thought and planning are inherent in the interior design, a functional design can be beautiful.

It is very important that libraries are designed for users in order to continue to attract people to use them. While we are still far from being a paperless society as Lancaster (1982) and others predicted, the computer is revolutionizing services to the public. Library users are being offered alternative information services beyond the walls of the local public library. An extreme example of alternative services is that of the Catawba Waterbee Health Education Consortium in rural South Carolina that has established a "library without walls" (Morgan, 1991, p. 125).

Libraries have a different appearance because of the integration of automation into the design as a whole. Many libraries—Carnegies, 1960s large open room, shopping center branches—have installed technologies and forever altered the existing design. Some are aesthetically appealing. To illustrate, the April 1990 *American Libraries* shows Yale University's Sterling Memorial Library's English Gothic design intermingled effectively with custom-designed tables and chairs for public access terminals. Similarly, the historic Pasadena Public library restoration boasts a refinished oak circulation desk that is authentic on the outside, while being modular on the inside. The visual display terminals work surprisingly well with the decor (American Libraries, 1990, p. 348).

Almost all library interiors are affected by the changes that technologies have brought to their facilities. It is now commonplace to walk into any kind of library and find computer workstations. The initial appearance of the library is sometimes similar to that of an automated office. Many special libraries rely heavily on computer access to in-house reports, CD-ROM products, database access, online catalogs, desktop publishing, and facsimile or electronic mail service to patrons. These libraries, or "information centers," are sometimes small, and largely composed of CD-ROM and online terminals. A few bookcases and journal shelves give one the clue that it really is a library. Libraries on most college and university campuses in the United States have visual display terminals (VDT) for the online or CD-ROM catalogs. School libraries and public libraries add computers and automation equipment as soon as their budgets permit.

With library technologies moving so rapidly there is a need for the technologies to be incorporated into the "fabric" of all new library interior design, and there is a need for guidelines for those who are renovating. The addition of technologies affects both library renovations and new library designs. Architectural considerations for lighting, wiring, telephone (including data and facsimile) lines, furnishings, workstations, and space considerations are all affected by the addition, or the incorporation of automation into a library building. It is imperative that early planning take place if the automated services are to be integrated smoothly into an existing or new library facility design. Automation has an impact on design, and design of the facility has an impact on how usable the technologies will be in any library.

From the general library space planning literature, one gets the picture that automation has not caused a significant change in the *total planning* process. Library design must begin with an understanding of the functional requirements of the facility. All planning, whether for a new building or for the renovation of an existing facility, is best done when it is founded on the mission statement and goals of the library organization. Planning for service is at the core of planning for technologies. Service is the most important ingredient in any library, and technologies are an enhancement to service. Computers give information seekers more access points to the literature than has ever been possible before with card catalogs and other indexes. Networks among libraries make the joint use of information resources possible. Online public access catalogs, circulation modules, network systems, dial-up catalogs, and CD-ROM products can greatly enhance public services.

While a networked system of information dissemination seems to be an alternative to paper, books will probably be the mainstay of the public library for some time to come. Therefore, planning for automation does not mean planning a smaller area, or planning for less growth.

Public libraries have perhaps been "caught up" in the wake of the technological wave more than any other library group. They are at the mercy of public funding as well as public demands for library services. Sometimes several years pass from the beginning architectural plans until ground is actually broken for construction to begin. Some public libraries that were in the architectural planning stages during the early phase of the availability of library automation now find that plans have to be revised again and again as even newer products are marketed. Still others, housed in historic buildings for which electricity and running water was the last major improvement, now find an even greater interior design challenge as technologies are incorporated into the facility.

Libraries have integrated technologies for public service into the interior design of the public library. California libraries were surveyed in order to answer some questions regarding interiors and automation: (1) How have public libraries, constructed as recently as the late eighties, planned ahead? (2) What lighting solutions, with regard to visual display terminal (VDT) screens, have been utilized by public libraries; and how successful are these lighting arrangements? (3) Have public libraries in California retained card catalogs in tandem with online public access catalogs? (4) Do public libraries have patron dial-up access to their catalogs? (5) Are all departments, including children's introducing the online public access catalog at once? (6) How many patrons can access the online catalog at once; and what criteria, if any, is being used to determine how many terminals are installed? (7) Are people waiting in line to use technologies? (8) Is electronic media beginning to replace books? (9) Are libraries depending on premanufactured furniture for workstations or automation equipment, or are they having these furnishings custom made? (10) When libraries choose online catalog workstation furniture, are they providing wheelchair access?

Answers to the foregoing questions reveal to some extent the library's responsiveness to patron's needs as interiors change to accommodate automation for public services. The way the lighting is handled in screen areas could determine whether or not a patron accepts technologies for public service. It could have a lot to do with staff acceptance and job satisfaction. Whether or not a workstation is comfortable could be a deciding factor on whether a patron wants to use the library at all. Convenient spacial arrangements, an uncrowded atmosphere, and logical department "flow" are very important to library user and staff satisfaction. From the general questions, some specific survey questions which hope to answer some of the concerns were formulated (see *Appendix B*). How California public libraries are handling space planning, furnishings, and lighting for the addition or incorporation of technologies for public service is the subject of the survey.

A background study of literature on the subject of library automation and interior design precedes the survey findings. The topics highlighted are: space planning, planning for access and traffic, planning for electricity, furniture, furniture workstations, furniture ergonomics, and lighting.

## THE LITERATURE

Automation brings with it a set of interior design problems that can seriously affect whether or not the workstation and other areas are comfortable and efficient to use. Space planning, furnishings, and lighting related to technologies for public service are specifically detailed herein. Other issues that are an outgrowth of the study are ergonomics and electrical wiring. These issues are of primary importance for the increased usage of technologies for public service in public libraries in the "Information Age."

"Historically, libraries were designed with a deep appreciation for achieving a balance between function and beauty" (Sherer, 1990, p. 312). Designs demonstrated a reverence for the past and respect for the future. Many libraries built in the 1960s demonstrated a lack of balance between aesthetics and function. Eric Rockwell (1989), in the "Seven Deadly Sins of Architects," writes that architects are more interested in creating a *look* or making a *statement* than they are in providing a functional library building. He recounts libraries with a number of architectural ills: "Too many libraries are built without adequate provision for computer networks and other signal distribution systems" (Rockwell, 1989, p. 341). Hidden light switches have been introduced by designers because they thought light switches weren't attractive (Cohen and Cohen, 1979). Cohen (1982) also writes about architects who are more concerned with architectural highlighting than lighting. From these articles one gets the message that in the past librarians may have not been involved in the architectural planning process, or may have allowed architects to tell them how the interiors should look.

In the special libraries literature one can find some detailed information on planning for technologies. Hodge and Lawrence

(1983) in "Planning for the Electronic Library," have a special library, rather than public library in mind. The planning advice seems to fit the public library as well: "The first (step) is to develop a strong background knowledge of potentially useful technology and design resources" (Hodge and Lawrence, 1983). Second, one should set objectives for the library of information center based on user requirements, and third, one should define the facilities and services to meet these objectives. From user and plant surveys, plans are formed for work and task flow. Details such as antistatic carpeting and "an abundance of electrical outlets," modular furniture, ergonomic factors for chairs and workstations, telephone outlets, emergency power backup, facsimile, and photocopy equipment are filled in from surveys taken at the subject plant or corporation. The best piece of advice seems to be, "Behave as if you are the construction project manager" (Hodge and Lawrence, 1983, p. 14). Space planning is a good place to begin.

## Space Planning

The planning process for interior design for automation is perhaps the most important aspect, because it is, in effect, the foundation for all the details. Space consideration in particular is impacted in many ways by automation. Everything just seems to take up more room. The "Wheeler-Githens Formula" of .55 square feet per capita is no longer the accepted rule for determining the size of the library, and it is more appropriate to allot .75 square feet or more even than 1 square foot per capita (Holt, 1987, p. 273). Simply because of increased book publishing (largely due to technologies and new knowledge), book collections are growing rapidly. Automated library systems have shifted work flow and require a more complex arrangement of the total library.

Authors in the literature discuss new library facility planning at length. While some authors such as Dahlgren (1985) touch on the subject of technology planning, even the newest editions of books on facility planning do not seem to have a lot of *detailed* information about planning for the incorporation of technologies into the public areas of the library. Perhaps the reason could be, as Thompson (1989) says, that changes are taking place at such a speed that anything that is written today is bound to be out of date by the time a book is printed. He further states that "drastic changes will come ... the rate of change will depend less on the ability of thinkers than on the funding which will be approved." To illustrate, some of the recent literature still refers to card catalogs within the scheme of things. "The traditional card catalogue is still used world-wide" (Thompson, 1989, p. 13). Fraley and Anderson (1990), in *Library Space Planning*, write, "During the space assessment, measure all card catalog cabinets and complete a furniture record for each section)" Fraley and Anderson, 1990, p. 92). No mention was made in these writings about running card catalogs in tandem with the online public access catalog.

Measuring everything is important so that final arrangements can work. Room for chairs and open space to move people around equipment areas is important. Due to automated equipment for data searching, more room is required at the reference counter and circulation desk. Of course, special patron areas for searching the online catalog must be carefully planned.

At least one writer is concerned about flexibility, or the ability to change the way things are arranged as it becomes necessary. Flexibility is an important aspect of planning for space. The trend is toward library buildings with enhanced electrical and communications capabilities, which includes planning for easy access to power sources. According to Holt (1987, p. 275), "... flexibility has taken on a new meaning as public libraries attempt to provide appropriate space for nonprint media and replace manual operations with automated systems."

A planning document, *Checklist of Library Building Design Considerations*, is available from the American Library Association. Section 3, "Interior," and Section 14, "Communication Equipment and Electrical," are both applicable and useful checklists (Sannwald, 1991). Location of service desks and PAC relationship to the service area is an important planning feature. The first question on the checklist, "Interior," is an important design consideration. "Are all public service elements of the building easily located from the entrance" (Sannwald, 1991, p. 7)? New users could become confused if confronted by corridors, machines, or anything other than some kind of service desk or guiding signage. To further highlight Section 3, the question, "Is the catalog easily accessible from all parts of the library and/or PAC's distributed throughout the collection?" is important to interior design regarding PAC implementation (Sannwald, 1991, p. 9). While access to the catalog is discussed here, the authors don't discuss how libraries establish the correct number of online public access terminals for a given library.

All of these space planning questions relate to function. While some users only want a comfortable place to read, many of today's users want to quickly find a specific piece of information and then leave. Automation seems to promise the patron that that can happen. To further illustrate, some questions from Section 14 are: "Are workstations or carrels used for electronic equipment staggered to enhance noise control and privacy?" and, "Are the areas where electronic equipment is used well ventilated and comfortable?" Both questions demand a "yes" answer if the library is to be all it can be for the user (Sannwald, 1991, p. 41).

*Library Space Planning*, is another general reference source for library space planners. The advice is, "If planning is an ongoing process, the framework for implementing a space reconfiguration will be in place" (Fraley and Anderson, 1990, p. 27). Eleven pieces of information are essential to the planning process.

1.  Institutional mission statement.
2.  Library mission statement.
3.  Institutional and library budget information copies of justifications, and so forth. Energy uses and changes.
4.  Space utilization reports and studies done in past.
5.  Photographs of the past.
6.  Collection housing measures and notes.
7.  Equipment and furniture inventory.
8.  Building blueprints.
9.  Institutional space inventory.
10. Outline of present work flow.
11. Budget information, proposals, bids, specifications of earlier work (Fraley and Anderson, 1990, p. 28).

These eleven pieces of information relate to planning for automation as well as planing in general. (1, 2,) the mission statements will define the function of the facility that will in turn clarify the need for automation, or expansion of existing technologies. (3, 11) Budget and energy uses are a consideration. These pieces of information will determine what the library can afford in terms of the whole renovation for technology, or plans for a new facility. (4, 5) Past studies on space utilization and photographs are good ways to determine what worked well and where improvements can be made in terms of space utilization. (6, 7) Collection, equipment, and furniture inventories are essential to the smooth transition. Some pieces may work well in the new interior and even find a new function, while some simply may no longer be usable. Some part of the collection may do well to be weeded, moved, or even replaced with new media. (8) Building blueprints of the existing facility are essential for renovations to show where electrical wiring, telephones, load bearing walls, and the like are located. For new buildings, it helps to show how everything fit together in the older facility. (9) If the library is part of an institution, an institutional space inventory would be valuable to show where the library might expand, or be located more effectively. (10) An outline of the present work flow may provide a guide to work reassignments or other administrative concerns due to a new way of providing services once automated features are installed (Fraley and Anderson, 1990, p. 28).

## Planning: Access/Traffic

Lushington and Kusack (1991, p. 24) state that "Planning a library building must start with an understanding of people's aesthetic needs and functional requirements of being able to quickly and easily gain access to an increasingly bewildering array of materials and services." Each service area is unique in some way (such as children's reference services) yet has some relationship to other services. Rohlf (1989) has likened service desks to a series of spokes and hubs, each one touching each other. Staff work areas should be connected with service points, with machines in view of staff, and service points in view of patrons who enter the area. Holt (1989) proposes a method of bubble diagrams that indicate relationships of areas as a useful way to begin planning the total library.

Spaces should be designed so that people can move easily around and through various areas of the library. The impact of circulation space on square footage is that 15 percent of the area is required just to move people (Hensley, 1991). Aisle space for book shelving has been established at 36 inches, and that standard should also apply for movement through or around an equipment area. Whenever lines are anticipated around machine areas such as photocopy machines, extra space should be allowed for the typical number of people waiting in line. Lines can be directed to one side of the equipment or in some other direction by means of roping, especially in areas such as the circulation desk during peak hours. Thoughtful placement of equipment is dependent on how well one plans for electrical requirements.

## Planning for Electricity

Electricity requirements are impacted considerably by technologies for public services. Wiring, location of outlets, switches, lighting configuration, telephones, and data lines are all important aspects of the plan for automation. Fraley and Anderson (1990) write about electrical requirements for technology. Location of equipment is important, particularly when some electrical equipment may require 220 wiring. The decision to locate or move equipment should be done with the power and grounding requirements thoroughly understood and noted on architectural drawings. Contractors will normally follow the current *National Electrical Code* (1993). "The amount of power coming into the building, the amount available to the library, and the load on each line is of prime importance" (Fraley and Anderson, 1990, p. 84).

Dahlgren (1985), who devotes six paragraphs to "computerization" in *Planning the Small Public Library*, writes, "Running conduit for electrical service and data cable to 10 projected terminal locations is expensive, more so if several of those locations are never used" (Dahlgren, 1985, p. 16). A particular concern with this advice is the expense of re-wiring, running conduit and cables to add terminals at a later date. Dix (1990, p. 64), on the other hand, states that planners can opt for flexibility and "plan to bring power and data wiring to every conceivable point in the building." Dowlin (1991), who is involved in planning the large San Francisco Public Library says that wiring will be run there under the floor in a grid pattern every four feet. Electrical wiring plans also play an important role in furniture placement.

## Furniture

Furnishings are impacted by automation. Circulation desks, as well as other public service desks must now be planned as automated workstations that provide for the associated wiring and computer equipment. Patron terminals must be located on counters, carrels, workstations or desks that are appropriately designed and safely, aesthetically wired. Since both library workers and patrons will sit at visual display terminals, sometimes for long periods of time, ergonomic design has to be taken into consideration.

In *The Design and Evaluation of Public Library Buildings*, Lushington and Kusack (1991) devote a chapter to "Planning for the Future." They say that microfiche, CD-ROM, and other optical disc technology will access huge amounts of recently published materials in greatly reduced space, but with considerable additional machine workstation space and electrical needs. They refer to "stand-up access" because of the speed of searches. Predictions for the 1990s are that public access computerized catalogs will replace card catalogs; there will be a proliferation of local area networks to access other local and regional libraries; and there will be public terminals to use CD-ROM databases, such as encyclopedias. The general trend, as they see it, is a gradually decreasing need for book storage, and an increasing need for electronic workstations and cable transmission systems.

In the Lushington and Kusack (1991, p. 51) chapter on, "Library Functions Related to Library Roles," there is a brief discussion of requirements for seating, desks, work surfaces, computer equipment and screens for staff, but not the patron areas. Andrea Michaels (1988, p. 55) says that library furniture is replaced no more frequently than about every twenty years. Her statement raises the question of how libraries are coping with the rapidly changing computer environments, and consequently the changing furniture needs.

## Furniture: Workstations

Cohen and Cohen (1987, pp. 310-311) have researched and written about planning furniture for computer workstations. The potential location of each terminal should be indicated on the architectural drawing. An individual workstation area takes up about 35 square feet, a microform reader-printer takes up 30 square feet, and a freestanding computer workstation often requires 60 square feet. A design which would be conducive to privacy for the online public access catalog searcher is featured in a picture of the William H. Hall Free Library in the *American Libraries* "Interiors Showcase" (1990, p. 346). It is almost completely enclosed in a cubicle with an entrance opening to one side, which is not the screen side. The cubicle appears to take up approximately 5 by 7 feet, which is a 35 square feet area as Cohen and Cohen (1987) describe. One wonders whether or not online public access catalogs which are not a part of groupings or clustered arrangements require 35 square feet for each terminal.

New equipment, as well as furniture such as counters, carrels, or workstations to put it on, should be carefully thought out and measured. Workstation furniture should be sturdy, ergonomic, and should assure a patron's privacy. Public libraries need durable furniture, and traditional library furniture manufacturers have provided that kind of product for traditional furnishings for many years.

When the computer first became a regular piece of library equipment, workstations were only available from office equipment manufacturers. The kind of wear resistance needed by libraries was not inherent in those workstations or systems furnishings. The alternative was to have counters or workstations custom made, which many libraries did. Over the past couple of years the library manufacturers have come up with a line of computer furniture that begins to fill the need.

There are a number of "rules of thumb" for determining the needed number of OPAC terminals.

1. One OPAC terminal for each 15,000 circulations.
2. One OPAC terminal for each 100 to 150 persons who enter the library on days of heaviest use.
3. Ten OPAC terminals for each OCLC terminal.
4. Four OPAC terminals for each circulation terminal.
5. An activity index can be created by adding together:
   A. Registration of patrons per year (in thousands);
   B. Circulation per year (in thousands);
   C. Number of square feet in floor space (in thousands);
   D. Reference questions per year (in thousands);
      along with a constant 41.64 to provide a floor number for small branches. The formula $41.64 + A + B + C + D =$ the activity index. The activity index number divided by 100 gives the minimum number of online catalog terminals needed.

6. Another formula is: number of OPAC terminals $= 1.23$ multiplied by the number of people checking out books per hour $+ 11.53$ (Main, 1989).

## Furniture: Ergonomics

The ergonomics of computer workstations as a separate topic was not addressed extensively in the reviewed *library* literature. All of the many tasks applied to a workstation environment require a different set of ergonomic considerations. According to Veatch (1987, p. 372), "If the element supports the task, it is ergonomic; if it inhibits the task it is poorly designed." In a multimedia environment, the furniture should be ergonomically designed, with the human-machine interface in mind. Chairs, tables, carrels, counters, and workstations should provide comfort for large and small people. Child-sized units should be available in the children's section of the library, and the biggest man should be able to sit or stand at the terminal without getting a backache, neck strain, or eye strain. Keyboards should be at a comfortable height, that is, the arm bent at a 70 percent angle when working to avoid wrist, elbow, and hand strains. A person in a wheelchair should be able to use the public access catalog. Adjustable workstation units are recommended to accommodate the variable sizes of users.

One of the ways librarians can assure that the human-machine element is taken into consideration is to comply with the standard that specifies the correct measures for workstations (seated) with (VDTs). The *American National Standard for Human Factors Engineering of Visual Display Terminal Workstations, ANSI/HFS 100-1988* specifies standards for human factors engineering principles for the design of VDTs (based on CRT technology) and associated furniture. The VDT applications are described as "text processing, data entry, and data inquiry." This standard is intended for use by professionals who have technical responsibility for the design, installation, and setup of VDTs, the associated furniture, and the work environments. The standard is for seated users and does not apply to standing (American National Standards Institute, 1988, p. 5).

## Lighting

Another aspect of patron comfort is associated with lighting. Lighting is one of the prime considerations for planning for automation. The quality of lighting from fenestration (windows) and luminaries (electrical lighting fixtures) greatly affects whether a screen area is usable. Waters and Winters (1987) write that, until recently, library lighting was planned by electrical engineers and designers who generally used a "quantitative" approach. The emphasis was placed on general quantities of illumination, with little consideration for an individual user's comfort, color rendition of the source, aesthetics, or energy conservation. Typical public institution layouts consisted of fluorescent luminaries equally spaced across the ceiling. Lighting for the library should place an emphasis on the "qualitative" approach in order to emphasize the quality of the light being provided, provide a pleasing atmosphere and result in an energy efficient system design (Waters and Winters, 1987, p. 327).

Lighting in screen areas, with reference to concern for glaring and light that is too bright or too dim, is discussed very briefly by Lushington and Kusack (1991). While lighting in general is covered, nothing is said about lighting screen areas for patrons. In their summary of lighting considerations they recommend that one select lenses or louvers that diffuse light and prevent glare (Lushington and Kusack, 1991). While Thompson (1989) devotes a chapter to "lighting" in his work, he does not go into any detail about lighting for online public access catalogs in the public areas.

The problem for libraries is that both reading tasks and screens are usually under the same lighting system. One lighting strategy is to provide uniform fluorescent lighting throughout the library, and task lighting for areas where more illumination is needed. Cohen and Cohen (1979, p. 5) state that one wants to achieve a visual comfort probability (VCP) index of 70 or better. That means that 70 out of 100 people are comfortable in light from a particular fixture. Illumination over a visual display terminal should not be more than 50 footcandles according to consultant Silver (1991). Ramsey and Sleeper (1989, p. 52) write that the Illuminating Engineering Society (IES) recommends 70 footcandles for general writing and reading. In *Guide for Educational Facilities Lighting*, the IES recommends that the general reading range should be from 50 to 100 footcandles, but the screen area range should be from 5 to 10 footcandles. The footnote to the table where the information for screens is found reads, "Especially subject to veiling reflections. It may be necessary to shield the task or reorient it" (IES RP-3-1988, p. 10).

Kaser (1985) writes that there are three pressures that "muddle what should be a simple issue." These pressures result from aesthetics, economics, and market forces. Market forces can result in the over lighting of library spaces. Task lighting, while aesthetic and seemingly economical, can be costly in terms of bulb replacement, or even entire fixture replacement due to vandalism or theft. As for aesthetics, some designers look at uniform lighting as uninspired or even ugly and institutional. Designers see illumination as a vital part of the aesthetic composition of the interior design. Contrasts in light and shadow are utilized for effect. What is overlooked in this "effect" is that heavy contrasts of light and dark can produce a poor reading environment, and can even cause disorientation. It can also produce undesirable glaring, which can be temporarily blinding to anyone, but is especially hazardous to older patrons (Cohen and Cohen, 1979).

As the human eye ages, lenses begin to thicken and discolor, making it more difficult to focus on reading materials. The eye's ability to deal with light intensity, glare, and contrasts is affected as well. Greater light intensities are needed in order for people to see. Bifocals and trifocals are worn by many library patrons. Since libraries as yet have not come up with a "seeing standard," it is important to take these sight problems into consideration when planning for lighting libraries (Cohen and Cohen, 1979, p. 127).

Waters (1987, p. 329) says that some task lighting systems produce undesirable glaring from ceiling and/or wall reflections. Luminaries should be chosen that are glare free. One should not be able to see the light source from the normal working position, or passing area. Task lighting in visual display terminal screen areas should be positioned in a way that no veiling reflections are present on the screens, nor glaring in the user's eyes. In reading areas a desk lamp should not light the printed page more than three times the level of the adjacent desk top, or five times the level of the room (Cohen and Cohen, 1979, p. 132).

"Direct glare is produced by excessive luminance in the visual field that affect the visual systems as the individual looks around the environment. It is usually associated with the luminary zone" from 45 to 90 degree zone (Ramsey and Sleeper, 1989, p. 52).

Daylight is thought to be free, which is why it is so often chosen as part of a lighting system for public services. In a comprehensive energy analysis, heat losses and gains through glass and air infiltration around window frames generate some energy costs that may begin to offset the savings of using natural light to augment artificial light. "Daylight produces less interior heat per unit of illumination, however, than do most forms of electric light" (Kurz, 1986, p. 124). Sharma (1970) discusses natural lighting for general library lighting. He writes that in the evolutionary process, the human eye has developed and adjusted itself to natural light, making it the best light. Defects listed for natural light are uneven distribution, glaring, temperature control, wall space consumption, and the expense of installation and maintenance. Daylight is not as controllable as artificial lighting sources. Blinds and shades are necessary to perform as barriers and filters to prevent glaring.

Lighting for visual display terminals is discussed in the library literature by Cohen and Cohen (1987), Kaser (1985), and others, as well as in lighting standards relating to lighting for screen areas. The important variables that the literature addresses are: library space planning; planning for access/traffic; electricity; furniture; workstations; ergonomics; and lighting. The literature partially answers some of the questions regarding interiors and automation. What lighting solutions with regard to VDT screens have been utilized by public libraries? Is daylight a part of the lighting solution? According to the literature, lighting for screen areas is important, because the screen location in relationship to light sources has an impact on screen usage. Glaring and veiling reflections can result from poor choice of location. Lighting, both daylight and electrical, is frequently used by architects as a design element. The literature indicates that windows and glass may be planned more as an artistic or aesthetic part of the architectural creation, than a source of light for library activities. Further study is indicated to determine what is happening in actual library design.

In the question, "How have public libraries constructed in the 1980s planned ahead for automation?" the keyword is "planned." According to the planning literature one needs to go through the planning process for space, electricity, lighting, and furniture before any automated system can successfully be installed either in an existing or a planned facility. Space relationships and work flow are important design considerations inherent in this question. When design elements for automation are not taken into account during the planning phase of a new building, the results could be less than desirable.

Are libraries using premanufactured or custom made workstations and other furniture for automation? There seems to be a fairly reasonable selection of premanufactured furniture for automation.

The problem is whether or not the particular furniture system meets a particular need. Each automated system has its own set of specifications for size, and they are not always the same. One library may need space for printers in a workstation, while another library has no need for a printer stand next to every computer. The importance of this subject is a matter of "fitting" a system to some particular style of furniture, or vice versa.

Is electronic media beginning to replace books? Predictions have been made (Lushington, 1983) that raise the question. Given the availability of encyclopedias and other books on CD-ROM media, public libraries could very well retrieve valuable shelving space. On the other hand, CD-ROM products could be an added service, rather than replacement of bound copies. Some factors involved in the decision to retain both formats could be the availability of space, the kinds of services patrons expect, or even administrative or staff preference. The implication for public libraries is the need to maintain the flexibility to go either way.

How many patrons can access the online catalog at one time, and what criteria, if any, is used to determine how many terminals are installed? The literature answers the question in part (see notes on "rules of thumb," page 17). The ratio of patrons to OPAC or CD-ROM terminals is a critical question when one is looking at the degree of acceptance and satisfaction of users with an online system. More study on this subject is indicated. If some libraries have found a good method for determining the ideal number of terminals to install for the OPAC, then that information will benefit other libraries as well.

Some questions were not answered by the literature. Are people waiting in line to use technologies? This question is directly related to the previous one regarding the number of terminals needed. When lines must form for any reason, library traffic patterns are impacted. Some areas which can be affected are terminals for CD-ROM products which index journals, copy machines, automated circulation desks, and public access catalog terminals. Where do public service areas need to expand to remain current with the increased demands placed on the system due to automation?

Have public libraries in California retained card catalogs in tandem with the public access catalog? Nothing in the literature addresses this question, so further study is indicated. The literature does not answer whether or not public libraries have patron dial-up access to their catalogs? When the answer is, "yes," one design implication for some communities could be that fewer terminals are needed at the library site itself. Perhaps the biggest implication for this question is whether or not public libraries are financially able to take advantage of some technologies that are available.

Are all departments, including those offering services to children, introducing the public access catalog at the same time? The literature does not address the question. The design implication here is the location and size requirements for workstations as well as staff locations in relationship to online public access terminals. When workstations are located conveniently in particular departments rather than in one large central bank of terminals, the wiring and furniture requirements will be different. Child-sized units would be indicated in the children's department as would one or more convenient adult-sized unit for parents and staff.

Are libraries providing wheelchair access to terminals? Are libraries aware of their responsibilities to these patrons; and are they finding ways to accommodate them? These questions are of prime concern because of the *Americans with Disabilities Act*, which was signed into law July 26, 1990, which brings the access requirements into effect January 26, 1992.

Since the literature raised some questions, and does not answer others, further study is indicated. A survey of public libraries is covered in the next sections. Responses to space planning questions hope to reveal what public libraries have been doing to plan for automation in general. The benefit should be to learn from the experience of others what worked well, as well as what did not work at all. Survey answers are important for both functional and aesthetic design reasons, and can be expected to find that the specialized needs of automated public service areas are addressed in actual library design.

## SURVEY OF PUBLIC LIBRARIES

In order to further study how technologies for public service have impacted the interior design of public libraries, a questionnaire was developed to survey subject libraries on the way they have handled interior design problems related to automation. The author wanted to see, hear, and write down the experiences of the selected libraries so that others might learn useful interior design information for their libraries. It is assumed that it is helpful to hear success stories as well as those which were not so successful.

## Selection of Survey Subjects

For the purpose of this study on how technologies for public service have affected the interior design of public libraries in California, eleven California libraries were selected, ranging in original date of building construction from 1959 to future completion in 1995. The California public libraries were chosen as research subjects based upon their appearance in *Library Journal's* (December 1988, 1989, 1990) annual architectural issue, or based upon the author's knowledge of local libraries. Local libraries were selected as much as possible so that more libraries could be observed by the author.

The reason for selecting both new and renovating libraries as a representative sample of California public libraries was twofold. (1) The author wanted to see the contrast, if any, between the interior design problems encountered because of automation being added to an existing building, and those that occur when one plans them into the facility before it is built. (2) With the existence of new construction being limited, including the renovated libraries provided the opportunity to observe more libraries. Since most of these libraries have similar public service requirements, mild year-round climate, and the availability of sunshine for lighting purposes, the assumption was made that these libraries would have similar design needs and adopt similar solutions.

Libraries constructed within the last three years or libraries planning construction completion within the next three to four years were selected to give the study a sense of how public libraries are now incorporating technologies for public service into interior design. Newer libraries, or libraries under construction: Fremont, Oxnard, Pleasanton, Sacramento, San Francisco, and a composite of Los Angeles branches[1] were chosen based on the recent date of construction or projected date of completion. Older libraries that have incorporated technologies for public service were chosen in order to get a more balanced view of how libraries in general are handling interior design solutions for automation. Existing libraries: Concord, Cupertino, Dublin, Livermore, and San Ramon were interviewed, because they had similar demographics, and were near enough for the author's personal observation of how renovation for technologies had been accomplished.

Demographics and the general economic climate of the community can make a difference on the kinds of library services supported by the community. The eleven libraries which were selected for the survey represent communities with a population spread of from 23,229 to more than 400,000. Library sizes range from 12,640 square feet to a projected 361,960 square feet. Two larger cities: San Francisco and Sacramento are represented in the new library group. Sacramento's main public library is being completed in 1992, and San Francisco's main public library is planned for 1995. In the older libraries, the fast growing communities of Concord and Dublin are included.

## SURVEY RESULTS

The results of the survey can be reduced to three major variables: *space planning*, *furniture*, and *lighting*. Within space planning, the areas of planning for *access/flow*, and planning for *electricity* are included; and within furnishings, the areas of *workstations* and *ergonomics* are included.

The data collected in this survey is reported in five tables. Renovated library survey results for space planning and furniture, except the Los Angeles branches, are in Table 1. Space planning and furniture results for all new libraries in the survey except major cities, San Francisco and Sacramento are in Table 2. Los Angeles branches composite answers, Sacramento and San Francisco are compared in Table 3. Lighting results are compiled in Table 4 for renovated libraries, and Table 5 for new libraries.

### Space Planning

General planning for technologies by the surveyed public libraries has been common considering all of the variables involved in the process. Concord, Cupertino, Dublin, and Livermore all have added technologies. All of these libraries have renovated except one. New libraries, except one, in this survey have all planned for technologies during the architectural planning phase. When technologies are not included in a new library's architectural plan, but added after the fact, the result is that the library almost needs renovation before it can install an automated system. The major difference between the four libraries in Table 2 is that technologies were added in San Ramon without the benefit of being integrated into the original architectural plan. Even though this is a new building, there aren't enough outlets and wiring for all of the equipment. Technologies were not included in the architectural plans of this library, and the resulting design is difficult for librarians as well as patrons. Both Pleasanton and Fremont planned for technologies as the facility was being planned. Oxnard and Sacramento couldn't be compared as they were not yet open at the time of the survey. Both have planned technologies into the architectural construction plans.

Planning for the space that hardware for automation and its associated furniture will occupy seems to be an inexact science. Libraries in the survey generally do not know the percentage of assignable space which is devoted to automation. Estimates of from 1 percent to 20 percent are given by a few, who admit it is only a guess. Hardware involved in the technologies for public service for renovated libraries takes the same amount of space as had been anticipated for two libraries, and "more" space than anticipated for two libraries. Part of the problem is unfamiliarity with what is available, or getting a different, newer product by the time the requisition is finally filled. For example, one of the newer libraries had furniture which would not fit the equipment when it finally arrived. They had to remove the side partitions from the workstation carrels in order to accommodate printers. Pleasanton, in contrast, built for growth in this area. Most new libraries have planned for and measured to allow the necessary room for equipment, hardware and associated furniture.

One of the planning differences among the surveyed libraries is the ratio of online public access catalog workstations to the number of users. Among these libraries, the number of PAC or OPAC terminals varied, and so far there does not seem to be a formula that relates the number of terminals to the number of square feet of library space, or the number of terminals to the population served. No true analysis can be done on the size of the library versus the population due to the fact that some communities also have branch libraries. Cupertino has one catalog terminal for every 1,000 people in the community; Concord 1 per 13,000; Dublin 1 per 3,000; Fremont 1 per 5,000; Livermore 1 per 5,000; Oxnard 1 per 4,700; Pleasanton 1 per 3,000; Sacramento 1 per 1,200; San Ramon 1 per 3,000. The average is 1 terminal for each 4,237 population in these cities. The trend seems to be to provide an average of 1 per 3,000. The rationale for using population versus cardholders is that everyone in the community is a potential library user, whether or not that person has a library card.

Newer libraries, regardless of size, are planning for more online public access catalog terminals than are renovated libraries. The number of OPAC terminals ranges from 11 to 35, with an average of 24 terminals. Twenty online catalog terminals will be placed adjacent to the First Stop Reference Desk on the first floor of the San Francisco Main Library. All public service departments throughout the building will contain additional smaller groupings of terminals (the total number is yet to be determined). Compare Pleasanton (population of 50,553), a new library, with 16 terminals, to Livermore (population of 56,741), an older library, with 8 public and 2 staff terminals. In the surveyed libraries, the renovated *main library* in a similar sized community with similar demographics has half the number of terminals of a new main library. This seems to result from the fact that it is almost impossible to include more terminals in an older facility without a considerable amount of expensive rewiring.

The libraries that have a more adequate number of PAC terminals per potential user experience better patron traffic flow. Generally speaking, those libraries having only 8 to 10 public access catalogs find patrons waiting to use the catalogs during peak hours. In Table 1, the answers to the number of OPAC terminals (line 5) to population (line 1), and size (line 2) have some relationship to flow problems (line 17). Concord, with a population of 111,348 and 12,640 square feet floor space with 8 terminals experiences formation of lines and obstructed aisles. Dublin, with a smaller population, 23,229, and 15,000 square feet library facility also has 8 terminals, and experiences line formation, not so much at the OPAC, but at the CD-ROM product terminals. (Dublin plans to have about 50 terminals when they renovate.) In contrast, Cupertino with a population of 40,263 and 24,000 sq. ft. library facility has a projected 40 terminals (now microfilm) and does not normally experience line formation for catalog usage. Livermore (population 56,741), with 10 OPAC terminals and dial-up access *does not report line formation* for the OPAC terminals. For the renovated libraries surveyed, the number of online public access catalogs (OPAC) or CD-ROM based public access catalog (PAC) terminals ranges from 8 to a projected 50 terminals. Space constraints and budget constraints are limiting factors for the renovated libraries.

The renovation date in relationship to the addition of technologies, along with the ratio between the number of OPAC terminals and the population seems to have an affect on line formation. Concord (lines form) has added technologies without the benefit of facility renovation, while Cupertino (lines generally do not form unless the equipment has broken down) has renovated prior to the addition of an automated system. While Cupertino had not yet installed OPAC terminals at the time of the survey, the 40 available microfilm workstations now serving as the public catalog could be equated to OPAC workstations. Concord has experienced some inconvenience as a result of having added technologies without the benefit of renovation, although renovation is planned. Little or no space planning was done prior to the implementation of the public access catalog and other technologies. The library went through a progression from card catalog to book catalog, to microfilm catalog, to CD-ROM catalog. Concord replaced the microfilm stations one-on-one with the CD-ROM catalog.

CD-ROM products and associated hardware are making an impact on the interior design of public libraries, particularly in the journal areas. All new libraries, except one, and all older libraries, except one, have chosen InfoTrac CD-ROM index for journals and its associated microfilm subscription. An area must be devoted just for this product, because it usually consists of one or more CD-ROM workstations and one or more microfilm reader-printers. Parts of the collection in one library had to be shifted to accommodate the change. In one library, a counter in the reference section was sacrificed to house the InfoTrac system. The CD-ROM is centrally located at mid-building and can be seen from both reference and circulation desks. It is important for two reasons: security, and assisting patrons with the equipment, or teaching patrons how to use it. Since bound journals are no longer needed with this system, some libraries such as Pleasanton and one of the Los Angeles branches report a space savings there.

The public access catalog was introduced in all departments at once in all of the libraries in this survey. The children's area catalog is a complete catalog, and not restricted to children's literature. In most of the surveyed libraries there is at least one child-sized workstation as well as a regular sized unit for the librarian or for adults who accompany children. This arrangement seems to work well. The children's area has not really been greatly changed by the advent of the computer. It generally looks bright and cheerful as always, with child-sized furniture, block, or cushion type arrangements for story time.

## Planning: Access/Flow/Traffic

In some libraries, peak time will find adults and children in queue at the circulation desk. Patron traffic flow problems exist in the renovated libraries to varying degrees. When the same terminal is used for both check-outs and returns, libraries experience a bottleneck at the circulation desk. Concord and Livermore both report congestion at the circulation desk during peak hours. Pleasanton, in contrast, has more terminals and has little or no waiting during a peak period.

Line formation affects the aisle space and spaces around equipment which were planned in the original architectural design. The affect is both on the functional aspect of being able to move people through areas, and the negative aesthetic affect of a crowded appearance. During this study, a line of patrons waiting for a photocopy machine was measured. The test was only performed once, and is not meant to be scientific. But it does give an idea of a space requirement that many designers seem to have overlooked. The total standing area taken up by the average individual was approximately 20 inches wide by 18 inches deep, with a range of 10 to 20 inch space between people. Others who wanted to use the machine saw the line of people and moved on to other areas of the library until the line had diminished, because the line already impacted the flow to another area of the library.

While the copy machine lines and "peak time" circulation lines in some libraries are a problem, a somewhat smaller problem occurs when equipment or products are placed wherever they seem to fit. Some stand-up use catalogs are placed at the ends of bookcase sections. When two people are standing at the terminal, one using and one waiting, the walk way is blocked.

All surveyed libraries are aware of the need for access to the OPAC for the handicapped person. San Francisco Public Library has handicapped access planned for the entire five story building. Whether renovated, or in the newly completed or planning stages, all libraries surveyed report that they have "wheelchair access" to at least one public access catalog terminal. Some libraries are counting on using an existing terminal by removing the regular chair. An observation by the author is that if one moved a regular chair away from a workstation, a wheelchair patron could get to the keyboard, but not necessarily comfortably. Some wheelchairs bump against the structure of the workstation and impede the wheelchair from sitting comfortably beneath the work surface.

The San Francisco Main Public Library is planning to maximize access and flow. This will be an "intelligent building" which will measure the flow of people within it. The First Stop Reference Desk staff will assist patrons with the catalogs on the first floor and direct them to the department holding the library materials they want. The interlibrary loan department is placed in a logical spatial relationship, adjacent to the First Stop Reference Desk. Relationships between the functions that occupy each space and the spaces that adjoin it are taken into consideration so that users can function in a comfortable manner in an environment that encourages study. User traffic areas and cross aisles between the stacks and seating are planned to minimize distraction caused by those moving through the book stacks. Special attention is given to the visual control of entrances, exits, public rest rooms, meeting rooms, the spaces for children and the small study and meeting rooms. The library and furnishings layout are planned to provide considerable visual control of the several building spaces and areas with minimal staff.

## Furniture

It was originally thought by some that the OPAC terminals would take up less space or about the same area as the card catalog. While the days of providing a special air-conditioned computer room for a huge main-frame is no longer an issue, computers still require special attention and take up more space than card catalogs. But one librarian reports that, before they actually had computers, they were told that computers could be put almost anywhere as long as one had an electrical outlet and a desk to put them on. Architect Bob Callori (1991) of Hornberger Worstell reports that he had done only slight remodeling for computer installation in some offices, usually placing computers on existing work surfaces.

Computer furniture has forever altered the appearance of public library interior design. The area required for computer terminal installations largely depends on the number of terminals, choice of arrangement, and style of the workstations. The most economic use of space seems to be the side-by-side and back-to-back arrangement of up to eight computers which is being referred to by librarians in this survey as an "electronic island." Every public access catalog terminal, including a small printer and a standard chair, takes up approximately a four by five foot area. In the "island" arrangement, printers are sometimes shared, and sometimes stools are used instead of chairs.

Electronic "islands" have emerged as a way of dealing with the public access catalog and keeping it largely contained within viewing distance of the information or reference desk, and readily available as well as recognizable to library patrons entering the library. Newer libraries (Sacramento, Pleasanton, Fremont, and San Francisco) all have, or have planned, groupings of OPAC terminals. San Ramon's OPAC area consists of eight study carrels attached to each other, and placed in the back of the library near the reference area. Some of the renovated libraries manage smaller groupings of terminals.

CD-ROM products for some items such as encyclopedias or indexes are beginning to be utilized, but there does not seem to be a significant change in shelving requirements as a result of CD-ROM technologies. No library surveyed has gotten rid of the bound text equivalent, or bought the CD-ROM product in place of bound texts such as encyclopedias. Bound journals are not kept in most libraries surveyed, and fewer magazine racks are needed as a result of a CD-ROM and microfilm magazine and journal product usage. InfoTrac (a CD-ROM index with microfilmed journal subscription) is used by seven of the nine libraries (Los Angeles and San Francisco are excluded).

Furniture in all libraries (Tables 1, 2, 3; line 14) is a combination of custom made and pre-manufactured pieces. Not all automated systems will fit all workstation furniture. Some libraries have custom made furniture for the online public access catalogs, because there was no suitable computer furniture available from library manufacturers at the time they began looking for it. Many kinds of workstation arrangements are now available from the major library furniture manufacturers.

***Table 1.*** Renovated Library Space Planning and Furniture Survey Results

|  |  | Concord 1959 | Cupertino 1971 | Dublin 1979 | Livermore 1966 |
|---|---|---|---|---|---|
| 1 | Population | 111348 | 40263 | 23229 | 56741 |
| 2 | Library Size Square Feet | 12640 | 24000 | 15000 | NR |
| 3 | Renovation Date | Future | 1988 | 1992 | 1989 |
| 4 | Technologies added | Yes | Yes | Yes | Yes |
| 5 | PAC Terminals | 8 | 40 projected | 8 | 10 |
| 6 | Wheelchair access to PAC | Yes | Yes | Yes | Yes |
| 7 | Children's Dept. | 1 | 3 | 2 | 1 |
| 8 | Depts. Introduced | All | All | All | All |
| 9 | Did hardware take up more, less or same area anticipated | Same | Same | More | More |
| 10 | CD-ROM Products | No | InfoTrac, Grolier, Guinness | InfoTrac, Worldbook | InfoTrac |
| 11 | Network | No | No | No | Dial-up access |
| 12 | Public Fax | No | No | Staff use | Staff use |
| 13 | Public Computers | No | 3 | 1 | 2 |
| 14 | Furniture: C. Custom P.Premanufactured. | NR | P, C | P, C | P, C |
| 15 | Does any CD or online product replace paper | No | Not yet | No | No |
| 16 | Commercial Databases such as BRS, Dialog | No | No | No | RLIN, staff use |
| 17 | Flow problems? | Lines form; obstruct aisles. | Yes, some, but not usually | Aisles obstructed by CD-ROM, etc. | Circulation desk during peak hours. |

**Note:** For the sake of brevity in all tables, abbreviations have been used:
NA = Not applicable; NR = No response.

## Furniture/Ergonomics

Ergonomics is a separate subject which was not considered in this survey. One library reports that their patron chairs are high-backed, "spoked" chairs. These chairs are not ergonomic. However, their staff chairs are reported to be ergonomic. The ergonomic relationship of keyboard to arm, and eyes to VDT, as well as seating for library computer workstations is addressed in standards of the American National Standards Institute (see Appendix A).

**Table 2.**    New Library Space Planning and Furniture Survey Results

|    |                                                      | Fremont                                        | Oxnard           | Pleasanton           | San Ramon                   |
|----|------------------------------------------------------|------------------------------------------------|------------------|----------------------|-----------------------------|
| 1  | Population                                            | 180000                                         | 142216           | 50553                | 35303                       |
| 2  | Library Sq. Ft.                                      | 60000                                          | 72000            | 30000                | 18238                       |
| 3  | Completion Date                                      | 1988                                           | 1992             | 1988                 | 1989                        |
| 4  | Technologies in plan                                 | Yes                                            | Yes              | Yes                  | No, added                   |
| 5  | PAC Terminals                                        | 35                                             | 30               | 16                   | 11                          |
| 6  | Wheelchair access to PAC                             | Yes                                            | Yes              | Yes, some            | NR                          |
| 7  | Children's Dept. PAC                                 | 6                                              | Yes              | 5                    | 1                           |
| 8  | Depts. PAC Introduced                               | All                                            | All              | All                  | All                         |
| 9  | Did hardware take up more, less or same area anticipated | More                                     | Same             | Less, built space for growth | Same               |
| 10 | CD-ROM/Products                                     | InfoTrac, Worldbook, Kurzweil Reader           | Ebsco,B.I.P      | InfoTrac, Graingers  | InfoTrac                    |
| 11 | Network                                             | No                                             | No               | No (RFP)             | PC LAN staff                |
| 12 | Public Fax                                          | No                                             | Staff            | Staff                | Not yet                     |
| 13 | Public Computers                                    | 5                                              | No               | 2                    | No                          |
| 14 | Furniture: Custom (C) Premanufactured (P)           | Tech. all on custom                            | C, P             | C, P                 | C, P                        |
| 15 | Does any CD or online product replace paper         | No                                             | NR               | Graingers            | InfoTrac, Old Journals      |
| 16 | Commercial Databases such as BRS, Dialog            | No                                             | NCLS, OCLC       | No                   | No                          |
| 17 | Flow problems?                                      | No                                             | None anticipated | No                   | Yes, lines at peak time     |

## Furniture/Equipment

Facsimile machines (FAX), and local area networks have made little impact on the public libraries surveyed. While some libraries have a network for their personal computers for staff and Livermore has a port for community dial-up catalog access, most libraries surveyed do not yet have community network access. Some anticipate a network in their cooperative, or locally, in the future. Pleasanton reports that a request for procurement of a local network for community dial-up access has been placed. FAX machines are generally available for the use of the staff in some libraries, they are not yet widely available for the public.

The change that personal computers for patron usage has made on the interior design is that in some libraries, study rooms are set aside for computers. These arrangements were never needed in pre-computer days. Six of nine libraries have personal computers available for the public to use (refer to Tables 1, 2 , 3; line 13). The number of computers that are available ranges from one to five.

## Electricity

Planning for the electrical aspect of automation is of major importance and all of the requirements for power should be assessed and carefully spelled out before equipment is ordered and installed. Electrical wiring for automation is more of a problem for older

**Table 3.** Los Angeles Branches, San Francisco Main, and Sacramento Main Library Space Planning and Furniture Survey Results

|    |                                                        | *Los Angeles* | *San Francisco* | *Sacramento*     |
|----|--------------------------------------------------------|---------------|-----------------|------------------|
| 1  | Cardholders                                            | NA            | 405,000         | 369365           |
| 2  | Library Gross Sq. Ft.                                  | NA            | 361,960         | NR               |
| 3  | Completion Date                                        | NA            | 1995            | 1992             |
| 4  | Technologies in plan                                   | Yes           | Yes             | Yes              |
| 5  | PAC Terminals                                          | 6-12          | 30              |                  |
| 6  | Wheelchair access to PAC                               | Yes           | Yes             | NR               |
| 7  | Children's Dept. PAC                                   | Yes           | Yes             | Yes              |
| 8  | Depts. PAC Introduced                                  | All           | All             | All              |
| 9  | Did hardware take up more, less or same area anticipated | Same        | Same            | Same             |
| 10 | CD-ROM/Products                                        | Yes           | Yes             | Yes              |
| 11 | Network                                                | NR            | Planned         | No               |
| 12 | Public Fax                                             | Planned       | Planned         | Yes              |
| 13 | Public Computers                                       | 1-2           | NR              | 3 or 4           |
| 14 | Furniture: Custom(C) Premanufactured (P)               | C, P          | C, P            | C, P             |
| 15 | Does any CD or online product replace paper            | No            | NR              | NR               |
| 16 | Commercial Databases such as BRS, Dialog               | 1             | Planned Ref.    | Dialog, staff use |
| 17 | Flow problems?                                         | NA            | NA              | Don't know yet   |

**Notes:** Abbreviations are used in the tables for the sake of brevity.

NA = Not applicable; NR = No response.

Lighting Key:
1. Diffused
2. Natural
3. Incandescent
4. Fluorescent
E. Excellent
S. Satisfactory
In. Inadequate

libraries than newer ones. Librarians in this survey have learned that they cannot merely run another extension cord and plug things in. One library reports that it cannot run two particular pieces of equipment at the same time, because doing so will overload the electrical system. Of the new libraries, three out of four (Table 5) report that the wiring is adequate for automation. Of the renovated libraries, three out of the four (Table 4) report that electrical wiring and outlets are inadequate. San Francisco plans to run conduit every four feet beneath all floors so that electrical lines can be accessed almost anywhere in the building.

One library is switching from a microfilm-based catalog which has been in place since 1964 to an online system. The advantage is that the electrical conduit for workstations is already in place, so that the workstations can be replaced almost one-on-one.

*Table 4.* Renovated Library Lighting and Wiring Results

|  | Circulation Area | VDT/PAC Area | Glare Problems | Ceiling/ Wall Colors | Wiring |
|---|---|---|---|---|---|
| Concord | 1, 2, 4/E | 2, 4/S to In | Yes | Light | Inadequate |
| Cupertino | 1, 4/S | 4/S | Yes, Little | Light Gray | Adequate |
| Dublin | 1, 2, 4/S | 2, 4/In | Yes | White & Wood | Inadequate |
| Livermore | 1, 2, 3, 4/E | 1, 2, 4/S | Very little | Light | Inadequate |
| Los Angeles Branches | 2, 4/NR | 2, 4/NRNR | Light colors mostly | Various Solutions | |

*Table 5.* New Library Lighting and Wiring Results

|  | Circulation Area | VDT/PAC Area | Glare Problems | Ceiling/ Wall Colors | Wiring |
|---|---|---|---|---|---|
| Fremont | 2, 4/S | 1, 2, 4/S | Little | White | Inadequate |
| Oxnard | 3, 4/NR | 2, 4/NR | NR | Light; Dk.trim | Adequate |
| Pleasanton | 2, 3, 4/S | 2, 4/S | Little | Light | Adequate |
| San Ramon | 2, 4/S | 2, 4/S | NR | Light | Inadequate |
| Sacramento | 2, 4/NR | 1, 4/NR | NR | Light | Adequate after rewire |
| San Francisco | 2, 4/NR | 1, 4/NR | NR | Light | Adequate/ Planning |

## Lighting

The survey answers seem to say that, besides choice of lighting sources, an important interior design element should be screen placement relative to light sources and light spill. All of the surveyed libraries use a combination of fenestration (natural light) and luminaries to light the general public service areas of the library. The most frequent lighting-related complaints are veiling reflections and glaring on screens. Optimum placement of the visual display terminal (VDT) in relationship to the light source in existing buildings is often hindered by constraints such as wiring, or other fixed furnishings.

Lighting solutions which are chosen for VDTs in public access catalog (PAC) areas in determining whether glaring and/or veiling reflections are a problem. Screen areas in renovated libraries generally experience some glaring and veiling reflections. New libraries report "some" to "very little" glaring in VDT areas. Lighting solutions for the screen areas for renovated libraries (Table 5) are combinations of natural light and fluorescent fixtures; diffused, fluorescent, and natural lighting; and just fluorescent lights. Libraries with a natural and fluorescent combination lighting solution report that it is generally inadequate (or unsatisfactory) due to placement of screens relative to natural (window) light. The other three renovated libraries, one of which also has a natural and fluorescent combination, report satisfaction with screen areas. New libraries utilize combinations of diffused, natural, and fluorescent; natural and fluorescent (3 libraries); and diffused-fluorescent lighting (2 libraries) for their VDT areas. Two of the new libraries report a "little" problem with glaring or veiling reflections on screens (Table 5).

Circulation desk lighting solutions which are utilized by all libraries in the survey are combinations rather than single lighting solutions, and are rated by the survey participants from satisfactory to excellent. Renovated libraries (Table 4) rate their circulation desk areas as satisfactory to excellent. Combinations rated as excellent are "diffused, fluorescent, and natural," in Concord, and "diffused-incandescent, fluorescent, and natural" in Livermore. Satisfactory combinations are "diffused, fluorescent" in Cupertino and "diffused, fluorescent, and natural" in Dublin. When Livermore renovated to move its circulation desk, more lighting had to be installed in order for the barcode readers to function.

New libraries (Table 5) report lighting solutions for the circulation desk which are: natural and fluorescent (4 libraries); incandescent and fluorescent; and natural, incandescent, and fluorescent. New libraries (which are open) report satisfactory results with these lighting combinations. Variables in these combinations such as placement of fenestrations and luminaries in relationship to the workstation or desk, bulb wattage, and light spill are not apparent in this report.

Libraries are finding various solutions to the problems of the veiling reflections and glaring on VDT screens. Use of remote control shades on clerestory windows in the Fremont Public Library is one solution for daylight variations. Screen guards are another way to handle the problem of veiling reflections. Screens that tilt and rotate can be moved to avoid a reflection or glare. Tinted or treated glass is used for windows in the newer constructions to screen out damaging ultraviolet rays. Some older libraries report that poor lighting conditions are a result of inadequate planning for the installation of automation.

The colors of ceiling, wall, flooring, and furnishings are taken into consideration for the purpose of lighting by most of the surveyed libraries. The use of antistatic carpeting in muted tones to prevent floor glare, is a common choice for newer libraries. Wall treatment (Tables 4 and 5) varies, but generally the ceilings and walls are done in pastels or white, with wood trim. Only the Los Angeles composite report of several branch libraries indicates that some libraries in the group are historical buildings with darker interior walls which may not be changed. Some of these historical branches are planning to add task lighting.

## CONCLUSION

Technologies for public service have made an impact on the interior design of public libraries. The interior designs for public service areas of new and recently renovated public libraries in California are being heavily influenced by lighting, furnishing, and space planning considerations for automation. In the area of space planning the biggest impact is on areas which are now planned for workstations for staff and for support of the online public access catalogs (OPAC). The specialized furniture and electrical wiring required for the "electronic island" of public access terminals is another impact of automation. Lighting solutions now take computer screens into consideration.

Perhaps one of the most significant impacts of the "Information Age" on public libraries is on how the library itself is perceived by both librarians and patrons. Interiors are becoming more focused on the library user. The library is no longer only a place to check out books, or review journals and references. A diverse range of services is often accommodated. Someone who needs a personal computer to type a term paper may find one available for use in the public library. The public library is the place for all kinds of people, be they senior citizens or youngsters looking for audio tapes, videos, or compact disks, or business people reviewing journal article citations from an online database search. New American citizens looking for ethnic materials or a place to learn English may satisfy their information needs at their local library. Hearing impaired users may find a telecommunications device for the deaf (TDD); or sight impaired patrons might turn to the public library for braille publications and talking books. The public library is often the place where exhibits influence and educate, where local history is archived, and so much more. These services are not especially an outgrowth of emerging technologies, but the embracing of those technologies has been a direct result of the same *user* focus that inspires these and many other services.

The typical California public library in this survey is both functional and aesthetic, and it is definitely the place to go for the information seeking community. The public library utilizes technologies for public service in order to provide information to their communities in the most expedient manner. Some libraries in this study have information desks in clear sight as a patron enters the library. At the same time, there is a feeling of spaciousness and orderliness. High clerestory windows stream natural light onto the reading areas, and signage gives clear directions to the business area, children's area, and the like. The online catalog "electronic island" is in view, with users perched on stools, busily searching for information. The facilities which are built or renovated are there to serve the library users. The books, journals, reports, videos, and so forth, in the public library, are the most available source of most kinds of information for the masses.

Space planning is probably the single most important aspect of facility planning, whether one is planning a new facility, or renovating

an older library building to accommodate automation. Space
planning involves the entire facility and how everything, including
automation, works together to present a viable resource for the
community. Flexibility within the spaces allocated for all the areas
that make up a library is necessary, because the information industry,
automation and its associated equipment is like a living organism,
growing and changing even as this paper is written.

According to the survey, libraries built prior to the sixties and even
into the eighties were ill prepared for automation. The struggle with
inflexible facilities is an ongoing battle for some. Some identified
problems with renovation of public libraries are: slab flooring which
causes problems for running electrical wiring; asbestos removal; not
enough terminals so that people wait in line, causing traffic flow
problems and congestion; line of sight problems due to terminals
being placed where they can be hooked up rather than the ideal spot;
poor ergonomics for workstation or computer users; and printer
noise control.

The design of a new building project or a renovation project best
begins with the mission statement. Consideration of the goals of the
library as a whole and also the goals and plans of the various areas
of the library follows its mission. How the various areas relate to
each other and what services are to be performed in the various areas
of the building should be determined before any layout can be drawn.
Here follows an example, which is the mission statement for the San
Francisco Public Library.

> The mission of the San Francisco Public Library is to be the focal institution
> for public supported access to information and knowledge in San Francisco.
> Special emphasis should be placed upon meeting the needs of San Francisco's
> economically and culturally diverse, and multilingual community, utilizing the
> most up-to-date technologies available (HBW Associates, 1990).

Ken Dowlin (1991), of the San Francisco Public Library, speaks
of the library as a "cultural anchor in the electronic age." He sees
the library as a community information and communication center.
The planned library ideally shall serve as a central computerized
database for access by constituents' home computers, and
disseminate information to the public through cable programs,
meetings, and electronic mail. In comparing the present library
building, which was built in 1916 to the building plan for 1995, the

major difference is that the old building is "building focused" while the newer building will be "user focused." The old building, like so many other older libraries, is inflexible, crowded, confusing, with a lack of flow, a lack of program space, impossible security, and only fifty percent of the building space assignable. The newer plan is for a facility that is flexible, and that allows for ease of access, handicapped access, and a controlled environment. An integral graphics design for flow will make moving from one area to another a natural course and will maximize technology. Focused centers will include: art and music, book, business, and technology center, government center, San Francisco history archives, service to the visually impaired, and service to the hearing impaired. The plan has a complete telecommunications system, and an infrastructure with the capacity to expand. Seventy-five percent of the building space will be assignable (HBW Associates, 1990).

A work flow scheme as well as establishment of patron traffic flow patterns is essential groundwork for planning. For each area, questions to ask include: what will be the major function or service performed; who will be the typical person performing this function; how many people will be at this place at the same time; what specifically will they be doing; does this person have specialized needs such as wheelchair access, hearing impairment, or sight impairment; how much time will the person spend at one sitting in this place; where will patrons and/ or staff be standing or sitting as they perform this research task, and what amount of space shall be allocated? Answers to these questions can help formulate a task-oriented sketch of each area.

While space planning must take flow, logical sequence of library operations, and patron traffic into consideration for the general plan, the final drawing of the area cannot be accomplished without a measurement of the equipment, shelving, and furniture that will occupy any given area. An equipment and furniture inventory, with an indication of the condition of the items and their expected useful life, as well as careful measurement of each piece is an important beginning. Equipment and associated peripherals such as number of computer terminals, screens, printers may be hypothetically drawn into place during the rough sketch phase. Placement and requirements for lighting, wiring and cabling, electrical outlets, telephone outlets for data communications, acoustics, and furniture space requirements are best determined even in the earliest stages of a plan.

Electrical outlets, data communications, phone outlets, and wiring for computerized services is an integral part of the space planning, regarding location of workstations, electronic islands of OPACs, and circulation desks. One cannot have enough telecommunications access planned for the future. Plans for future expansion of services should also be anticipated and worked into the total concept. While most libraries do not usually electrically wire the whole book stacks, reference areas and reader areas should have more electrical flexibility built in. A single CD-ROM jukebox may serve several workstations, serviced from a single desk. This means there could be cabling all over the place. Designers have to allow for that kind of maximum flexibility, so as to be able to move things around later on without major rewiring, which can be fairly costly.

Electricity for the various hardware components that are needed today may not be necessary tomorrow because of advances in microwave and fiber optics. Possibly, the electrical needs for the future could be even greater, if history is any guide. A number of wiring solutions are available: cellular floors with built-in channels for wiring, so one could merely punch a hole in the floor to access the wires to equipment at any future time. (San Francisco Public Library is planning that type of wiring solution.)

Other wiring solutions are flat cabling. Flat cabling is of somewhat limited value and can be costly to move around. It almost requires carpet tiles, can be easily abraded, and is difficult to splice. Initially it is less expensive than a cellular floor, but it is less flexible in terms of access. Power poles can be made reasonably attractive and are another option for retrofits. "Colorful" cable drops from the ceiling can also work aesthetically and may be the least expensive solution, with the only drawback being some loss of open ambience (Silver, 1991).

One of the most important findings in this survey regarding lighting for public libraries is that there should be a standard for lighting the VDT areas of the library. Placement of VDT screens in relationship to light sources should be an exact art, not something left to chance as it now appears to be. Librarians are interested in glare-free lighting, but don't always know how to achieve it. Whereas an office worker often has the ability to change or adjust lighting for a VDT, the patron areas of the library are not usually that flexible. Librarians did not seem to know how many footcandles were generally needed in the library for reading purposes.

The quality of lighting seems to be more important than the quantity. The Illuminating Engineering Society's 1988 standards drastically changed the amount of lighting recommended for reading. Where they used to specify 100 footcandles, now 50 footcandles is more often specified, with 75 footcandles specified in some areas of more intense work.

Lighting solutions are varied in the California Public Libraries. Use of energy conserving fluorescent lighting and clerestory windows seems to be an emerging trend for new California libraries (refer to Table 5). The most common electrical lighting for new public buildings uses dropped ceiling recessed, parabolic, diffused fluorescent lights in the stacks, the ideal place for lighting is parallel over the aisle center (Silver, 1991). None of the public libraries in the survey had used lights attached to stacks. Another style emerging is high intensity lamps on top of stacks designed to bounce light off of the ceiling. In older buildings, lights were placed in strips perpendicular to stacks so that they did not have to be changed if stacks were moved. Sometimes, fixtures are suspended over the stack aisles if the ceiling is too high.

*California Administrative Code, Title 24, of the State Building Code* states that the minimum handicap aisle is 36 inches. This factor was not present 10 years ago. The federal government is now adopting laws concerning the physically disabled which affect library facilities. The *Americans with Disabilities Act*, which was signed into law July 26, 1990, brought the access requirements into effect January 26, 1992. These laws make the strip fluorescent over the dead center aisle a sound construction practice, because the likelihood of stacks being moved or changed once in place is minimal, to not at all.

There is some movement toward task lighting, with wiring and light controls at each seat in some reading areas. The general lighting is softer, diffused to prevent glaring on screens and areas of high contrast. Table lamps or carrel lamps are sometimes integrated into plans to bring light to the work surface. The trade-off for using a table lamp is that the table has less work surface. Some libraries use technology plug strips at reader tables for laptop computer use, or individual portable reading lamps.

Furniture for automation for public libraries is a problem which the library furniture manufacturers have only recently begun to address. Meanwhile, several libraries in the survey had service desks and OPAC units custom made. But, there are now a number of manufacturers of computer furniture which accommodate library automated system arrangements.

One of the most important aspects concerning library furniture for automation is that *the furniture must be coordinated to fit the equipment*. In one library that the author visited, there was a computer on a *regular desk* in the staff area. It definitely appeared to be an ergonomic problem. A difficulty was encountered by another library when the computer furniture was ordered without taking into consideration their specific automated system. Needless to say, the furniture had to be altered to accommodate the equipment.

The "electronic island" seems to work well in public libraries for a number of reasons. The group of OPACs are usually situated in view of a reference or other staff area for the purpose of patron assistance and equipment security. This arrangement makes more efficient use of staff than when terminals are scattered throughout the library. Electrical wiring and cabling is less expensive to install for an electronic island in a renovated library, because it is centralized. The disadvantages of the electronic island are lack of privacy for patrons, noise, sometimes a lack of adequate wheelchair access, and sometimes the distance from actual references. A more conscious effort to insure a patron's privacy needs to be made on the part of those planning public access catalog terminals. Patrons strike up conversations at the OPAC or observe each other's searches. The accelerated conversational noise, combined with printer noise is something that public libraries did not have to deal with before automation. More needs to be done in order to insure the privacy of those searching for titles on the public access catalog. In all the libraries observed, none seem to have addressed that issue. No screening is available to prevent someone looking over another's shoulder while they search on the VDT screen for information. One library has side-screening in individual carrels, but someone might still view the screen from behind.

The interior designs for public service areas of new public libraries in California are being influenced by lighting, furnishing, and space planning considerations for automation. New interiors are becoming more focused on the library user, and librarians are finding that they must become more knowledgeable and more actively involved in the planning stages of new facility building. How public libraries are handling space planning, furnishings, and lighting for the addition or incorporation of technologies for public service are answered in part by the study. While the results of the interior design strategies of public libraries is the subject of this survey, the underlying emphasis in the responses of all the librarians is not so much *technology*, but *public service.*

## APPENDIX A

### Ergonomics

Seating, as well as adjustment ability of the seat, influences user comfort at a workstation. Stability and support of the back is the primary objective of an ergonomic chair. Posture, effort to maintain posture, back strain experienced, circulation, and freedom of movement are all affected by the design of a chair or seat. Chair components should allow for flexibility, adjustability, and safety. Whenever armrests are provided, they should not interfere with the ability to maintain posture. The seat depth should be between 15 and 17 inches and the width shall be at least 18.2 inches to accommodate average sized people. To avoid excessive pressure just behind the chair occupant's knee and lower thigh area, the front edge of the chair should ideally have a contoured relief design (ANSI X5.1-1985).

The seat height should allow the user to place their feet on the floor or on a support surface. Seat height adjustment range is ideally 16 to 20.5 inches (40.6 to 52.0 cm), and a foot support should be provided as an alternative for less than average height individuals. The range of seat height is based on the 5th percentile female height and the 95th percentile male height. Shoe heel height should be factored into the total measurement. The foot rest may be a part of the chair, the workstation, or a separate item (ANSI X5.1-1985).

In Section 8 of the ANSI/HSF-100 standard the minimum parameters needed to accommodate postures of most users when seated and performing tasks at a VDT is addressed. The fifth percentile female dimensions through the ninety-fifth percent male dimensions are the minimum parameters.

The minimum leg clearance under the work surface at the level of the knee should be the buttock-to-knee length minus the torso depth. Diffrient, Tilley and Bardagjy (1974) indicate torso depth for the 95th percentile male to be approximately 40 percent of the buttock-to-knee length. Therefore, the minimum leg clearance under the work surface at the level of the knee should

be approximately 60 percent of the buttock-to-knee length (ANSI /HSF Std.
No. 100-1988).

Care should be taken to place keyboards at a comfortable level
for library tasks. Keyboards are raised about two inches above desk
top. Keyboards should be about 24-26 inches from the floor. Placing
computer terminals on a standard desk top can produce ergonomic
problems. Visual display terminals should be positioned at the
operator's eye level, and the operator's elbows should be flexed at
a 70 degree angle to the keyboard.

In upright posture chairs for conventional CRT-based VDT
workstations, the maximum floor-to-seat height is determined by the
seated fifth percentile female operating a keyboard at a fixed-height
work surface. Under the most extreme circumstances, a seat height
greater than 52 cm (20.5 inches) may be necessary for the small female
to achieve an acceptable keyboard-to-forearm relationship (ANSI/
HSF Std. No. 100-1988, pp. 52-53).

Minimum viewing distance of the screen is equal to or greater than
30 cm (12 inches). Greater viewing distances are allowed, and some
people may require additional corrective or multisegmented lenses
to view text. The typical eye-to-keyboard distance when the VDT
user is seated in the upright position has been estimated to be about
45 to 50 cm (17.7 to 19.7 inches).

## APPENDIX B

### Survey Questions

Library:                              Year built/year renovated:
Population:
Facility contact; phone number:
  1.  In general, how do you think technologies for public service
      have affected the interior design of libraries?
  2.  Size of library: Overall assignable space.
  3.  Do you think that the age of building is a hindrance when
      retrofitting for technologies?
  4.  Does the interior design of the new library facility accommo-
      date, or have you changed the interior of an older library to
      handle electronic technologies which are available to the public

such as:

online public access catalogs (  )     Number (  )

computers(  )                    "           (  )

CD-ROMs(  )                  "           (  )

facsimiles(  )                 "           (  )

telecommunications(  )       "           (  )

commercial online databases(  )  "           (  )

or other technologies(  )      "           (  )

Yes _____ No _____ No, but in the planning stages.

_____

5. Approximately what percentage of total library (square footage) area is devoted to technologies for public service?

6. Did the hardware for the system take up
more (  )     less (  )
about the same amount of space anticipated (  )

7. If the new technologies take up more area than anticipated, what has been given up to accommodate it? (i.e. card catalog, reading tables, etc.)

8. In what department was the technology introduced? Check all, or note all that apply. Give the number of units (OPAC, etc.) installed for each area?
All (  )

Reference (  )              Number             (  )

Circulation (  )            "                  (  )

Children's (  )             "                  (  )

Any others, please list.      "                  (  )

9. When the library was renovated, what specific changes, if any, took place in the public areas? Why did these changes take place?

10. What codes, laws, or standards were referenced?

11. Traffic patterns in the library. Does the new technology affect the flow? Anticipated? Unanticipated?

12. What kind of lighting is utilized?
(1.) Parabolic or diffused
(2.) Natural
(3.) Incandescent
(4.) Fluorescent
Why?

What kind of lighting is used in the reading area? (1) (2) (3)
(4)

(A) At the circulation desk? (1) (2) (3) (4)

(B) In the stacks? (1) (2) (3) (4)

(C) Any task lighting under shelves? (1) (2) (3) (4)

(D) Where CRTs or Terminals are located? (1) (2) (3) (4)

For each, is the lighting inadequate? satisfactory? excellent?

| | | | |
|---|---|---|---|
| (A) | ( ) | ( ) | ( ) |
| (B) | ( ) | ( ) | ( ) |
| (C) | ( ) | ( ) | ( ) |
| (D) | ( ) | ( ) | ( ) |

How many footcandles, if known, are normal for each area?

(A)          (B)          (C)          (D)

13. Are windows taken into consideration for any lighting reason?
    Describe.

    Are wall or ceiling colors taken into consideration for the
    purpose of lighting?

    No ( )     Yes ( )        If yes, please explain.

    Were CRT screens taken into consideration when lights were
    placed?

    Discuss electrical wiring and outlets if applicable.

14. Briefly describe the furniture in the public areas.

    Custom made ( )or pre-manufactured furnishings ( )
    combination ( )

15. Does the technology in any way affect the type or amount of
    shelving in the library? Was shelving removed or omitted to
    make room for computers or other technologies?

    Approximate linear footage removed _____ .

    What took its place?

    Was it circulating or reference shelving?

16.If CD-ROM and online databases were added, were larger
   paper volumes of the same information discarded, or retained?

    If discarded was it for space consideration?          ( )

    If discarded was it for outdated material?            ( )

    Didn't replace paper.                                 ( )

17. If you had a chance to do it over, what would you change?

    What worked well?

    What could have worked better?

## NOTE

1. Some Los Angeles branches are renovations.

## REFERENCES

American Libraries Editorial Staff. 1990. "Interiors Showcase." *American Libraries* 22 (April): 346-48.

American National Standards Institute. 1985. *American National Standard for General Purpose Office Chairs-Tests.* ANSI X5.1-1985, New York: American National Standards Institute.

American National Standards Institute. 1988. *American National Standard for Human Factors Engineering of Visual Display Terminal Workstations.* ANSI/HSF Standard No. 100-1988, Santa Monica, CA: Human Factors Society, Inc.

Callori, B. 1991. Telephone Interview by Author, 8 October, Livermore, CA.

Cohen, A., and E. Cohen. 1979. *Designing and Space Planning for Libraries.* New York: R. R. Bowker.

Cohen, E. 1982. *Automation, Space Management and Productivity.* New York: Bowker.

Cohen, E., and A. Cohen. 1987. "Trends in Special Library Buildings." *Library Trends* 36 (Fall): 299-316.

Dahlgren, A. 1985. *Planning the Small Public Library.* Chicago: American Library Association.

Dix, W.S. 1990. "Space Planning for Technology." *American School and University* 62 (February): 64a-64b.

Dowlin, K. 1991. "A Presentation of the Plans for the New Main Library in San Francisco." California Library Association Conference Presentation, November 18, 1991, Oakland, CA.

*Encyclopaedia Britannica.* 1988. "The Art of Architecture." Chicago: William Benton. S. v.

Fraley, R.A., and C.L. Anderson. 1990. "Library Space Planning." In *How-to-do-it Manuals for Libraries,* edited by B. Katz. New York: Neal-Schumann, Inc.

HBW Associates, Inc. 1990. *A Building Program Prepared for the San Francisco Public Library.* Dallas, TX: HBW Associates.

Hensley, R.J. 1991. "Designing Libraries for the Twenty-first Century." California Library Association Conference Presentation, November 18, 1991, Oakland, CA.

Hodge, P., and B. Lawrence. 1983. "Planning for the Electronic Library." Pp. 13-24 in *Managing the Electronic Library: Papers of the 1982 Conference of the Library Management Division of Special Libraries Association,* edited by M. Koenig. New York: Special Libraries Association.

Holt, R.M. 1987. "Trends in Public Library Buildings." *Library Trends* 36 (Fall): 267-285.

_____. 1989. *Planning Library Buildings and Facilities: From Concept to Completion*. Metuchen: Scarecrow Press.

Horny, K. 1982. "The Electronic Library at Northwestern." Pp. 1-7 in *Managing the Electronic Library: Papers of the 1982 Conference of the Library Management Division of Special Libraries Association*, edited by M. Koenig. New York: Special Libraries Association.

Illuminating Engineering Society of North America. 1986. *Nomenclature and Definitions for Illuminating Engineering*. New York: Illuminating Engineering Society. IES RP-16-1986.

Kaser, D. 1985. "The Role of the Building in the Delivery of Library Service." Pp. 13-24 in *Access to Scholarly Information Issues and Strategies*. Ann Arbor, MI: Pierian Press.

Kurz, N.D. 1986. "Energy's Future." *Progressive Architecture* (April): 124-27.

Lancaster, F.W. 1982. *Libraries and Librarians in an Age of Electronics*. Arlington, VA: Information Resources Press.

*Library Journal*. 1988. 113 (Dec.): 51, 53, 60.

*Library Journal*. 1989. 114 (Dec): 54.

*Library Journal*. 1990. 115 (Dec):.60.

Lushington, N. 1983. "Designed for Users." *Wilson Library Bulletin* 58 (Nov): 204-5.

Lushington, N., and J.M. Kusack. 1991. *The Design and Evaluation of Public Library Buildings*. Hamden, CT: Library Professional Publications.

Main, L. 1989. *Advanced Microcomputer Applications in Libraries*. San Jose, CA: San Jose State University.

Michaels, A. 1988. "Design Today." *Wilson Library Bulletin* 62 (April): 55-57.

Morgan, E.L. 1991. "Implementing a Library Without Walls." In *Conference Proceedings of the Sixth Annual Computers in Libraries '91 Conference, Oakland, California, March 10-13, 1991*. Westport, CT: Meckler.

*National Electrical Code*. 1993. Quincy MA: National Fire Protection Association.

Ramsey, C.G., and H.R. Sleeper. 1989. *Ramsey/Sleeper Architectural Graphic Standards*, Student edition abridged from the 7th ed., edited by S.A. Kliment. New York: Wiley.

Rockwell, E. 1989. "Seven Deadly Sins of Architects." *American Libraries* 20 (April): 307, 341-42.

Rohlf, R.H. 1989. "Public Service Points." *American Libraries* 20 (April): 304-306.

Sannwald, W.W. 1991. *Checklist of Library Building Design Considerations* (2nd ed.). Chicago: Library Administration and Management Association a division of the American Library Association.

Sharma, H.D. 1970. *Library Building and Furniture*. Jullundur: Indian Bibliographic Centre.

Sherer, J.A. 1990. "Function vs. Beauty." *American Libraries* 21 (April): 312.

Silver, S. 1991. Telephone interview by author, 8 October, Livermore, California. Notes.

State Building Standards Commission, State and Consumer Services Agency. 1985. *California Administrative Code. Title 24, State Building Code*. Sacramento, CA: State of California Documents Section.

Thompson, G. 1989. *Planning and Design of Library Buildings* (3rd ed.). London: Butterworth Architecture.

Veatch, L. 1987. "Toward the Environmental Design of Library Buildings." *Library Trends* 36 (Fall): 371-373.

Waters, B.A., and W.C. Winters. 1987. "On the Verge of a Revolution: Current Trends in Library Lighting." *Library Trends* 36 (Fall): 327-349.

Waters, R.L. 1987. "The Library Building Tomorrow." *Library Trends* 36 (Fall): 455-473.

# TRANSFORMATIONAL LEADERSHIP IN ACADEMIC LIBRARIES:

## AN EMPIRICAL STUDY OF THE MODEL AND ITS RELATIONSHIP TO PERCEIVED ORGANIZATIONAL EFFECTIVENESS

Rosie L. Albritton

## INTRODUCTION

### A New Model of Leadership

As technological and societal changes continue to influence librarianship, higher education, and the nature of library services in academic libraries, there will be a corresponding need for leaders with vision and energy to foster the development of new paradigms (models) for library administration and management. In order to develop leadership potential in future library administrators and to promote the success of incumbents, it is necessary to determine

Advances in Library Administration and Organization, Volume 13, pages 57-110.
Copyright © 1995 by JAI Press Inc.
All rights of reproduction in any form reserved.
ISBN: 1-55938-931-1

leadership effectiveness and its relationship to organizational outcomes in academic libraries. Very little has been done on the study of leadership, as a researchable concept, in the field of library and information science.

Administration/management in librarianship has been well-covered in the literature, while there is a noticeable scarcity of material on library leadership. Dragon (1976) stated: "Leadership, although recognized by management theorists as an element in the management process, is generally neglected in the literature of library administration" (p. 1). Although researchers have reported findings on many aspects of leadership behavior over the past three decades, these studies have almost always been conducted in industrial, corporate, or military settings, and their relevance to libraries is unknown. This study is designed to provide data that will be useful in (1) making comparisons between leadership in university libraries and leadership in other formal organizations; (2) evaluating effective organizational leadership in university libraries; and (3) testing the feasibility of replicating research previously conducted in other fields.

Management and leadership are explained in the recent literature (Bass, 1990a) as two separate hemispheres. Managers tend to work within defined bounds of known quantities, using well-established techniques to accomplish predetermined ends. The leader's task is to provide all persons connected with an organization, some vision of what its mission is and how it can be reached more effectively. Bennis (1973) distinguished leadership from administration/management:

> Leadership is the capacity to infuse new values and goals into the organization, to provide perspective on events and environments which, if unnoticed, can impose constraints on the institution. Leadership involves planning, auditing, communicating, relating to outside constituencies, insisting on the highest quality of performance and people, keeping an eye out for forces which may lead to or disable important reforms. Administration is managing given resources efficiently for a given mission. Leaders question the mission (pp. 83-84).

Researchers usually define leadership according to their individual perspective and the aspect of the phenomenon of most interest to them. After a comprehensive review of the leadership literature, Stogdill (1974) concluded that "there are almost as many definitions of leadership as there are persons who have attempted to define the concept" (p. 259).

The focus of much of the study and research on leadership models has been on the determinants of leadership effectiveness. Leadership has been defined in terms of individual traits, behavior, and influence over other people, interaction patterns, role relationships, occupation of an administrative position, and perception by others regarding legitimacy of influence. Behavioral and social scientists have attempted to discover what traits, abilities, behaviors, sources of power, or aspects of the situation determine how well a leader is able to influence followers and accomplish group objectives. The reasons why some people emerge as leaders and the determinants of the way a leader acts are other important questions that have been investigated, but the predominant concern has been leadership effectiveness.

## Leadership Research and Theory

Historically, the study of leadership shifted from trait theory (1920s-late 1940s) to behavioral theories (late 1940s-to early 1960s) to contingency theories (late 1960s to the present). During the trait and behavioral eras, researchers were seeking to identify the "best" leadership style. Chemers (1984) explained that earlier researchers failed to recognize that no single style of leadership is universally best across all situations and environments. Emphasis was placed on the leader and somewhat less on leader-follower relations and the situation. The multimodel approach of contingency theory (Fiedler, 1967; House, 1971; Vroom and Yetton, 1973) introduced the idea that the most appropriate leadership in terms of follower outcomes was a function of situational factors (i.e., subordinate, task, and/or group variables). With House's path-goal theory (1971) and Hollander's definition of leadership (1978), authors introduced the idea that the leader offered the inducement as a reward in exchange for the exertion of effort on the part of the followers. Burns (1978) called this transactional leadership; one person taking the initiative in making contact with others for the purpose of the exchange of valued things. The willingness of followers to accept leader influence depended upon a process of exchange in which the leader gave something and received something in return (Hollander, 1978). This type of leadership emphasized follower satisfaction and acceptance of the leader (path-goal theory) and stressed an approach that considered the quality of the relationship between the leader and followers. Just as the rejection of the trait emphasis in favor of behavioral models may have led to an inappropriate de-emphasis of individual differences, so the subsequent shift to contingency models tended to minimize the importance of interpersonal trust (Yetton, 1984). According to Chemers (1984), the contingency approaches provided a secure foundation for a new leadership era, one focused on values, needs, and motives of both leaders and followers.

Each new era of leadership research represents a higher stage of development in leadership thought processes than the preceding era. The study of leadership, as described earlier, has evolved through eight eras before reaching the transformational leadership level: personality, influence, behavioral, situational, contingency, transactional, anti-leadership, and the culture era. The transformational era represents the latest phase in the evolutionary development of leadership theory. Its dramatic improvement over the previous eras lies in the fact that it is based on intrinsic, as opposed to extrinsic motivation. Also, in comparison with the transactional era, leaders must be proactive rather than reactive in their thinking; radical rather than conservative; more innovative and creative; and more open to new ideas (Bass, 1985a). Here, leadership exercises influences to produce enthusiastic commitment by subordinates, as opposed to reluctant obedience or indifferent compliance (Yukl, 1989). Tichy and Ulrich (1984) additionally state that transformational leadership is essential during organizational transition, by creating visions of potential opportunities and instilling employee commitment to change.

Burns (1978) differentiated carefully between transactional and what he called transformational leadership; the latter "occurs when one or more persons engage with others in such a way that leaders and followers raise one another to higher levels of motivation and morality" (p. 20). This transformational leadership approach has received increasing attention in the literature.

Transformational leadership, as defined by Burns (1978) and Bass (1985a), represents an important addition to previous conceptualizations of leadership. Researchers in search of a new leadership paradigm have reanalyzed the concept of transformational leadership, as described by James MacGregor Burns in his Pulitzer prize-winning book, *Leadership* (1978). Burns defined leadership as "inducing followers to act for certain goals that represent the values and the motivations—the wants and the needs, the aspirations and expectations—of both leaders and followers" (p. 19). For Burns, the essence of leader-follower relationships become the interaction of persons with different levels of motivation and power potential in pursuit of a common or at least a joint purpose.

*Research on the Bass Transformational Model and the MLQ*

In 1985, Bernard Bass proposed a *new model* of leadership, based on the work of James M. Burns (1978), in which he described leaders as *transformational or transactional*. Bass theorized that there is a certain kind of leader who is capable of inspiring subordinates to heights they never intended to achieve. He referred to these leaders

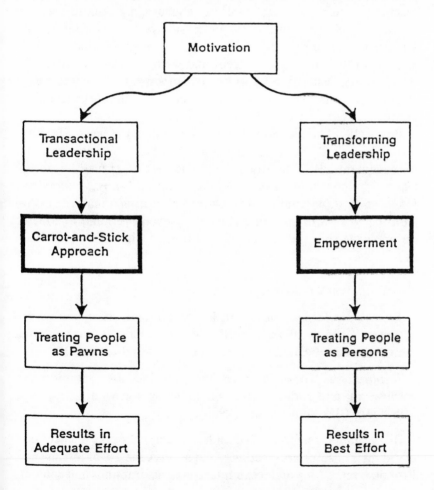

**Figure 1.** Transformational versus Transactional Leadership

as transformational. The transactional leader, on the other hand, is rooted in two-way influence: a social exchange in which the leader gives something and gets something in return (Bass, 1985a), as illustrated in Figure 1.

In his book, *Leadership and Performance Beyond Expectations*, Bass (1985a) stated that the transactional leader recognizes what subordinates want to derive from their work and provides appropriate rewards for expected performance. That is, he or she responds to subordinates' immediate self-interest (p. 11). He described the transformational leader as: (a) motivating subordinates to do more than they ever expected to do by raising their level of awareness and consciousness about the importance and value of reaching designated outcomes; (b) encouraging subordinates to transcend their own self-interest for the sake of the organization; and (c) altering subordinates' need levels on Maslow's hierarchy or expanding their portfolio of needs and wants (p. 20). For Bass "the transactional leader works within the organizational culture as it exists; the transformational leader changes the organizational culture" (p. 24).

Burns (1978) had identified these two types in the field of political leadership, and Bass applied the concepts to organizational management. He identified four factors of transformational leadership (*charisma, inspiration, individualized consideration, and intellectual stimulation*), two factors of transactional leadership (*contingent reward and management by exception*) and one factor on nonleadership (*laissez-faire*), as shown in Figure 2, and defined as follows.

### Transformational Leadership Factors

*Idealized influence* (*charisma*). The leader has a vision and a sense of mission. Gains respect, trust, and confidence. Acquires strong individual identification from followers (Bass and Avolio, 1990b).

*Inspirational.* The leader gives pep talks, increases optimism and enthusiasm, and communicates his or her vision with fluency and confidence (Bass and Avolio, 1990b).

*Intellectual stimulation.* The leader actively encourages a new look at old methods, fosters creativity, and stresses the use of intelligence. Provokes rethinking and reexamination of assumptions and contexts on which previous assessments of possibilities, capabilities, strategies, and goals were based (Bass and Avolio, 1990b).

*Individualized consideration.* The leader gives personal attention to all members, making each individual feel valued and each individual's contribution important. Coaches, advises, and provides feedback in ways easiest for each group member to accept, understand, and to use for personal development (Bass and Avolio, 1990b).

## Transactional Leadership Factors

*Contingent reward.* Contracts for an exchange of rewards for effort and agreed upon levels of performance. Gives individual a clear understanding of what is expected of them (Bass and Avolio, 1990b).

*Management-by-exception.* Intervenes only if standards are not met or if something goes wrong (Bass and Avolio, 1990b).

## Laissez-Faire (Nonleadership Factor)

Indicates the absence of leadership, the avoidance of intervention, or both. There are generally neither transactions nor agreements with followers. Decisions are often delayed; feedback, rewards, and involvement are absent; and there is no attempt to motivate the followers or to recognize and satisfy their needs. The leader is uninvolved, withdraws when needed, is reluctant to take a responsible stand; believes the best leadership is the least leadership (Bass and Avolio, 1990b).

The instrument developed by Bass (1985a) to quantitatively assess the constructs of his model is the *Multifactor Leadership Questionnaire* (*MLQ*). The MLQ has been found to be reliable and valid as the result of exhaustive research since the early 1980s. A detailed description of the MLQ, including scale and factor structure, items associated with each factor of the model, and psychometric data on reliability and validity is provided in the Methodology section of this paper.

Since Bass published his research results (1985a), a number of studies have been conducted investigating the effects of transformational/transactional leadership in organizations. "The results are encouraging both in terms of the basic propositions of the model and

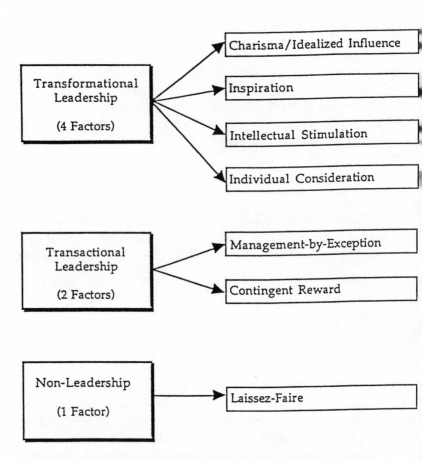

**Figure 2.** Transformational versus Transactional Leadership Model: Seven Factors as Measured by the Bass MLQ

in regards to the overwhelming evidence supporting the notion that transformational leadership seems to exist at many levels in a variety of organizational settings" (Avolio and Bass, 1988, p. 29).

Evidence of transformational leadership has been found in the military as well as in industrial and educational settings. Singer (1985) had 38 randomly selected New Zealand company managers complete the MLQ. Two ratings were obtained: one of an ideal leader followed by a rating of the immediate superior. For ratings of the real leader, the mean ratings on the transformational factors were more highly correlated than those on the transactional factors with perceived leader's effectiveness and job satisfaction.

Seltzer and Bass (1987) asked 294 part-time MBA students to complete the MLQ describing their superior. Additionally 73 managers (near MBAs) were described by their subordinates. "Hierarchical regressions for Bass' (1985) transformational leadership model show that it adds to initiation and consideration in explaining the variance of subordinate's satisfaction and rating of leader's effectiveness" (p. 2).

In a study done in a corporation specializing in the express delivery of goods and information, Hater and Bass (1988) found support for the hypothesis that managers identified as top performers would be rated higher on transformational leadership of subordinates than a randomly chosen group of managers.

Bass, Avolio, and Goodheim (1987) examined how world-class leaders differed on the five transformational and transactional leadership factors. The subjects in this study were 149 undergraduate business students who completed the multifactor leadership behavior questionnaire as if they were subordinates of one of the 68 world-class leaders whose biography they had read. Additional ratings were done by persons who had not read the biography of their chosen person. This study provided empirical verification that "respondents were able to reliably differentiate between transformational and transactional qualities of different leaders" (p. 14).

In terms of the application of the model to practice, Bass and his associates have focused on the inspirational processes of leadership, aspects of learning to share the visionary outlook, developing transformational leadership beyond the decade of the 1990s; confirmation studies that further support the augmentation effect of transformational factors beyond transactional factors; emphasis on the four I's of the model—Inspirational motivation, Intellectual stimulation, Individualized consideration, and Idealized influence (Charisma), (Bass, 1989; Bass, 1990b; Bass and Avolio, 1990b; Seltzer and Bass, 1990; Seltzer, Numerof, and Bass, 1989; Avolio, Waldman, and Yammarino, 1991).

The transformational leadership model represents a significant qualitative step beyond previous leadership models, and is changing the focus of leadership research in two ways. First, research is moving away from the issue of solely rational models of supervisory behavior. Earlier leadership models were generally rational approaches and prescriptions as to how a supervisor should deal with a subordinate. Second, transformational models, starting with the work of Burns

(1978) and Bass (1985a), are pursuing the issue of using and dealing with emotion in the leadership process. For many the issue is equated to the distinction between leadership and management (Clover, 1990).

Bennis and Nanus (1985) stressed that leadership is the pivotal force behind successful organizations and that, in the creation of vital and viable organizations, a new vision is required. They further stated the following:

> Nothing is more central to modern organizations than their capacity to cope with complexity, ambiguity, uncertainty—with spastic change. In an era of rapid change, it becomes necessary for organizations to be more future-oriented...This makes leadership all the more necessary today as compared with more stable times when the relationship between organizations and the environment was better understood... (Bennis and Nanus, 1985, pp. 226-227).

Tichy and Devanna (1986) supported many of the same themes; they described transformational leadership as being about "change, innovation, entrepreneurship" (p. 27). In-depth interviews with 11 corporate organization executives demonstrated that transformational leadership can be likened to a discipline with predictable steps and that corporate transformation can be seen as a drama in three acts: (1) recognizing the need for revitalization; (2) creating a new vision; and (3) institutionalizing change. Characteristics of the Tichy-Devanna transformational leader included: (a) identification of self as a change agent; (b) courage; (c) belief in people; (d) being value driven; (e) willingness to admit mistakes; (f) ability to deal with complexity, ambiguity, uncertainty; and (g) being a visionary.

Fiedler and House (1988) in their review of leadership theory and research cited several studies conducted by Bass and his associates using the MLQ (i.e., Hater and Bass, 1988; Avolio and Bass, 1988; Pereira, 1986; Bass, 1985a; Bass, Avolio, and Goodheim, 1987) and concluded the following:

> ...findings are impressive because they have occurred in India as well as in the United States (Pereira, 1986), and because the correlations between transformational leader behavior, followers' performance and satisfaction are significantly higher under transformational than transactional leaders. Finally, the correlations between transformational leader behaviors and ratings by followers and superiors are consistently above 0.50 and often as high as 0.70...empirical studies lend support to the charismatic and

transformational theories...correlations between follower satisfaction and performance are consistently high compared with prior field study findings concerning leader behavior (pp. 81-82).

Bass and Avolio (1990c) further explain the impact of the new model on current leadership research:

> The constructs of transformational and transactional leadership form a new paradigm for understanding the effects of leadership on individual, team and organizational development. This new paradigm builds on earlier paradigms of autocratic versus democratic leadership, directive versus participative leadership, task versus relationship-oriented leadership, which have dominated research on leadership selection, training and development for the past half century (p. 231).

## A New Model of Organizational Effectiveness

The emerging shift in leadership research (Cummings, 1981) accompanied a similar shift in organizational behavior research. The literature of organizational effectiveness is devoted to determining what denotes effectiveness for an organization, how to measure it, and ultimately, how to increase it. Cameron (1981a) was the first to identify indicators of organizational effectiveness in college and university settings. Over the past two decades, little agreement has existed regarding the meaning and proper assessment of organizational effectiveness.

In studying organizational effectiveness in academic libraries, researchers have primarily focused on developing specific, practical output measures for evaluating library services to users. However, the larger issues of the conceptual basis for such measures, with appropriate statistical methods for developing and validating effectiveness studies have rarely been addressed.

McDonald (1987) conducted a study of library-wide organizational effectiveness in academic libraries, and selected Cameron's comprehensive framework for addressing organizational effectiveness from several competing theoretical models. McDonald then constructed a model of library organizational effectiveness upon which further research and theory development can build; by establishing criteria for assessing academic library organizational effectiveness and developing an instrument, the *Academic Library Effectiveness Questionnaire* (ALEQ), to measure the construct.

McDonald's ALEQ was found to measure twenty dimensions of effectiveness in small academic libraries. Thirteen of these were designated as major dimensions, and these were organized into four *Domains of Library Effectiveness* (see Appendix A-1). These were:

- *Domain I: Major Resources*—library collection adequacy; staff size and diversity; and institutional (college or university) support for the library.
- *Domain II: Services*—use of external library collections; cooperative associations; and professional service by librarians.
- *Domain III: Library Stake-Holder Interaction*—library/user's shared goals; staff development; librarian/faculty relations; shared organizational direction; and evaluation of the library.
- *Domain IV: Access*—use of library collections and physical organization of the collection.

The remaining seven factors (see Appendix A-2) revealed by McDonald's study were designated as *Minor Dimensions of Library-Wide Organizational Effectiveness*. These were staff morale; collection development; facilities; library perception of college needs; management techniques; materials control; and faculty involvement in materials selection.

The ALEQ instrument for assessing academic library effectiveness will be described later in greater detail under Methodology.

## Statement of the Problem

The theoretical constructs presented by Bass and his colleagues, such as, Bass and Avolio (1990), provide a model of organizational leadership that seeks to explain differences in outstanding and ordinary leadership. Based on earlier research findings, as described earlier, transformational and transactional leadership both appear to be related to organizational outcomes such as effectiveness, satisfaction, and extra-effort of subordinates. However, transformational factors seem to have incremental effects on these outcomes, above and beyond that of transactional factors, thus suggesting that differences in transactional and transformation leadership may also differentiate outstanding and ordinary leaders. The transformational model seems to have research potential for studying academic library management by providing the following: (1) a systematic approach for exploring leadership behavior as a means of enhancing the overall administration and management of libraries and (2) a conceptual link between the behavior of library administrators and performance outcomes related to organizational effectiveness. But it does not appear that the transformational model has been tested in libraries. Any possible application of the model to library and information science would be limited by this lack of empirical investigation.

Exactly how and to what degree a leader affects the organization has been the subject of some research and much speculation. Even though the problem is yet to be resolved, any additions to the body of knowledge of leadership contributed by research should be of value to both those who administer libraries and to those who educate future library administrators, because of the importance of leadership as a key element in the understanding of the functioning of the organization.

Researchers, as noted earlier, have gathered results using the Bass *MLQ* that have been encouraging in establishing the basic propositions of the transformational model. Findings on the model indicate that transformational leadership has been positively correlated with how effective the leader is perceived to be by subordinates, how much effort subordinates say they will expend for the leader, how satisfied the subordinates are with the leader, and how well subordinates performed as rated by the leader. In the same studies, transactional leadership was also positively correlated with these outcomes, but in general, the correlations were considerably less clear than those found for transformational leadership. Studies also indicate that transformational leadership is not uncommon in different organizational settings, nor is it limited to executives and world-class leaders. Some degree of transformational leadership was being practiced at the most senior levels down to first-level management in industrial settings, among students, and from lieutenant to lieutenant colonel in the military (Bass, 1985a; Avolio and Bass, 1987).

An exploratory pilot-study of the transformational versus transactional leadership model in academic libraries was conducted by Albritton (1990). Data were collected from seven medium-sized academic libraries. The pilot-study was designed to answer the following research question: Will transformational and transactional leadership patterns, as defined by the Bass Multifactor Leadership Questionnaire (MLQ), appear in academic libraries in a similar configuration as found in studies of other organizations? The results revealed that the leadership profiles were typical of patterns in the model, with minor differences observed when compared with norms from previous studies.

## Purpose of the Study

The overall purpose of this research was to increase the base of knowledge that concerns the development of leaders and leadership processes in university libraries. It was presumed that the outcomes of this study could ultimately influence how library administrators and managers facilitate and promote the improvement of library organizational effectiveness. Toward that end, this study tested the Bass and Avolio (1990c) transformational versus transactional model to determine if it would appear in university libraries, and further sought to determine if the leadership model was related to perceptions of organizational effectiveness as defined by Cameron (1981a) and McDonald (1987).

The study was designed to determine whether perceptions of transformational leadership were present in the sample from medium-sized university libraries, and if these perceptions were related to perceived library organizational effectiveness (see Detailed Research Model in Appendix B). The components of this new leadership model were investigated by testing the transformational factors for any incremental effect in organizational effectiveness beyond that produced by the transactional leadership factors. The study also examined the influence of selected demographics of the respondents on their perceptions of leadership behavior and organizational effectiveness. Therefore, the major research objective of this study was to determine whether transformational leadership was associated with dimensions of organizational effectiveness by respondents from an academic library setting, and if their perceptions were influenced by selected demographics.

While the primary intentions of this study were to focus on the exploration of a model of transformational versus transactional leadership and an organizational effectiveness model, the secondary intentions of the study were: (1) to apply theoretical and methodological foundations of recent developments in leadership research to the study of leadership in library and information science; and (2) to validate and extend the use of the MLQ instrument to leader/follower behavior in university libraries.

## Research Questions and Hypotheses

*Research Questions*

1. Will the transformational versus transactional leadership model of organizational leadership appear in a sample from a group of university libraries in configurations similar to those found in studies of other formal organizations?

2. Will the academic library effectiveness model of organizational effectiveness appear in a sample taken from university libraries in a configuration similar to the McDonald (1987) model?

3. What is the relationship between perceptions of transformational leadership and perceived organizational effectiveness in university library settings?

4. Will selected demographic characteristics of respondents influence their perceptions of transformational versus transactional leadership, and perceived organizational effectiveness in university libraries?

Based on the reports of prior research on the transformational leadership and organizational effectiveness models that led to the formulation of the research questions stated previously, the following hypotheses were derived and tested.

*Hypotheses*

**Hypothesis 1.** The transformational versus transactional model of leadership, as measured by the MLQ, will appear in a sample from a group of university libraries in configurations similar to those found in studies of other formal organizations. This includes four transformational factors— Charisma, Inspiration, Intellectual Stimulation, and Individual Consideration and two transactional factors— Contingent Reward and Management-by- Exception.

**Hypothesis 2.** The academic library effectiveness model of organizational effectiveness, as measured by the McDonald Academic Library Effectiveness Questionnaire (ALEQ), will appear in a sample of university libraries in configurations similar to those found in McDonald's (1987) study. Twenty

organizational effectiveness dimensions—13 major dimensions and 7 minor dimensions—can be identified.

**Hypothesis 3.** Transformational leadership as perceived by
respondents to the MLQ will be more highly correlated than
transactional leadership with perceptions of library
organizational effectiveness, in university libraries, as
measured by the Bass MLQ leadership factors, and
dimensions of organizational effectiveness from the
McDonald ALEQ.

Research question 4 was not developed into a testable hypothesis
in this study. This question was approached as a means of extending
and supporting findings and results from testing the four stated
hypotheses. In order to interpret the findings and to assess possible
causal priorities of the investigated variables, other variables in the
form of demographic "controls" were introduced into the research
models for further analysis.

## Scope and Limitations of the Study

The primary theoretical limitation of this study was the restriction
of the concept of leadership to that found in formal organizations.
This investigation explored the relationship between transformational leadership (Bass, 1985a), and organizational effectiveness
(Cameron, 1978; McDonald, 1987) in selected university library
settings. Other limitations of the study resulted from the fact that
respondents were members of the administration and management
teams of the university libraries from which the sample was drawn;
the philosophical and historical positions of the libraries studied were
not examined and their effect, on both leadership and organizational
effectiveness, was not measured. The use of a mail-questionnaire to
gather the data; the manipulation of data limited to answering only
questions raised; and results of other similar studies, weighed heavily
in confirming the findings of the study.

It should also be noted that the group of respondents selected for
this study, including the library directors, were viewed for purposes
of this study as representatives of the major subunits of an academic
library who influence direction and functioning of the organization

in terms of decisions concerning library resources and operations. Faculty, university administrators, students, and other potential recipients of library services were omitted from the study since its focus was on investigating perceptions of leadership and organizational effectiveness held by the "internal dominant coalition," as defined by Thompson (1967).

The study was also limited by the static nature of the data. That is, no attempt was made to gather information on changes within the libraries over time. Rather, the data represent conditions as they existed in the libraries at the time of the survey. It is possible that over time effectiveness profiles may change in response to environmental influences, internal decisions to emphasize certain dimensions, and changes in the universitys' strategic emphases. But questions such as how did the libraries develop their leadership and effectiveness profiles and how their profiles changed over time will not be answered by this study.

In addition, although the sample of university libraries chosen represented a wide range of demographic indicators, the presence of additional demographic factors in other institutions may hinder some aspects of generalizability.

## Assumptions Underlying the Study

1. Transactional and transformational leadership as defined are distinct; because they are different, they have the potential of having different impacts on organizational effectiveness. Since change is an implicit goal of transformational leadership, the assumption that change is desirable is implicit.

2. Perceptions of the respondents are useful measures of both leadership behavior and the presumed outcomes. Samples will be assumed to reflect those of the constituencies from which they are drawn in university libraries at large.

3. The respondents will respond truthfully and accurately to the instruments and their questions.

4. Members of the internal dominant coalition and their subordinates in each library will have sufficient knowledge to make meaningful judgments regarding characteristics of leadership and effectiveness.

## LEADERSHIP RESEARCH AND LIBRARIES

Even though the transformational model has been cited and referred to in the library and information science literature, (i.e., Albritton and Shaughnessy, 1990; Carver, 1989; Riggs, 1988a, 1988b, 1993; Sheldon, 1991), it does not appear that this leadership model has been empirically tested in libraries. The present study represents the first attempt to apply the transformational versus the transactional models of leadership to the study and research of organizational leadership and management development in libraries. As mentioned earlier, there is currently a paucity of research on formal organizational leadership in the field of library administration and management. A survey of the literature revealed ten dissertations that studied some aspect of formal managerial leadership in libraries, from 1968 to 1989. Only seven of these studies investigated leadership behavior in academic libraries. Most of these dissertations applied well-known leadership theories and instruments. (i.e., the Ohio State Leadership studies model that generated the Leadership Behavior Description Questionnaire (LBDQ), or Fiedler's contingency model and his leadership effectiveness instrument, the Least Preferred Co-Worker (LPC) Scale).

During the 1970s and early 1980s, library leadership research followed the trend of leadership theory and development as described earlier, and most of the research was implemented using the Leadership Behavior Description Questionnaire (LBDQ) developed by Stogdill and Coons (1957) that emerged from the Ohio State Studies during the 1940s. Research studies using the LBDQ began with a study on public libraries by Schneider (1968), and continued through the study done in academic libraries by Young (1980). Other studies in academic libraries using the LBDQ include Binder (1973) and Comes (1978), and in public and state libraries respectively by Dragon (1976) and Rike (1976). Other major theories and instruments applied to the study of library leadership include the application of the Contingency Theory of Lawrence and Lorsch (1976a, 1976b), and Fiedler's Leadership Effectiveness theory (1967). Benson (1977) examined the applicability of the Lawrence and Lorsch (1976a, 1976b) contingency theory in six academic libraries.

Other recent studies on leadership roles and organizational effectiveness in the academic library were conducted by Euster (1986) on the role of the academic library director within an environmental framework; by Mitchell (1987) who tested the validity of Fiedler's Contingency Model of Leadership Effectiveness for predicting the effectiveness of academic library department heads; and by Carlson (1989) who studied the perceptions of administrative leadership of five directors of large research libraries using a qualitative case study approach.

Also during the late seventies to mid-eighties, six dissertations were completed that focused on the managerial aspects of the library director's role. Three of these studies focused on academic libraries. Metz (1977) investigated the differences among academic directors in their basic orientations to management. He used a survey instrument to measure the behavioral and attitudinal dimensions of the question. Lee (1981) studied the role of the academic library director in the organization by applying the framework of role theory and interviewing 20 directors and Holmes (1983) examined the academic library director's perceived power and its correlates. The management behavior focus of these studies are all relevant to the history of the study of leadership theory in libraries, when they are viewed as describing implicit leadership behaviors of library administrators.

## METHODOLOGY OF THE STUDY

This study was designed as a correlational (ex post facto) field study. Correlational research is defined by Meyers and Grossen (1974) as follows:

> In correlational research, the investigator enters the to-be-sampled population with two or more dependent measures. His intent is to determine the degree to which these various measures are related to one another...The issue, then, whether variations in X correspond or correlate with variations in Y (pp. 190-191).

The correlational design is most often identified with survey research in many social science fields. Survey research involves asking a random sample of individuals to respond to a set of questions about their backgrounds, past experiences, and attitudes considered relevant to the research topic. Data were collected for this study within the existing library settings, with two survey questionnaires, one measuring Transformational Leadership, the other Organizational Effectiveness.

## Transformational Leadership Instrument

The instrument used to assess perceptions of transformational and transactional leadership behavior was the *Multifactor Leadership Questionnaire - 5R* [*MLQ*] (Bass and Avolio, 1990c). The questionnaire contains 80 items, 70 of which require a rating-scale. Individuals completing the MLQ Rater Form evaluate how frequently, or to what degree, they have observed their leader engage in a specific behavior. Leaders completing the MLQ Self-Rating Form similarly evaluate how frequently, or to what degree, they believe they engage in the same types of leadership behavior toward their supervisees. Directions for completing the survey, and the questions on both the Leader and Rater forms are identical, except for the use of pronouns to designate the status of the respondent.

A five-point ratio-based rating scale for rating the frequency of observed leader behaviors is used for both forms and bears a magnitude estimation-based ratio of 4:3:2:1:0, according to a tested list of anchors provided by Bass, Cascio, and O'Connnor (1974). The five response choices ranged from "frequently, if not always" to "not at all."

Four of these factor subscales (charisma, individualized consideration, intellectual stimulation, and inspiration) are measures of transformational leadership. Two of the factor subscales, contingent reward and management-by-exception, measure transactional leadership. A seventh factor, laissez-faire, is considered to measure nonleadership. In addition to these 70 items, respondents were asked to give biographical and demographic information. The remaining four items address biographical data and allowed respondents to rate the degree of confidence they have that the MLQ identifies and measures the appropriate range of leadership behaviors. To date, data collected on the MLQ indicate substantial support for the construct validity of the theoretically and empirically based factors that comprise it (Bass and Avolio, 1990b). The scales have been found internally consistent, and test-retest reliability over a six-month interval has been good.

## Organizational Effectiveness Instrument

McDonald (1987) defined effectiveness as "successful organizational transactions" as perceived by a group of specified library decision makers. The results of his study showed that library effectiveness may be a multidimensional construct. Thirteen major dimensions and seven minor dimensions were identified. McDonald selected Cameron's comprehensive framework from among the competing theoretical constructs of organizational effectiveness as the most suitable reference for addressing academic library organizational effectiveness. He then constructed an empirically defensible model upon which further research and theory development can build by establishing criteria for assessing academic library organizational effectiveness and developing an instrument to measure the construct. A list of questions was then developed from the criteria suggested by Cameron and Whetten (1983). The intent of this questionnaire is to measure the trait indicators of effectiveness as perceived by the defined set of library decision makers. Each criterion is keyed to the question or questions used to assess the presence or extent of the effectiveness trait embedded in it. In most cases, more than one question was used to capture the full meaning of a particular criterion. All of the questions asked for the respondent's perceptions.

The questionnaire that emerged has 95 items that represent thirteen major dimensions and seven minor dimensions of academic library effectiveness. A seven-point ratio-based rating scale for rating the perceived frequency and amount of observed library organizational effectiveness characteristics is used and bears a magnitude estimation-based ratio of 6:5:4:3:2:1:0, according to a tested list of anchors provided by Bass, Cascio, and O'Connor (1974). The seven response choices are as follows: "extremely important to not at all important"; "very successful to unsuccessful"; "very true to very untrue"; "highly typical to highly untypical"; "more than adequate to inadequate"; and from "all to none."

## Subjects

The subjects used in the study were university library directors, members of their administrative/management teams, and other library staff members randomly selected from medium-sized U.S. academic libraries holding membership in the Association of College and Research Libraries (ACRL) or the Association of Research Libraries (ARL). The selection of medium-sized university library settings was the result of a preferential choice of the researcher,

primarily due to extensive experience and educational background
in these libraries as an administrator, management intern, and
research investigator. The *ACRL University Library Statistics: 1987-
88* (1989), and the *ARL Statistics: 1989-90* (1991), were used to
develop a list of 104 medium-sized U.S. university libraries that had
a total staff size of between 80 to 300 people and a full-time appointed
library director. Medium-sized libraries were identified by combining
Rank Order Tables for Staff Size from the ARL and the ACRL
Statistics, and selecting those libraries from the bottom 50 percent
of the ARL list and the top 50 percent of the ACRL table.

## Sample Size and Data Collection

In terms of sample size for generating results from the application
of correlational statistical procedures, that is, descriptive correlations,
multiple regressions, and factor analyses, the number of respondents
(cases) available for this study were considered acceptable. From pilot
data and the literature review on the MLQ and the transformational
leadership model, the range of correlations (r), multiple correlations
(R), and coefficients of determination (Rsq) were estimated, as
described by Cohen and Cohen (1983).

Letters and consent forms inviting participation in the study were
sent to 90 library directors by applying proportional stratified
random sampling to the sampling frame of 104 medium-sized
libraries. The characteristics of these libraries are shown in Table 1.
Ninety letters of invitation were mailed in order to obtain as close
to 30 directors as possible (the sample size determined by the Cohen
and Cohen [1983], power analysis calculations). Pilot study data
collected prior to the study indicated a volunteer acceptance rate of
approximately 35 percent.

Twenty-three directors agreed to have their libraries participate.
From each of the 23 lists of library staff, six were randomly selected
to evaluate leadership behavior and organizational effectiveness. The
two questionnaires were mailed along with a cover letter to the 23
directors and 138 library staff reporting to them (a total of 161
potential cases). Of the 322 questionnaires (161 MLQ and 161 ALEQ)
distributed, 292 (91%) were returned, and 291 were useable for data
analysis. The 23 libraries in the sample provided responses from 146
individuals, well within the acceptable sample size range established
by power analysis, for the quantitative data analysis needed for

**Table 1.**   Profile of 90 University Libraries Invited to Participate
in the Study*

*Campus Data:*

| | |
|---|---|
| Enrollment: | |
| Total Full-Time** | 3,300-22,800 |
| Total FTE (Part-Time)** | 360-18,000 |
| Graduate Full-Time | 300-5,500 |
| Graduate FTE (Part-Time) | 20-7,400 |
| Faculty: | 300-1,600 |
| Ph.D. Fields: | 5-90 |
| Ph.D.'s Awarded: | 10-280 |
| *Library Statistics:* | |
| Volumes in Library: | 470,000-3,100,000 |
| Current Serials (Total): | 4,000-26,000 |
| Professional Staff (FTE): | 20-90 |
| Non-Professional Staff (FTE): | 30-150 |
| Total Staff: | 80-300 |

**Notes:**   *All data reported in this profile are estimates, as a result of rounding statistics reported to ACRL or ARL.
**Includes both undergraduate and graduate students.

**Table 2.**   Profile of 23 Participating University Libraries*

*Campus Data:*

| | |
|---|---|
| Enrollment: | |
| Total Full-Time** | 3,300-22,100 |
| Total FTE (Part-Time)** | 450-14,000 |
| Graduate Full-Time | 700-4,800 |
| Graduate FTE (Part-Time) | 150-5,600 |
| Faculty: | 300-1,600 |
| Ph.D. Fields: | 10-80 |
| Ph.D.'s Awarded: | 20-250 |
| *Library Statistics:* | |
| Volumes in Library: | 504,000-2,300,000 |
| Current Serials (Total): | 4,000-22,800 |
| Professional Staff (FTE): | 20-80 |
| Non-Professional Staff (FTE): | 40-150 |
| Total Staff: | 100-300 |

**Notes:**   *All data reported in this profile are estimates, as a result of rounding statistics reported to ACRL or ARL.
**Includes both undergraduate and graduate students.

testing the hypotheses addressed in this study. Table 2 indicates the characteristics of the 23 libraries in the sample.

## Analysis of Data

Both the leadership and effectiveness data were entered into a *SPSS-X* (Norusis, 1988) Release 4.1 IBM vm/cms mainframe computer statistical analysis program to determine associations between variables, that is, correlations, multiple regressions, means tables and ANOVA. Factor analysis and principal components analysis were applied to both questionnaires to confirm the presence of the models and the variance of the associated factors and dimensions.

Multiple regression models were used to determine the incremental contribution of transformational leadership above that of transactional leadership; to predict extra effort; satisfaction, and effectiveness in university library settings, as well as the ability of transformational and transactional leadership factors to predict organizational effectiveness in terms of dimensions of effectiveness in university settings. Selected "background" or "status" variables (type of respondent-self or rater; respondents' institutional support-private or state funded; respondents' library governance style-faculty status or other; respondents' library type-research or college) were added to the analyses as control variables. Descriptive statistics were calculated for questionnaire items and demographic data from both survey instruments.

# RESULTS AND FINDINGS OF THE STUDY

**Hypothesis 1.** The transformational versus transactional model of leadership, as measured by the MLQ, will appear in a sample from a group of university libraries in configurations similar to those found in studies of other formal organizations. This includes four transformational factors—Charisma, Inspiration, Intellectual Stimulation, and Individual Consideration, and two transactional factors—Contingent Reward and Management-by-Exception.

Hypothesis 1 was supported by results of this study. The university library sample tested in this study displayed perceptions of transformational and transactional leadership behaviors that are similar to the Bass model and other previous research on transformational and transactional leadership.

In testing hypothesis 1, the factor analysis of the MLQ were compared with other factor analyses of the MLQ in order to discover whether similar factors could be accounted for in the library sample. The results of the factor analyses accounted for 67 percent of the common variance measuring the initial six factors extracted, and represented all of the Bass transformational and transactional leadership factors, as indicated in Table 3. Some factor-groupings revealed slight deviations from the original Bass findings, but were almost identical to results obtained in settings similar to libraries, that is, colleges, universities, private and public secondary educational institutions. Overall, the university library sample displayed perceptions of leadership behavior that were very similar to the Bass model. Transformational and transactional leadership characteristics were confirmed and measured by six factors: charisma, inspiration, individualized consideration, and intellectual stimulation representing perceptions of transformational behaviors; and contingent reward and management-by-exception, representing perceptions of transactional behaviors. See results of factor analyses of the MLQ, with factor loadings and items representing each factor for the university library sample in Appendix C.

***Table 3.***   MLQ Factor Analysis: 6 Factors-Initial Statistics

*Principal-Components Analysis (pc)*

*6 Factors Extracted with Varimax Rotation:*

Initial Statistics: (Factors with eigenvalues above 1.00)

| Factor | Eigenvalue | % of Common Variance | Cumulative % |
|---|---|---|---|
| 1 | 25.56 | 44.8 | 44.8 |
| 2 | 4.00 | 7.0 | 51.8 |
| 3 | 2.96 | 5.2 | 57.0 |
| 4 | 2.32 | 4.1 | 61.1 |
| 5 | 1.97 | 3.4 | 64.5 |
| 6 | 1.53 | 2.7 | 67.2 |
| 7 | 1.35 | 2.4 | 69.6 |
| 8 | 1.27 | 2.2 | 71.8 |
| 9 | 1.09 | 1.9 | 73.8 |
| 10 | 1.04 | 1.8 | 75.6 |

**Table 4.**   Internal Consistency Reliabilities of the Scales Forming the
University Library Transformational Leadership Model

| Scale | Number of Items | Cronback Alpha |
| --- | --- | --- |
| Charisma | 11 | 0.954 |
| Inspiration | 8 | 0.899 |
| Individualized Consideration | 9 | 0.924 |
| Intellectual Stimulation | 9 | 0.894 |
| Contingent Reward | 10 | 0.885 |
| Management-by-Exception | 10 | 0.474 |
| Laissez-faire | 10 | 0.709 |
| Effectiveness | 3 | 0.872 |
| Extra-Effort | 3 | 0.740 |
| Satisfaction | 2 | 0.925 |
| (N = 140) | | |

*Note:*   Defived from the Multifactor Leadership Questionnaire

Cronbach alphas were computed for each of the six subscales of the University Library Model derived from the factor analysis to test reliability and internal consistency of the measures. As shown in Table 4, with the exception of the scale for management-by-exception, reliability coefficients are well within the acceptable range of .70 and above. This suggests that the MLQ factors as derived from this sample are composed of items with high internal consistency. The subscales were computed by summing response-items (variables) of the MLQ that loaded on each of the six factors.

The results of the factor analysis of the MLQ and the reliability coefficients of the scales derived from the factor loadings confirmed the suitability of the model for this sample, and indicated perceptions of transformational as well as transactional leadership behaviors. The results further indicated that the university library sample tested in this study displayed perceptions of administrative leadership behavior that are were similar to the transformational model described by Bass and his colleagues.

**Hypothesis 2.**   The academic library effectiveness model of organizational effectiveness, as measured by the McDonald Academic Library Effectiveness Questionnaire (ALEQ), will appear in a sample of university libraries in configurations similar to those found in McDonald's (1987) study. Twenty organizational effectiveness dimensions—13 major dimensions and 7 minor dimensions—can be identified.

Hypothesis 2 was also supported. Academic library organizational effectiveness was perceived by the respondents from the sample of university libraries tested in this study as a multidimensional construct, similar to the McDonald (1987) model.

A principal components "confirmatory" factor analysis was conducted on the questionnaire items of the ALEQ to determine if perceptions of the McDonald dimensions of library organizational effectiveness were present in the university library sample. An examination of the initial statistics revealed that the same variables that McDonald noted as being excluded from his final factor model would need to be also "deleted" from the library data. The criteria-rationale for dropping 27 ALEQ variables from further analysis included: variables with communalities below .4000; high intercorrelations with similar variables—above .7500. The remaining sixty-eight variables were re-factored using maximum likelihood extraction and oblique rotation. The resulting initial statistics are shown in Table 5. These results revealed nineteen factors with eigenvalues approaching 1.00, that accounted for 75.7 percent of the common variance.

**Table 5.** ALEQ Factor Analysis-Initial Statistics

| | Maximum Likelihood Extraction (ml) 19 Factors Extracted with Oblique Rotation: | | |
| Factor | Eigenvalue | % of Common Variance | Cumulative % |
| --- | --- | --- | --- |
| 1 | 16.30 | 24.0 | 24.0 |
| 2 | 5.70 | 8.4 | 32.3 |
| 3 | 3.31 | 4.9 | 37.2 |
| 4 | 2.88 | 4.2 | 41.5 |
| 5 | 2.65 | 3.9 | 45.4 |
| 6 | 2.50 | 3.7 | 49.0 |
| 7 | 2.05 | 3.0 | 52.0 |
| 8 | 2.03 | 3.0 | 55.0 |
| 9 | 1.81 | 2.7 | 57.7 |
| 10 | 1.58 | 2.3 | 60.0 |
| 11 | 1.50 | 2.2 | 62.2 |
| 12 | 1.45 | 2.1 | 64.3 |
| 13 | 1.27 | 1.9 | 66.2 |
| 14 | 1.26 | 1.9 | 66.2 |
| 15 | 1.18 | 1.7 | 69.8 |
| 16 | 1.10 | 1.6 | 71.4 |
| 17 | 1.03 | 1.5 | 72.9 |
| 18 | .96 | 1.4 | 74.3 |
| 19 | .95 | 1.4 | 75.7 |
| 20 | .90 | 1.3 | 77.0 |
| 21 | .88 | 1.3 | 78.3 |

As an indicator of the reliability of the Academic Library Effectiveness Questionnaire (ALEQ) with this sample, Cronbach alphas were computed for each of the 19 subscales derived from the factor analysis. The subscales were computed by summing response-items (variables) of the ALEQ that loaded on each of the 19 factors. As shown in Table 6, with the exception of five minor subscales (Faculty Selection of Materials, Cooperative Associations, Librarian/User Relations, and Materials Control) the reliability coefficients are within the acceptable range of .70 or higher; Continuing Education of staff at .672 is also acceptable when rounded to the nearest tenth at .70. These coefficients are either equal to or exceed the alphas reported by McDonald.

The nineteen factors were separated according to McDonald's approach into two groups. Factors with two variables were designated as "minor," while those with three or more variables were designated as "major." McDonald followed Thurstone's (1947)

**Table 6.** Internal Consistency Reliabilities of the Scales Forming the University Library Effectiveness Model

| Scale | Number of Items | Cronback Alpha |
| --- | --- | --- |
| Organizational Planning | 7 | .886 |
| Adequate Collection & Budget | 7 | .915 |
| Organization of Collection | 4 | .769 |
| Staff Size & Diversity | 4 | .870 |
| Library/Faculty Relations | 4 | .740 |
| Evaluation of Library | 4 | .848 |
| I.L.L. Services | 4 | .700 |
| Use of Library Collections | 3 | .714 |
| Access to Research Resources | 4 | .773 |
| Administrative Leadership | 6 | .835 |
| Staff Moral | 2 | .867 |
| Professional Development | 2. | 746 |
| Faculty Selection of Materials | 2 | .482 |
| Collection Development Policy | 2 | .847 |
| University Support for Library | 2 | .756 |
| Cooperative Associations | 2 | .425 |
| Librarian/User Relations | 2 | .638 |
| Continuing Education of Staff | 2 | .672 |
| Materials Control | 2 | .579 |

(N = 146)

**Note:** Derived from the McDonald Academic Library Effectiveness Questionnaire

**Table 7.** Comparison of Academic Library Effectiveness Models

| Albritton Medium-Sized University Libraties | | McDonald Small Academic Libraries | |
|---|---|---|---|
| 19 Dimensions | | 20 Dimenions | |
| 10 Major Dimensions | #Items | 13 Major Dimenions | #Items |
| Adequate Library Collection | | Library Collecltion Adequacy | 7 |
| and Budget | 7 | Use of Collections | 3 |
| Organization of Collection | 4 | Use of Outside Coll. | 5 |
| Staff Size & Diversity | 4 | User's Shared Goals | 4 |
| Faculty Relations | 4 | Staff Development | 4 |
| Evaluation of Library | 4 | Staff Size & Diversity | 5 |
| I.L.L. Services | 4 | Faculty Relations | 5 |
| Use of Library Collections | 3 | Evaluation of Library | 4 |
| Access to Research Resources | 4 | Cooperative Assoc. | 3 |
| Administrative Leadership | 6 | College Support | 4 |
| | | Shared Organizational Direction | 6 |
| 9 Minor Dimensions | | Librarian Prof. Serv. | 4 |
| Staff Moral | 2 | Collections' Physical Organization | 4 |
| Professional Development | 2 | | |
| Faculty Select Materials | 2 | 7 Minor Dimensions | |
| Collection Development | 2 | Staff Morale | 2 |
| University Support | 2 | Collection Development | 2 |
| Cooperative Associations | 2 | Facilities | 2 |
| User Relations | 2 | Perception of College Needs | 2 |
| Continuing Education | 2 | Faculty Involvement | 2 |
| Materials Control | 2 | Management Technique | 2 |
| | | Materials Control | 2 |

suggestion that there be at least three variables for each factor in exploratory analysis. The nineteen-factor library model revealed in this study was compared with the distribution of the twenty factor library effectiveness model produced by McDonald, as shown in Table 7.

The oblique rotation of the matrix produced a configuration of factors that were similar to McDonald's results in its general overall structure: total number of factors extracted from ALEQ; number of major versus minor factors, and replication of approximately 50 percent of McDonald Dimensions in the Library Model. See Appendix D for detailed results of the factor analysis of the ALEQ, with factor loadings and items representing ten major and nine minor factors that emerged from the university library sample.

**Hypothesis 3.** Transformational leadership as perceived by respondents to the MLQ will be more highly correlated than transactional leadership with perceptions of library organizational effectiveness, in university libraries, as measured by the Bass MLQ leadership factors, and dimensions of organizational effectiveness from the McDonald ALEQ.

Hypothesis 3 was also supported by the results of this study. Transformational leadership was perceived as having more effect than transactional leadership by respondents from the sample of university libraries tested with the McDonald ALEQ on the following dimensions of effectiveness: evaluation of the library, adequate collection and budget, university support, organizational planning, administrative leadership, professional development, organization of collections, staff morale, and continuing education.

This hypothesis was tested by applying hierarchical multiple regression analysis. A series of multiple correlations were computed and the relationships between the leadership factors from the MLQ and the organizational effectiveness dimensions from the ALEQ were analyzed using a hierarchical multiple regression analysis. Independent measures were transactional and transformational leadership factors measured by the Bass *Multifactor Leadership Questionnaire (MLQ)* (1990c). Dependent variables used were the academic library organizational effectiveness dimensions measured by the McDonald *Academic Library Effectiveness Questionnaire (ALEQ)* (1987). Nineteen multiple regression analyses were computed, entering first the control variables, then the transactional factors and finally the transformational factors to test the increment added by the latter set of predictors.

Each of the nineteen dimensions of McDonald's effectiveness dimensions were used as dependent variables in separate multiple regression analyses, with the values of the transactional leadership factors (management-by-exception and contingent reward) and the values of the transformational factors (charisma, individualized consideration, intellectual stimulation, and inspirational leadership) as independent variables. All four control variables (position, support, faculty status, and library type) were significantly related (correlated) with at least one or more of the ALEQ dimensions, and were entered into the regression analyses.

Table 8 presents a summary of the results of the hierarchical multiple regressions of the four control variables and the MLQ

**Table 8.** Summary of Significant Hierarchical Regressions of Selective Demographics and MLQ Leadership Factors as Predictors of ALEQ Effectiveness Dimensions
(With Controls)

| | MultR | Rsq | F | SigF | SigFch |
|---|---|---|---|---|---|
| *Organizational Planning* | | | | | |
| Position | .337 | .113 | 18.16 | .00 | .00** |
| Faculty Status | .387 | .150 | 12.40 | .00 | .02* |
| Transactionals | .411 | .169 | 4.64 | .00 | .49 |
| Transformationals | .504 | .254 | 4.52 | .00 | .01** |
| *Administrative Leadership* | | | | | |
| Position | .357 | .127 | 20.72 | .00 | .00** |
| Support | .424 | .180 | 7.62 | .00 | .01** |
| Transactionals | .435 | .189 | 5.32 | .00 | .47 |
| Transformationals | .498 | .248 | 4.39 | .00 | .04* |
| *Professional Development* | | | | | |
| Faculty Status | .201 | .040 | 2.97 | .05 | .03* |
| Management-By-Exception | .348 | .121 | 3.80 | .00 | .01** |
| Contingent Reward | .348 | .121 | 3.14 | .01 | .96 |
| Transformationals | .439 | 1.93 | 3.18 | .00 | .02* |
| *Organization of Collection* | | | | | |
| Position | .194 | .038 | 5.54 | .02 | .02* |
| Library Group | .310 | .096 | 4.96 | .00 | .00** |
| Transactionals | .375 | .141 | 3.74 | .00 | .04* |
| Transformational | .436 | .190 | 3.12 | .00 | .02* |
| *Evaluation of Library* | | | | | |
| Position | .284 | .081 | 12.43 | .00 | .00** |
| Support | .357 | .127 | 5.06 | .00 | .03* |
| Transactionals | .360 | 1.29 | 3.39 | .00 | .62 |
| Transformationals | .411 | .169 | 2.71 | .01 | .04* |
| *Staff Morale* | | | | | |
| Position | .299 | .090 | 13.95 | .00 | .00** |
| Transactionals | .344 | .118 | 3.07 | .01 | .36 |
| Transformationals | .401 | 161 | 2.54 | .01 | .03* |
| *Adequate Collection* | | | | | |
| Faculty Status | 2.67 | .071 | 5.40 | .01 | .01** |
| Library Group | .338 | .115 | 6.03 | .00 | .01** |
| Transactionals | .356 | .127 | 3.31 | .01 | .45 |
| Transformationals | .393 | .154 | 2.43 | .01 | .05* |
| *University Support* | | | | | |
| Position | .244 | .060 | 9.01 | .00 | .00* |
| Support | .339 | .115 | 4.51 | .00 | .02* |
| Transactionals | .340 | .115 | 2.97 | .01 | .90 |
| Transformations | 3.87 | .150 | 2.34 | .01 | .03* |
| *Continuing Education* | | | | | |
| Control Variables (4) | .199 | .039 | 1.43 | .23 | .23 |
| Transactionals | .243 | .059 | 1.43 | .21 | .25 |
| Transformationals | .350 | .122 | 1.86 | .05 | .05* |

(continued)

***Table 8.*** (Continued)

|  | MultR | Rsq | F | SigF | SigFch |
|---|---|---|---|---|---|
| *Faculty Relations* | | | | | |
| Faculty Status | .742 | .551 | 86.42 | .00 | .00** |
| Support | .767 | .588 | 49.63 | .009 | .00** |
| Transactionals | .768 | .599 | 32.83 | .00 | .76 |
| Transformationals | .775 | .601 | 20.05 | .00 | .44 |
| *Materials Control* | | | | | |
| Position | .231 | .053 | 7.99 | .01 | .01** |
| Library Group | .469 | .220 | 13.12 | .00 | .00** |
| Transactionals | .484 | .234 | 6.99 | .00 | .30 |
| Transformationals | .504 | .254 | 4.53 | .00 | .27 |
| *User Relations* | | | | | |
| Position | .191 | .037 | 5.38 | .02 | .02* |
| Library Group | .363 | .132 | 7.08 | .00 | .00** |
| Transactionals | .378 | .143 | 3.80 | .00 | .95 |
| Transformationals | .399 | .159 | 2.52 | .01 | .45 |
| *Use of Collection* | | | | | |
| Support | .365 | .133 | 5.35 | .00 | .00** |
| Transactionals | .377 | .142 | 3.78 | .00 | .30 |
| Transformationals | .385 | .148 | 2.32 | .02 | .38 |
| *I.L.L. Services* | | | | | |
| Position | .257 | .066 | 10.02 | .00 | .00** |
| Library Group | .336 | .113 | 5.94 | .00 | .05* |
| Transactionals | .339 | .115 | 2.96 | .01 | .85 |
| Transformationals | .364 | .132 | 2.03 | .04 | .21 |
| *Cooperative Assoc.* | | | | | |
| Position | .266 | .071 | 10.80 | .00 | .00** |
| Transactionals | .339 | .115 | 2.96 | .01 | .45 |
| Transformationals | .357 | .127 | 1.94 | .05 | .75 |

$*p < .05$     $**p < .01$

*Transactional Factors Hierarchical Order:*                                    $(N = 144)$
Management-by-Exception
Contingent Reward
*Transformational Factors Hierarchical Order:*
Intellectual Stimulation
Individual Consideration
Inspirational Leadership
Idealized Influence (Charisma)

leadership factors on the ALEQ effectiveness dimensions. The control variables were entered into the regression equation first as additional independent variables to determine their effect on the variance of the dependent organizational effectiveness variable. They were then followed by the six leadership factors (transactionals and then transformational). The results indicate that of the 19 effectiveness dimensions analyzed as dependent variables, nine were significantly related to the leadership factors in association with one or more of the controls (organizational planning, organization of collections, professional development, administrative leadership, staff morale, continuing education of staff, evaluation of library, adequate collection/budget, and university support). Transformational leadership behavior, as measured by the MLQ, was perceived by the library sample as augmenting, or having more effect on the effectiveness dimensions than transactional leadership behavior. These findings suggest that perceptions of transformational leadership, by this sample, were associated with higher levels of planning, organizing, leading, evaluating, managing, and developing resources (collections, fiscal, and staff) in medium-sized university library settings.

All three hypotheses concerning the association of transformational versus transactional leadership with organizational effectiveness in medium-sized university libraries were supported by the findings from this particular sample. In general, the overall results of this study suggest that perceptions of leadership behavior (both transactional and transformational), by this sample, are associated with perceptions of library organizational effectiveness, satisfaction with the leader, effectiveness of the leader, and amount of extra effort by followers. The results of this study concerning the effectiveness of transformational versus transactional leadership model are quite similar to those found by previous research in other academic settings. (Kirby, King, and Paradise, 1992; Koh, 1991; King, 1989; Murray, 1988; Gillett-Karam, 1988; Hoover, 1987).

The present study also replicated and extended past research on academic library organizational effectiveness. The results largely confirmed previous conclusions reached by McDonald (1987) that library effectiveness may be a multidimensional construct, and that Cameron's (1978) model for effectiveness studies in educational institutions may be the most suitable reference for determining academic library organizational effectiveness.

## DISCUSSION OF FINDINGS

All three hypotheses concerning the association of transformational versus transactional leadership with organizational effectiveness in medium-sized university libraries were supported by the findings from this sample. As expected, "transformational" leadership was perceived by the library sample as augmenting, or having more effect on dimensions of organizational effectiveness, than did "transactional" leadership. While these findings agree with the conclusions of the research of Bass and his associates (Bass, 1985a, 1985b; Bass and Avolio, 1990; Hater and Bass, 1988; Seltzer and Bass, 1990; Waldman, Bass, and Yammarino, 1990), they have further substantiated that the model may have meaning and applicability to settings other than industrial and military settings investigated by earlier studies, and particularly to the academic library.

Based on the results of this study, the following conclusions may be drawn.

1. *The university library sample tested in this study displayed perceptions of transformational and transactional leadership behaviors that are similar to the Bass (1985a) model and other previous research on transformational and transactional leadership.*

All six of the Bass factors (charisma, inspiration, individualized consideration, intellectual stimulation, contingent reward, and management-by-exception) can be explained and accounted for in the six factor University Library Model of Transformational Leadership derived in this study. A definite clustering occurred, especially with charisma/inspiration (Factor I) and active/passive management by exception (Factors V and VI). This library model was found to consist of three "predominately" transformational factors and three "predominately" transactional factors as follows: Factor I—Charisma and Inspiration; Factor II—Individualized Consideration; Factor III—Intellectual Stimulation; Factor IV—Contingent Reward; Factor V—Management by Exception (active) and Factor VI—Management by Exception (passive). These results point out that charisma is the strongest component of this model. These findings appear to provide support for earlier research in academic settings by Murray (1988) and King (1989) that indicated the following: (1) a distinction between transformational leadership as depicted by charisma/inspirational leadership, and transactional leadership as displayed by management by exception; (2) contingent reward (a transactional factor by definition) tends to act as a "bridge" with transformational leadership; (3) intellectual stimulation (to a greater extent) and individualized consideration (to a lesser extent) share common themes with the dominant factor: charisma/ inspirational leadership.

The high intercorrelations of the transformational scales suggest that the scales are highly interrelated, so much so that they may be measuring a single construct rather than four. Correlations and factor loadings suggest that the charisma scale measures much of this single construct. The two transactional scales, contingent reward and management-by-exception, diverge, as evidenced by their weak correlation. While this confirms that two different factors are being measured, the correlation is so low that it could indicate the two factors do not converge into a solid measurement of the single construct of transactional leadership. Contingent reward actually correlates more highly with transformational scales than with the other transactional scale.

From an operational perspective, transformational scales of the MLQ are fairly adequate measures, especially as a measure of transformational leadership rather than as measures of distinct scales. Transactional measurement appears somewhat weaker and is somewhat more difficult to interpret and to use to support substantive interpretations and conclusions with confidence. The low internal consistency of the scale indicates a possible operational problem, although it is difficult to establish the source, and to determine whether the problem is operational, conceptual, or both. It appears that this study supports and confirms findings of other studies that have suggested that the management-by-exception scale adds little (or at least a lot less), to the exploration of transactional and transformational leadership.

Several researchers have reported low reliability coefficients for the management-by-exception factor (King, 1989; Murray, 1988; Bauman, 1988), as well as Bass and his colleagues. Bass and Avolio (1990c) cited consistently lower reliability for this factor across a variety of studies, and gave the following explanation: "...management by exception may be lower in reliability for reasons unique to that dimension...this construct may be represented by active and passive dimensions...management by exception also may be more situationally determined than the other scales, so individual differences are less consistent...however, since an item-by-item analysis is presented in the MLQ Profile for all factor scales, such slight decreases in internal consistency should pose no problems in using the respective scales for tasks such as training, counseling, and organizational development" (pp. 21, 23).

2. *Academic library organizational effectiveness is perceived as a multidimensional construct, similar to that described in the McDonald (1987) model, by the respondents from the sample of university libraries tested in this study.*

McDonald's (1987) research defined effectiveness as "successful organizational transactions" as perceived by a group of specified library decision makers. The results of his study indicated that academic library effectiveness may be a multidimensional construct as he identified thirteen major dimensions and seven minor dimensions. He summarized his research efforts as an attempt to "...measure library effectiveness in ways that will enable future investigators to predict effectiveness and subsequently to compare library with college organizational effectiveness...this research developed criteria for measuring library effectiveness, created and tested an instrument for measuring effectiveness" (pp. 28-29). McDonald tested and administered his questionnaire to small college libraries in several Middle Atlantic states. Sixty percent of the institutions had enrollments under 3,000, and only 10 percent of the 131 institutions had enrollments over 7,000. Approximately 83 percent of this sample had collections under 350,000, and only 7 percent had collections over 500,000. Thirty-two percent of his libraries were state supported, leaving 68 percent as private colleges (31% religious and 37% secular).

The present study replicated and extended McDonald's research on academic library organizational effectiveness to medium-sized university libraries. The results confirmed his finding that certain clusters of items pertaining to library characteristics related to acquisition of resources, the vitality of internal processes and practices, and organizational outcomes would emerge as factors, and that these could be grouped into dimensions for measuring effectiveness.

Beyond replication, this test of McDonald's model provided additional support for a multidimensional approach to assessing effectiveness in academic libraries while also producing a similar model for the larger university library. The respondents in this study represented libraries with collections ranging from 500,000 up to 2.3 million and with institutional enrollments up to 22,000. The sample consisted largely of state-supported universities with only 34 percent of the sample coming from privately-supported institutions. The University Library Effectiveness Model that emerged in this present study revealed nineteen dimensions: ten major and nine minor factors of effectiveness; compared to McDonald's twenty dimensions, represented by thirteen major and seven minor factors. Furthermore, the University Model which emerged in this study showed that all of McDonald's factors were accounted for either as "renamed" or "newly configured" dimensions: ten factors (53%) are replications of the original McDonald dimensions, and were not renamed; seven factors (37%) are new dimensions that required renaming; and two factors (10%) were renamed for clarity of interpretation.

The ten major dimensions identified in this research were: organizational planning, adequate library collection and budget, organization of collections, staff size and diversity, librarian/faculty relations, evaluation of library, I.L.L. services, use of library collections, access to research resources and administrative leadership. Of these ten major dimensions, the following five were found to be significantly related to, or influenced (either directly or indirectly) by the transformational and transactional leadership factors: organizational planning, adequate library collection and budget, organization of collection, evaluation of library, and administrative leadership. The nine minor dimensions identified by this investigation were: staff morale, professional development, faculty involvement in materials selection, collection development policy, university support, cooperative associations, user relations, continuing education, and materials control. Four of the minor dimensions were found to be also significantly related to, or influenced (directly or indirectly) by the leadership factors: staff morale, professional development, university support, and continuing education.

3. *Transformational leadership was perceived by respondents from the sample of university libraries tested with the McDonald ALEQ as having more effect than transactional leadership, on the following dimensions of effectiveness: evaluation of library, adequate collection and budget, university support, organizational planning, administrative leadership, professional development, organization of collections, staff morale, and continuing education.*

As mentioned earlier, these nine dimensions of university library effectiveness, as derived from the McDonald Academic Library Effectiveness Questionnaire, represent approximately 50 percent of the University Library Effectiveness Model, and were found to be related to the leadership factors. However, the substantive finding of this aspect of the results is that transformational leadership as perceived by this sample was more highly correlated than transactional leadership with library organizational effectiveness. In other words, perceptions of transformational leadership tended to augment, or have more influence on perceptions of organizational outcomes, and therefore had significant incremental effects on the predictability of organizational planning, organization of collections, professional development, administrative leadership, staff morale, continuing education, university support, adequate collection and budget, and evaluation of library. These findings suggest that perceptions of transformational leadership, as indicated in this sample, were associated with perceptions of higher levels of planning, organizing, leading, evaluating, managing, and developing resources (collections, fiscal, and staff), in medium-sized university library settings.

4. *The background, status, and other demographic characteristics of the respondents had a strong influence (direct and indirect) on the perceived effect of transformational and transactional leadership behaviors on leadership outcomes and dimensions of organizational effectiveness. The background characteristics found to have influence in this study were: leader versus follower; affiliation with privately or state supported institution; faculty status or other governance structure for librarians at the university; and affiliation with a research or college-level library.*

Several demographic variables identified in previous research as most likely to influence perceptions of leadership and effectiveness were tested as "controls" in the regression models with the six MLQ transformational and transactional leadership factors and dimensions of organizational effectiveness. The status variables given consideration were: gender, age, position, time in position, time in management or leadership position, size of staff, college or research library, faculty status of librarians, and privately or state supported institution. From this group of controls, only three demographic variables were significantly related to perceptions of organizational effectiveness: position of respondent in the library (management or staff); support of institution (private or state funded ); and faculty status of librarians. Gender of director, age of respondents, time in positions, time in management, size of staff, or type of university (whether college or research university), did not have significant relationships with either the leadership factors or the organizational effectiveness dimensions.

The results of the "controlled" investigations revealed the following:

1. *Leadership factors and demographics:* position (leader or follower) and support (private or state supported) were related to the respondents' perceptions (responses on surveys) of transformational and transactional leadership behaviors. This finding indicated that the position that the respondent held in the library (whether management or other) and the type of institution (whether private or state funded) where the respondent was employed may have influenced perceptions of transformational versus transactional leadership.

2. *Effectiveness dimensions and controls:* position (leader or follower) was related to the following effectiveness dimensions: perceptions of organizational planning, evaluation of library, administrative leadership, staff morale, and university support. This finding indicated that library directors and library staff varied significantly on their responses and that the "condition" of position did have some effect on perceptions of these five library organizational effectiveness dimensions.

Support (state or privately supported) was related to the following effectiveness dimensions: perceptions of administrative leadership, evaluation of library, and university support. This finding indicated that the type of institutional support (state or private) of the respondents' library had a significant effect on perceptions of library organizational effectiveness as measured by these three dimensions.

Faculty status (faculty status versus nonfaculty status) was related to: perceptions of organizational planning, adequate collection and budget, and professional development. This finding indicated that the respondents with and without faculty status varied significantly on their responses, and that the condition of faculty status did have some effect on perceptions of library organizational effectiveness as measured by these three dimensions.

## CONCLUSIONS AND IMPLICATIONS

The conclusions of this study are limited to the population of university libraries who participated in the study and are also limited by the use of perceptual self-report instruments rather than direct measures. Despite these limitations, the results of the study do suggest some implications for the practice of library management and administration, library education, staff development, and future research on leadership theories and libraries.

The ultimate objective of this research is to develop library leaders who would go beyond ordinary and expected performance, to engage in outstanding leadership. This study provides some evidence that certain factors of the transformational/transactional leadership model can indeed be used to enhance performance:

1.  The factor of charisma appears to be powerful in predicting satisfaction and effectiveness. This scale reflects the expression of enthusiasm, optimism, and confidence. Library leaders can be trained to develop these qualities and can be evaluated on their success in these areas.

2.  The personal attention measured by the individualized consideration factor and intellectual stimulation measured by that scale can also be taught as elements of leadership to library administrators. Since these concepts are important to the satisfaction and effectiveness of followers, individualized consideration and intellectual stimulation should be expected of library managers, and encouraged by library administration. The actual scales of the Bass MLQ may be suitable for evaluating the extent to which library managers and administrators employ transformational leadership skills and behaviors.

3.  In terms of transactional leadership, library administrators and leaders should be aware that rewards and contingent reinforcement may be transformational as well as transactional. They should be trained in using rewards to develop enhanced performance rather that using rewards which they control for only meeting the status quo or ordinary expectations. Academic libraries are labor intensive organizations whose most important resource is its staff.

The study also suggests guidelines to library educators who seek to improve the preparation of students for managerial and administrative library positions. Better understanding of theoretical foundations of leadership and management should improve the education given to new and potential leaders. This should also be of great importance for continuing professional development after library school.

This study of transformational leadership and leadership effectiveness is clearly only a beginning of further research on these models in libraries in general and in university libraries, in particular. Recommendations and suggestions for further research are as follows:

1.  Research should be conducted to further test, affirm, or expand the theoretical framework of transformational leadership in academic libraries with larger samples, and the application of recently developed analytical procedures for testing latent variables, that is, structural equation modeling, or causal modeling with LISREL (Joreskog and Sorbom, 1989) or EQS (Bentler, 1989).
2.  This study could be replicated by studying different types of libraries and information centers.
3.  The design of longitudinal studies should be encouraged to determine transformational leadership and effectiveness changes in libraries in general, and particularly university libraries, over time.
4.  Case studies and other forms of in-depth qualitative data collection and research methodologies should be conducted in libraries to determine similarities and differences in perceptions of transformational leadership and effectiveness and develop profiles from perspectives other than quantitative data and analyses.
5.  Studies should be designed that explore relationships between transformational leadership and other organizational concepts that are currently postulated as having important effects on leadership behaviors, that is, empowerment of followers, total quality management, power and status, creativity, innovative behavior, organizational culture, organizational climate, and self-managed groups.
6.  Studies should be designed that would look at antecedent conditions to the development of transformational leadership, such as, personality traits, values, attitudes, family and educational background, internal/external locus of control dispositions.

This study can also be the beginning of a body of research directed toward a clearer understanding of the critical characteristics and the multidimensional aspects of organizational effectiveness in libraries. As McDonald (1987) pointed out, in this broad area of organizational effectiveness research, little work has been done on the effectiveness criteria of university libraries. Researchers have focused on developing specific, practical output measures for evaluating library services to users, but the larger issues of the conceptual basis for such measures, or for library-wide organizational effectiveness with appropriate statistical methods for developing and validating measures have rarely been addressed.

Efforts to develop transformational leadership require that we do more than just increase specific skills. As this study and other related research indicates, transformational leadership is not a mysterious process, but a measurable construct, whereby the perceptions of identifiable behaviors such as the articulation of transcendent goals, demonstration of strong self-confidence and confidence in others, setting a personal example for followers, showing high expectations for followers' performance, and the ability to communicate one's faith in one's goals. Therefore, what is needed is training and education that promotes self-understanding, awareness, and appreciation of the range of potential leadership behaviors used by effective transformational and transactional leaders.

The theoretical framework of this study focuses on the effective leadership and management of libraries. The results of this study do not necessarily mean that university libraries have the same kind of leadership as industrial or corporate organizations, nor that one kind of leadership is better or worse than another. The study was designed to investigate one specific model of leadership, but leadership may indeed consist of more than transformational and transactional factors, and the author did not attempt to find one definitive strategy of leadership or of organizational effectiveness that could be universally be applied to all university libraries, or to other types of libraries. The model investigated was theoretical and represented a conceptual framework that attempted to describe relationships between organizational constructs which were operationalized as leadership factors, leadership outcomes, and effectiveness measures. However, since the study was guided by theory and tested under real conditions, the research should be helpful in bridging the gap between practice and theory. The patterns revealed by this study that appear to be similar to other research simply suggests that libraries and other formal organizations are similar in their patterns of perceptions of leadership behaviors and descriptions of effectiveness and outcomes. The findings of this research will help to increase awareness of the need to continue to investigate perceived leadership behaviors and their influence on perceptions of organizational and leadership effectiveness.

## APPENDIX A-1

### DOMAINS AND MAJOR DIMENSIONS
### of the
### Library-Level Organizational Effectiveness Model
### (Academic Library Effective Questionnaire: McDonald, 1987)

4 - Domains of Effectiveness          13 - Dimensions of Effectiveness

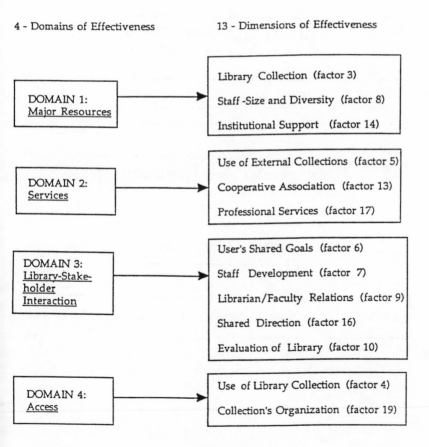

DOMAIN 1:
Major Resources

Library Collection (factor 3)

Staff -Size and Diversity (factor 8)

Institutional Support (factor 14)

DOMAIN 2:
Services

Use of External Collections (factor 5)

Cooperative Association (factor 13)

Professional Services (factor 17)

DOMAIN 3:
Library-Stake-
holder
Interaction

User's Shared Goals (factor 6)

Staff Development (factor 7)

Librarian/Faculty Relations (factor 9)

Shared Direction (factor 16)

Evaluation of Library (factor 10)

DOMAIN 4:
Access

Use of Library Collection (factor 4)

Collection's Organization (factor 19)

## APPENDIX A-2

MINOR DIMENSIONS
of the
Library-Level Organizational Effectiveness Model
(Academic Library Effectiveness Questionnaire: McDonald, 1987)

Staff Morale (Factor 1)

Collection Development (Factor 2)

Facilities (Factor 11)

Library Perception of Institution's Needs (Factor 15)

Management Technique (Factor 18)

Materials Control (Factor 20)

Faculty Involvement in Material Selection (Factor 21)

# APPENDIX B

## Detailed Research Model: Variables and Constructs

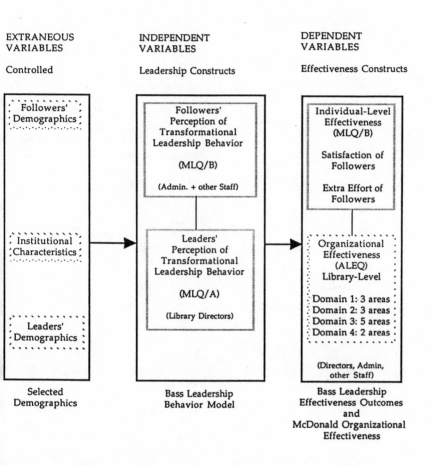

| EXTRANEOUS VARIABLES | INDEPENDENT VARIABLES | DEPENDENT VARIABLES |
|---|---|---|
| Controlled | Leadership Constructs | Effectiveness Constructs |

Followers' Demographics

Institutional Characteristics

Leaders' Demographics

Followers' Perception of Transformational Leadership Behavior

(MLQ/B)

(Admin. + other Staff)

Leaders' Perception of Transformational Leadership Behavior

(MLQ/A)

(Library Directors)

Individual-Level Effectiveness (MLQ/B)

Satisfaction of Followers

Extra Effort of Followers

Organizational Effectiveness (ALEQ) Library-Level

Domain 1: 3 areas
Domain 2: 3 areas
Domain 3: 5 areas
Domain 4: 2 areas

(Directors, Admin, other Staff)

Selected Demographics

Bass Leadership Behavior Model

Bass Leadership Effectiveness Outcomes and McDonald Organizational Effectiveness

# APPENDIX C

## Factor Analysis Results of MLQ Leadership Questionnaire
## (6 Factors)
## University Library Sample Configuration of Responses

| Factor | Bass's Factor | MLQ Items | forming university library model | Leadings |
|---|---|---|---|---|
| | | | Charisma: | |
| I | Charisma (Idealized | 29: | symbol of success | .769 |
| | Influence) | 15: | have faith in leader | .725 |
| | | 36: | has their respect | .714 |
| | | 8: | proud to be associated with | .701 |
| | | 64: | trust to overcome obstacles | .690 |
| | | 50: | communicates sense of mission | .671 |
| | | 57: | increases optimism for future | .636 |
| | | 22: | special gift for seeing what is worthwhile to consider | .593 |
| | Intellectual Stimulation | 17: | provides new ways of viewing puzzling situations | .730 |
| | | 10: | enables to think about old problems in new ways | .727 |
| | | 45: | aids in identifying key aspects of complex problems | .548 |
| | Inspiration | | Inspitation | |
| | | 16: | expresses purposes simpley | .750 |
| | | 9: | presents vision to spur on | .684 |
| | | 2: | sets high standards | .553 |
| | | 44: | communicates expectations of high performance | .504 |
| | Intellectual Stimulation | 24: | provides reasons to change thinking about problems | .513 |
| | | 3: | challenge to rethink old ideas | .453 |
| | Individualized Consideration | 11: | encourages to see problems as learning opportunities | .574 |
| | | 25: | treats each as individual | .527 |
| | | | Individualized Consideration | |
| II | Individualized Consideration | 39: | expresses appreciation for a good job | .806 |
| | | 18: | informs of progress | .665 |
| | | 32: | helps to get what is wanted | .514 |
| | | 4: | gives personal attention when seems neglected | .511 |
| | | 67: | gives help to newcomers | .429 |
| | Inspiration | 23: | develops ways to encourage | .639 |
| | | 37: | gives encouraging talks | .622 |
| | Charisma | 43: | enthusiasm for their jobs | .642 |
| | | 1: | makes them feel good | .504 |

(continued)

## APPENDIX C (Continued)

| Factor | Bass's Factor | MLQ Items | forming university library model | Leadings |
|---|---|---|---|---|
| | Contingent Reward | | *Contingent Reward* | |
| | | 68: | praises when good job done | .791 |
| | | 33: | commends when good work done | .777 |
| | | 12: | shows recognition for accomplishments | .610 |
| | | 5: | negotiates with subordinates for their rewards | .548 |
| | | 19: | agreement between expectations of subordinates & rewards | .534 |
| | Management by Exception (passive | 48: | no improvements if things going smoothly/as planned | .494 |
| | | 55: | corrective action if mistake occurs | .457 |
| III | Intellectual Stimulation | | *Intellectual Stimulation* | |
| | | 59: | encourages thought before action | .786 |
| | | 52: | stronge emphasis on problem solving before action | .665 |
| | | 66: | reasoning and evidence more than opinions | .643 |
| | | 31: | emphasizes intelligence to overcome obstacles | .573 |
| | | 38: | reasoning must back opinions | .480 |
| | Individualized Consideration | 60: | ready to instruct/coach when needed | .567 |
| | | 46: | coaches individuals in need | .513 |
| | | 53: | provides advice when needed | .484 |
| | Inspiration | 30: | uses symbols & images to focus efforts | .613 |
| IV | Contingent Reward | | *Contingent Reward* | |
| | | 40: | rewards in exchange for cooperation | .850 |
| | | 47: | subordinates get what they want in return for effort | .843 |
| | | 61: | indicates rewards for effort | .611 |
| | | 54: | agreement on rewards for effort | .582 |
| V | Management by Exception (active) | | *Management-by-Exception* | |
| | | 62: | concentrates on failures to meet expectations/standards | .747 |
| | | 41: | focuses on mistakes/deviations | .715 |
| | | 69: | arranges to know when things go wrong | .587 |
| | | 34: | avoid intervening except when failure to meet objectives | .564 |
| VI | Management by Exception (passive) | 6: | do same thing in same way | .725 |
| | | 20: | satisfied with old ways if they work | .636 |
| | | 13: | if no problem, status quo | .614 |
| | | 27: | "If it ain't broke, don't fix it" | .602 |

*Note:* The following items *not included* in this factor analysis:
Laissez-faire: 7,14,21,28,35,42,49,56,63,70
Extra-Effort: 51,58,65
Effectiveness: 71 to 74
Satisfaction: 75 and 76.

# APPENDIX D

## Factor Analysis Results of ALEQ Effectiveness Questionnaire: University Library Sample Configuration (19 Factors-ml/oblique)

| Major Factors | McDonald's Dimension | | ALEQ Items forming university library model | Leadings |
|---|---|---|---|---|
| | | | *Organizational Planning* | |
| III | 6: | Shared | 28: Library goals explicitly stated | .861 |
| | | Goals | 29: library goals agreed by mgmt & librarians | .836 |
| | | | 30: secure input from users to develop goals | .517 |
| | 15: | Perception of College Needs | 62: important than librarians support mission | .508 |
| | 18: | Management Techniques | 37: management techniques used by administration | .615 |
| | 16: | Shared | 41: policies/decisions jointly by adminis. & staff | .621 |
| | | Direction | 68: librarians participate in budget suggestions | .433 |
| | | | *Adequate Collection & Budget* | |
| IV | 3: | Collection | 13: acquires materials to support faculty research | .768 |
| | | Adequacy | 9: acquires materials to meet level of curricula | .769 |
| | | | 11: collection is large enough to meet user needs | .718 |
| | | | 6: existing collection meets level of curricula | .661 |
| | | | 59: acquire materials to meet anticipated curricula | .647 |
| | | | 27: users secure needed materials from collection | .540 |
| | | | 1: annual budget is adequate | .478 |
| | | | *Organization of Collection* | |
| VI | 19: | Collection | 22: organized so that it is readily accessible | .908 |
| | | Organization | 21: shelving and storage is efficiently used | .674 |
| | | | 23: heavily used materials are most accessible | .518 |
| | 11: | Facilities | 20: space provided to shelve all collections | .463 |
| | | | *Staff Size & Diversity* | |
| VII | 8: | Staff Size | 2: professional staff is adequate | .879 |
| | | and | 3: clerical staff is adequate | .865 |
| | | Diversity | 31: Library staff is large enough to cover work | .752 |
| | | | 32: library staff has sufficient diversity of skills | .470 |
| | | | *Faculty Relations* | |
| VIII | 9: | Faculty | 80: important that librarians are members of faculty | .826 |
| | | Relations | 95: librarians are members of university faculty | .738 |
| | | | 63: librarians actively involved in life of univ. | .508 |
| | | | 33: librarians & teaching faculty interact as professional colleagues | .438 |
| | | | *Evaluation of Library* | |
| X | 10: | Evaluation of Library | 74: important for collection to be evaluated by librarians | .845 |
| | | | 73: important for collection to be evaluated by comparisons with key lists of literature | .747 |

*(continued)*

## APPENDIX D   (Continued)

| Major Factors | McDonald's Dimension | ALEQ Items forming university library model | Leadings |
|---|---|---|---|
| | | 75:  important for collection to be evaluated by qualified faculty | .693 |
| | | 76:  important that services and programs be evaluated regularly | .473 |
| | | *I.L.L. Services* | |
| XI | 5:  Acess Use of Extramural Collections | 52:  able to obtain materials not owned promptly | .848 |
| | | 51:  maintains formal and publicized I.L.L. | .455 |
| | 13:  Cooperative Associations | 70:  maintains cooperative with neighboring colleges | .491 |
| | 6:  Shared Goals | 24:  library publicizes its services | .407 |
| | | *Use of Library Collections* | |
| XII | 4:  Access Use of Library's Collections | 26:  faculty regularly use materials & services | .793 |
| | | 25:  students regularly use materials & services | .609 |
| | | 49:  cataloging system is easily understood and used by faculty and students | .471 |
| | | *Access to Research Resources* | |
| XIV | 17:  Professional Service | 56:  formal efforts to teach skills | .829 |
| | | 55:  informal guidance in use of library | .611 |
| | 5:  Access Use of Extramural Collections | 54:  database searching is easily obtained | .497 |
| | | 50:  provides sufficient indexing material for users to identify resources on or off campus | .479 |
| | | *Administrative Leadership* | |
| XVI | 16:  Shared Direction | 78:  maintains formal communication between staff and management | .639 |
| | | 79:  maintains formal communication between library and users | .594 |
| | | 77:  develops innovative ways to perform task/service | .559 |
| | 5:  Use of Extramural Collections | 67:  participates in formal bibliographic cooperative | .425 |
| | 15:  Perception of College Needs | 64:  responsive to requirements of college's curicula | .498 |
| | 18:  Management Technique | 19:  provides opportunities and rewards for professional development | .380 |
| *Minor Factors* | | Staff Morale | |
| *I* | 1:  Staff Morale | 46:  clerical staff exhibit positive spirit | .980 |
| | | 47:  librarians exhibit positive spirit | .818 |
| | | *Professional Development* | |

*(continued)*

## APPENDIX D   (Continued)

| Minor Factors | McDonald's Dimension | ALEQ Items forming university library model | Leadings |
|---|---|---|---|
| II | 7: Staff Develpmt. | 90: librarians hold membership in professional associations | .985 |
| | | 91: librarians engaged in professional activities | .634 |
| | | *Faculty Involvement in Materials Selection* | |
| V | 21: Faculty Involvement in Materials | 85: faculty are involved in selection of materials | .933 |
| | | 66: important to library that faculty participate in selection of materials | .359 |
| | | *Collection Development* | |
| IX | 2: Collection Development | 38: collection development is well-planned and monitored | .742 |
| | | 39: makes strong effort to develop its collection in response to changes in curriculum | .716 |
| | | *University Support for Library* | |
| XV | 14: College Support for Library | 5: faculty support for programs and services is adequate | .718 |
| | | 4: university support for library innovation is adequate | .658 |
| | | *Cooperative Associations* | |
| XVII | 13: Cooperative Associations | 71: maintaining cooperative relationships with high school libraries is important | .535 |
| | | 72: maintaining cooperative relationships with neighboring public libraries is important | .459 |
| | | *User Relations* | |
| XVIII | 8: Staff Size and Diversity | 53: a librarian is always available to help users | .480 |
| | 17: Professional Services | 57: library staff provides prompt, courteous and reliable service | .456 |
| | | *Continuing Education* | |
| XX | 7: Staff Development | 93: clerical staff are involved in formal or informal continuing education | .680 |
| | | 92: librarians are involved in formal or informal continuing education | .618 |
| | | *Materials Control* | |
| XXI | 20: Materials Control | 40: catalog accurately represents the contents of the collections | .458 |
| | | 61: library is very successful at accurately accounting for all library materials | .426 |

# REFERENCES

Albritton, R. 1990. *Transformational and Transactional Leadership in Academic Libraries: An Exploratory Field Test of the Model.* A Report of Research for LIS 451. Unpublished manuscript. University of Illinois, Graduate School of Library and Information Science, Urbana.

Albritton, R., and T. Shaughnessy. 1990. *Developing Leadership Skills: A Sourcebook for Librarians.* Englewood, CO: Libraries Unlimited.

Association of College and Research Libraries. 1989. *ACRL University Library Statistics: 1987-88.* Chicago: ALA.

Association of Research Libraries. 1991. *ARL Statistics: 1989-90.* Washington, DC: ARL.

Avolio, B., D. Waldman, and F. Yammarino. 1991. "Leading in the 1990s: The Four I's of Transformational Leadership." *Journal of European Industrial Training* 15: 9-16.

Bass, B. 1985a. *Leadership and Performance Beyond Expectations.* New York: Free Press.

————. 1985b. "Leadership: Good, Better, Best." *Organizational Dynamics, 13,* 26-41.

————. 1989. "The Inspirational Processes of Leadership." *Journal of Management Development* 7: 21-31.

————. 1990a. *Bass and Stogdill's Handbook of Leadership* (3rd ed.). New York: Free Press.

————. 1990b. "From Transactional to Transformational Leadership: Learning to Share the Vision." *Organizational Dynamics* 18: 19-36.

Bass, B., and B. Avolio. 1990a. "The Implications of Transactional and Transformational Leadership for Individual, Team and Organization Development." Pp. 231-272 in *Research in Organizational Change and Development* (volume 4), edited by R. Woodman and W. Passmore. Greenwich, CT: JAI Press Inc.

————. 1990b. "Developing Transformational Leadership: 1992 and Beyond." *Journal of European Industrial Training* 14: 21-27.

————. 1990c. *Manual for the Multifactor Leadership Questionnaire.* Palo Alto, CA: Consulting Psychologists Press.

Bass, B., B. Avolio, and L. Goodheim. 1987. "Biography and the Assessment of Transformational Leadership at the World Class Level." *Journal of Management* 13: 7-19.

Bass, B., W. Cascio, and E. O'Connor. 1974. "Magnitude of Estimations of Frequency and Amount." *Journal of Applied Psychology* 59: 313-320.

Bauman, D. 1988. "Characteristics and Operational Styles of Transformational Leaders." Doctoral Dissertation, Brigham Young University. *Dissertation Abstracts* 49: 12A, 3559.

Bennis, W. 1973. *The Leaning Ivory Tower.* San Francisco: Jossey-Bass Publishers.

Bennis, W., and B. Nanus. 1985. *Leaders: The Strategies for Taking Charge.* New York: Harper and Row.

Benson, J. 1977. "Differentiation, integration, and leadership style in academic libraries." Doctoral Dissertation, Rutgers University. *Dissertation Abstracts* 38: 2390A.

Binder, M. 1973. "The Supervisory Behavior of Academic Library Cataloging and Processing Personnel: An Inquiry into Relationships with Certain Situational Factors." Doctoral Dissertation, University of Pittsburgh. *Dissertation Abstracts* 34: 3443A.

Burns, J. 1978. *Leadership.* New York: Harper and Row.

Cameron, K. 1978. "Measuring Organizational Effectiveness in Institutions of Higher Education." *Administrative Science Quarterly* 23: 604-632.

Cameron, K., and D. Whetten. 1983. *Organizational Effectiveness: A Comparison of Multiple Models.* New York: Academic Press.

Carlson, M. 1989. "Leadership in the University Library: Case Studies of Five Directors." Doctoral Dissertation, Columbia University. *Dissertation Abstracts* 50: 10A, 3095.

Carver, D. 1989. "Transformational Leadership: A Bibliographic Essay." *Library Administration and Management* 3: 30-34.

Clover, W. 1990. "Transformational Leaders." Pp. 171-184 in *Measures of Leadership*, edited by K. Clark and M. Clark. West Orange, NJ: Leadership Library of America, Inc.

Cohen, J., and P. Cohen. 1983. *Applied Multiple Regression/correlation Analysis for the Behavioral Sciences* (2nd ed.). Hillsdale, NJ: Erlbaum Associates.

Comes, J. 1978. "Relationships Between Leadership Behavior and Goal in Selected Academic Libraries." Doctoral Dissertation, Ball State University. *Dissertation Abstracts* 39: 5782A.

Cummings, L. 1981. "State of the Art: Organizational Behavior in the 1980s." *Decision Sciences* 12: 365-377.

Dragon, A. 1976. "Self-Descriptions and Subordinate Descriptions of the Leader Behavior of Library Administrators." Doctoral Dissertation, University of Minnesota. *Dissertation Abstracts* 37A: 7380.

Euster, J. 1986. "The Activities and Effectiveness of the Academic Library Director in the Environmental Context." Doctoral Dissertation, University of California, Berkeley. *Dissertation Abstracts* 47: 07A, 2350.

Fiedler, F. 1967. *A Theory of Leadership Effectiveness.* New York: McGraw-Hill.

Fiedler, F., and R. House. 1988. "Leadership Theory and Research: A Report of Progress." Pp. 73-92 in *International Review of Industrial and Organizational Psychology*, edited by C. Cooper and I. Robertson. Chichester, England: Wiley and Sons.

Gillett-Karam, R. 1988. "Transformational Leadership and the Community College President: Are There Gender Differences?" Doctoral Dissertation, University of Texas, Austin. *Dissertation Abstracts* 50: 02A, 314.

Hater, J., and B. Bass. 1988. "Superiors' Evaluations and Subordinates' Perceptions of Transformational and Transactional Leadership." *Journal of Applied Psychology* 73: 695-702.

Hollander, E. 1978. "Conformity, Status, and Idiosyncrasy Credit." *Psychological Review* 65: 117-27.

Holmes, R. 1983. "The Academic Library Director's Perceived Power and its Correlates." Doctoral Dissertation, University of Minnesota. *Dissertation Abstracts* 44: 11A, 319

Hoover, N. 1987. "Transformational and Transactional Leadership: A Test of the Model." Doctoral Dissertation, University of Louisville. *Dissertation Abstracts* 48: 12A, 3020.

House, R. 1971. "A Path-goal Theory of Leader Effectiveness." *Administrative Science Quarterly* 16: 321-339.

Joreskog, K., and D. Sorbom. 1989. *LISREL 7: A Guide to the Program and Applications* (2nd ed.). Chicago: SPSS, Inc.

King, M. 1989. "Extraordinary Leadership in Education." Doctoral Dissertation, University of New Orleans *Dissertation Abstracts* 50: 08A, 2329.

Kirby, P., M. King, and L. Paradise. 1992. "Extraordinary Leaders in Education: Understanding Transformational Leadership." *Journal of Educational Research* 85: 303-311.

Koh, W. 1991. "An Empirical Validation of the Theory of Transformational Leadership in Secondary Schools in Singapore." Doctoral Dissertation, University of Oregon. *Dissertation Abstracts* 52: 02, 602A.

Lawrence, P., and J. Lorsch. 1976a. *Organization and Environment*. Cambridge, MA: Harvard University Press.

_____. 1976b. "Differentiation and Integration in Complex Organizations." *Administrative Science Quarterly* 12: 1-47.

Lee, S. 1981. "The Role of the Academic Library Director: An Exploratory Investigation." Doctoral Dissertation, Simmons College. *Dissertation Abstracts* 43: 06A, 2071.

McDonald, J. 1987. "Academic Library Effectiveness: An Organizational Perspective." Doctoral Dissertation, Drexel University *Dissertation Abstracts* 49: 02A, 161.

Metz, P. 1977. "The Academic Library and its Director in their Institutional Environments." Doctoral Dissertation, University of Michigan. *Dissertation Abstracts* 38: 06A, 3750.

Meyers, L., and N. Grossen, N. 1974. *Behavioral Research: Theory, Procedure, and Design*. San Francisco: W. H. Freeman.

Mitchell, E. 1987. "Leadership Styles in Academic Libraries: A Test of Fiedler's Contingency Model of Leadership Effectiveness." Doctoral Dissertation, Rutgers University. *Dissertation Abstracts* 48: 08A, 1919.

Murray, M. 1988. "A Study of Transformational Leadership, Organizational Effectiveness, and Demographics in Selected Small College Settings." Doctoral Dissertation, Kent State University. *Dissertation Abstracts* 50: 07A, 1880.

Norusis, M. 1988. *SPSS-X User's Guide* (3rd ed.). Chicago: SPSS, Inc.

Pereira, D. 1986. *Factors Associated with Transformational Leadership in an Indian Engineering Firm*. Toronto: Administrative Sciences of Canada.

Riggs, D. 1988a. "Leadership vs. Management in Technical Services." *Journal of Library Administration* 9: 27-39.

_____. 1988b. *Libraries in the 90's: What the Leaders Expect*. Phoenix: Oryx Press.

_____. 1993. "The Time for Transformational Leadership is Now!" *Journal of Library Administration* 18: 55-68.

Rike, G. 1976. "Staff Leadership Behavior of Directors of State Library Agencies: A Study of Role Expectations and Perceived Fulfillment." Doctoral Dissertation.

Schneider, F. 1968. "A Study of the Leadership Role of Directors of Public Libraries as Reported by Selected Public Library Directors." Doctoral Dissertation, Arizona State University. *Dissertation Abstracts* 29: 1552A.

Seltzer, J., and B. Bass. 1987. *Transformational Leadership: Beyond Initiation and Consideration.* American Psychological Association Meeting. New York.
————. 1990. "Transformational Leadership: Beyond Initiation and Consideration." *Journal of Management* 16 (4): 693-703.
Seltzer, J., R. Numerof, and B. Bass. 1989. "Transformational Leadership: Is it a Source of More Burnout?" *Journal of Health and Human Resources Administration* 12: 174-185.
Sheldon, B. 1991. *Leaders in Libraries: Styles and strategies for Success.* Chicago: American Library Association.
Singer, M. 1985. "Transformational vs. Transactional Leadership: A Study of New Zealand Company Managers." *Psychological Reports* 57: 143-146.
Stogdill, R. 1974. *Handbook of Leadership.* New York: Free Press.
Stogdill, R., and A. Coons (Eds.). 1957. *Leader Behavior: Its Description and Measurement.* Columbus: Ohio State University, Bureau of Business Research.
Thompson, J. 1967. *Organizations in Action.* New York: McGraw Hill.
Thurstone, L. 1947. *Multiple Factor Analysis.* Chicago: University of Chicago Press.
Tichy, N., and F. Devanna. 1986. *Transformational Leadership.* New York: Wiley.
Tichy, N., and D. Ulrich. 1984. "The Leadership Challenge—A Call for the Transformational Leader." *Sloan Management Review* (Fall): 59-68.
Waldman, E., B. Bass, and F. Yammarino. 1990. "The Augmenting Effect of Transformational Leadership." Pp. 151-169 in *Measures of Leadership,* edited by K. Clark and M. Clark. West Orange, NJ: Leadership Library of America.
Yetton, P. 1984. "Leadership and Supervision." Pp. 9-35 in *Social Psychology and Organizational Behavior,* edited by M. Gruneberg and T. Wall. Chichester, NY: Wiley.
Young, E. 1980. "A Study of the Self-perception and Subordinate Perception of the Leadership Behavior of Black Library Directors." Doctoral Dissertation, George Peabody College for Teachers of Vanderbilt University. *Dissertation Abstracts* 42: 021A, 499.
Yukl, G. 1989. *Leadership in Organizations* (2nd ed.). Englewood Cliffs, NJ: Prentice-Hall.

# ETHICS IN PROFESSIONAL WORKLOAD ASSIGNMENT AND DELEGATION:
## MIDDLE MANAGEMENT DECISION MAKING DURING TIMES OF CHANGE

Tara Lynn Fulton

In her book, *Never Work for a Jerk!*, Patricia King describes various categories of problem bosses, including scoundrels, liars, snakes in the grass, bullies, vacillators, and cheapskates. None of us wants to believe we have ever been labeled as such. My working assumption is that middle managers do not set out with the intention to act immorally or amorally. Yet interest in this subject indicates that managers either frequently *do* act unethicly, or end up being *perceived* as having done so. While there is a myriad of reasons for both real and interpreted ethical misjudgments, frequently we fail to acknowledge the ethical elements and ramifications of the decisions

**Advances in Library Administration and Organization, Volume 13, pages 111-128.**
**Copyright © 1995 by JAI Press Inc.**
**All rights of reproduction in any form reserved.**
**ISBN: 1-55938-931-1**

we make on a daily basis. This paper provides examples of workload assignment and delegation situations in which ethical considerations are embedded, attempts to make library middle managers more aware of the ethical implications of their actions, and offers some pragmatic suggestions on how to take one's own "ethical pulse." It combines theoretical context with practical guidance.

In cases of ethical dilemmas, middle managers weigh and balance competing claims—for action, for direction, for services, for employee rights and needs. We juggle competing "goods," competing interests, and competing commitments (Guy, 1990). We feel pulled in several directions simultaneously. There are rarely clear "right" and "wrong" choices in middle management. As Pastin (1986) says, ethics "offers few black-and-white solutions; instead it offers complex problems, hard choices, and uncertain outcomes" (p. 33). The ideal solution is a chimera. If supervision did not require time- and energy-consuming thought, libraries would not pay us to be there. During times of transition and change, we as middle managers are particularly challenged to act with integrity and courage in moving our organizations forward.

## ORGANIZATIONAL VALUES AND MIDDLE MANAGEMENT INTEGRITY

Organizational culture is the set of assumptions, norms, values, and beliefs that are exemplified by daily life and decision making in the workplace. An "ethical culture is one in which core values are acknowledged and readily discussed in the context of the organization's actions" (Guy, 1990, p. 100). At the very minimum, it is imperative that there be congruence of values throughout the organization to serve as a framework for individual manager decision making. Mixed or muddled messages indicate a lack of harmony and can create role conflicts for managers (Liedtka, 1989). The American Library Association Library Administration and Management Association Task Force on the Library as a Humanistic Workplace (1991) argues that organizations must promulgate a simple message that reflects their articulated missions and goals so that managers in turn can exhibit consistent behavior and maintain consistent expectations, even during times of change (p. 4).

One complicating factor in contemporary, multicultural America is that standards of right and wrong are not universal and are continually shifting. The imperative to respect the customs and workstyles of others can become particularly complex, because "moral standards of behavior differ between groups within a single culture, between cultures, and between times" (Hosmer, 1991, p. 104). Middle managers are often forced to mediate between individuals and groups representing a variety of ethical frameworks both within the library and external to it.

Some institutions have code of conduct statements in addition to mission statements. Librarianship has its own professional code of ethics, a set of "commonly held standards of professional behavior" (Peterson, 1983, p. 132). Given these guidelines, we often focus on what is expected of us, our duty, our moral obligations, and what constitutes "right action." This proves problematic when we receive guidance or a directive from upper administration to handle a situation in a particular way with which we disagree. Sometimes we do not have a choice. Yet, it is easy to do what we are told to do, or to convince ourselves that we are doing what is right given our responsibility to the organization. On the other hand, we can "question, resist and challenge orders" when they are "inconsistent with known organizational or individual values" (Cooper, 1990, p. 228). If we do not rationalize away our responsibility to use what power we have to influence outcomes, if we take the personal risk to question authority (Toffler, 1986, p. 32), we have taken a first important step toward ethical action. As the saying goes, "If you don't stand for something, you'll fall for anything." "When leaders clarify the principles that will govern their lives and the ends that they will seek, they give purpose to their daily decisions. A set of ethical standards gives a point of reference for navigating the sometimes stormy seas of organizational life. It guides choices of action regardless of the situation and communicates personal integrity" (Webb, 1988, pp. 3-4).

There are many kinds of rulers.
The highest rule by virtue; their authority is invisible.
Those they rule are unaware of being ruled.
They may even believe that they are the ones who rule.
The next kind rule by love,
And those they rule praise and honor them.

The next kind rule by fear,
And those they rule become restless, agitated.
The lowest kind rule by muscle,
And those they rule wait for the moment to rebel.
(Japussy, 1990, p. 36)

## MANAGER/LEADER AS ROLE MODEL

Walton (1986) summarized the manager's ethical role when he said that we "absorb values, sift values, share values, and, if needed, impose values" (p. 103). "Employees emulate administrative and managerial behavior"; therefore, we must "lead by example" (Ziolkowski, 1993, p. 28). If there is one point that every manager/ leader must remember, it is that "actions speak louder than words." "Nothing loses the respect of staff as fast as inconsistencies between words and deeds" (Webb, 1988, p. 16). If we are to value ethical decision making, we must discuss ethics among the staff and show staff how to practice it. "[L]eadership must make individual leaders and followers accountable to their ethical responsibilities as human beings. Without that component, the ethical framework is not workable. Rather, it is dehumanizing" (Rost, 1991, p. 173) .

## ORGANIZATIONAL STRUCTURE AS
## WORKLOAD DELEGATION

To the degree that a middle manager has control over organizational structure, his ethical stance is reflected in the way he sets up and uses the chain of command. Strict adherence to line reporting is traditionally associated with a pessimistic Theory X perception of employees' capabilities and motivations. Matrix organizations, the use of "staff" and "specialist" positions outside the line authority, and the creation of work teams, on the other hand, reflect a shared leadership approach. "Librarians are moving away from the traditional, bureaucratic model and toward organic systems" in which "authority and power are delegated and dispersed, and managers are not viewed as omniscient" (White, 1985, p. 29). Hierarchical arrangements are simply "no longer supportive of the emerging functions and programs"; "effective library leaders will have to examine work flows, environments, positions, job requirements and tasks and find better structures and means to enable all employees to contribute their talents towards solving complex organizational problems" (Webb, 1988, p. 10).

## DEFINING PROFESSIONAL LEVEL ACTIVITIES: THE EFFICIENCY/EFFECTIVENESS DILEMMA AND MEANS-END ETHICS

As technology allows us to delegate more operations to support staff, librarians' jobs become primarily those of manager, computer expert, information broker. The management literature is replete with pleas to handle activities at the lowest possible level. The current financial climate is forcing managers to look carefully at how staff is utilized. There is a call for cost-benefit analyses. The end result is that employees often focus on doing things right rather than doing the right things. Middle managers are often forced to conclude that the net good is worth a certain number of negative side-effects. Unfortunately, a pragmatic approach can lead to either real or perceived conflict between service excellence and budgets, between quality and schedule deadlines. If we accept the utilitarian premise that the moral worth of our decisions is determined by the consequence of our actions, then cutting back too severely is obviously "wrong." It is incumbent upon us to take measures to reach our ultimate goals, but not at any price.

## THE UNIQUE CHARACTERISTICS OF SUPERVISING PROFESSIONALS

Make no mistake about it, supervising anyone involves control; it has a paternalistic dimension (Walton, 1986, p. 159). Managers hold enormous influence over their staff, and they have an obligation to exercise it judiciously (Shaughnessy, 1990, p. 131). "Liberty means we ought not to interfere, without special justification, in the chosen course of a rational being" (Cooper, 1990, p. 11). When supervising professionals, use of direct authority is often ineffective. Because they are involved in a wide and complex array of activities, their ability to act independently and take initiative are valued. While all "subordinates deserve the right to organize and perform their own work within the limits of prescribed guidelines" (White, 1985, p. 127), this right is even more essential for professionals. Intervening in a professional's project can actually "slow and confound the process" (Shapero, 1985, p. xv). Since so much of professional work is delegated rather than assigned, librarians need to have autonomy in designing aspects of their jobs; "freedom to fine tune job procedures (sometimes in consultation with others) and to reorganize or refocus their work flow" (Bechtel, 1993, p. 356). A Nietzschian "might makes right" mentality is likely to lead only to mutiny among professionals.

> Respect the realities of life.
> Do not try to squeeze two people through
> A space too small for even one to pass.
> Do not force an animal into a corner
> Where it must defend itself.
> When you meet resistance, understand it.
> It is part of the Way.
> Take it in stride, and you will find the way around it.
> (Japussy, 1990, p. 107)

For these reasons, it is essential that managers of professionals establish a climate of trust. The ALA LAMA Task Force on the Library as a Humanistic Workplace (1991) characterizes trust as follows: "Promises and commitments are honored. Staff feel safe in expressing their opinions. An absence of hostility or indifference exists...Staff feel the freedom to try, to experiment and sometimes to make mistakes" (p. 9). Leaders "gain the trust of their staff by demonstrating a common-sense handling of situations and having a reputation for fair play with a lack of double standards. [They] treat the employees with respect and have a willingness to take a stand on issues" (Ziolkowski, 1993, p.24).

## SICK TIME, VACATION TIME, PROFESSIONAL DEVELOPMENT TIME: DESCRIPTIVE AND PRESCRIPTIVE ETHICS

"The organizational climate refers to 'how we do things around here'—the ground rules that determine proper and improper conduct...may or may not exist in written form; nevertheless, they do exist and are communicated through words, actions, and impressions" (Hitt, 1990, p. 2). The ground rules are embodied in personnel policies, such as sick and vacation leave, grounds for immediate dismissal statements, and progressive discipline procedures. For librarians, written statements often do little more than describe usual practice and circumstances under which exceptions may be considered. Administrators find this vagueness convenient, for it allows more flexibility in handling individual cases; professionals often prefer it, because it reflects a higher level of autonomy. That is, until an individual case or two of abuse occurs. Suddenly, administrators find that they have no grounds upon which to enforce what almost anyone would consider a violation by a staff member, or professionals working in one department feel that their supervisor enforces different standards than others in the building or system. In such cases there is often pressure to prescribe and codify practice for professionals. In particular, "librarians and their employing institutions should recognize a dual responsibility in the allocation of time and resources to support research, publishing, and professional service activities" (Peterson, 1983, p. 135). "The question also arises about how much time during the regular work schedule may be spent," especially if it "imposes added work upon colleagues within the department" (Peterson, 1983, p. 135). Library employees have the right to participate in making rules for the community, but then they must consent to all rules made by that community.

## FAIRNESS IN ASSIGNING GOALS/TASKS TO INDIVIDUALS

Let us move now to the manager's responsibility to the individual employee when assigning work. Each staff member may play a number of service roles, and the roles they play are likely to shift over time. Staffing is based on "matching skills available to the tasks to be performed" (Myers, 1989, p. 40). It is essential that we define what needs we have in the organization, which are adequately covered, which will take future prominence, and so forth. Meanwhile we are charged with getting the job done well with existing staff. At the heart of this dilemma is the value of fairness.

In assigning work there are two forces that are often seen as being contradictory—(1) being consistent, and (2) recognizing individual talents, skills, and interests. The former force encourages us to have everyone do a little of everything; the latter encourages us to create

more distinct roles and opportunities. Reconciling individual goals/
motivations with the organizational agenda "requires the greatest
effort and sensitivity on the part of the manager" (White, 1985, p.
52).

"Fairness doesn't mean that everyone will be treated exactly the
same way. What it means is that the boss will give everyone the same
opportunities, and give each person the amount of direction and
attention he or she needs to keep up productivity, motivation, and
job satisfaction" (King, 1987, p. 40). It also involves "avoiding
arbitrary or capricious favoritism" (Guy, 1990, p. 16). For example,
altering a work schedule because of a personal circumstance may be
considered being a "good Samaritan" and therefore "humane" on one
occasion, but if others are not permitted the same when needed, or
when that individual receives other preferential treatment, then
workloads are not being fairly allocated. Middle managers must learn
to distinguish the smoke-screen complaints and belly-aching of self-
interested individuals (many of whom are frequently referred to by
middle managers as having a "9-5 mentality") from the legitimate
concerns and demands of those with inequitable or unreasonable
workloads. "Personnel policies and practices should operate to
promote the greatest good for the greatest number"; middle managers
must make a good faith effort to "consider the good of all" (Rubin,
1991, p. 15).

## DIVERSITY OR FRAGMENTATION

One professional's "plum" is "the pits" for another. Nowhere is this
more evident than in situations where individuals are expected to
perform a multiplicity of roles, especially if there are dual reporting
lines. Small libraries have always operated close to the "complete
librarian" model; even in large libraries, these days, narrow
specializations are a luxury. When individuals are members of several
overlapping groups, contradictory expectations almost inevitably
develop (Burns, 1978, p. 293).

Collection development is frequently the center of controversy over
workloads in libraries. Scott Bullard (1990) clearly articulated the
dilemma that librarians face on a daily basis—should they
demonstrate allegiance to the grand bureaucracy of functional areas
(e.g., cataloging), or spend time carrying out collection management

responsibilities? Bullard contends that hybridized authority "violates the principle of unity of command. This can enhance competition for personnel shared with other units, foster power struggles, increase stress, and oblige collection development librarians to accommodate sometimes incompatible demands" (p. 18). Particularly in cases of diversification and fragmentation, providing guidelines on quantity of work (e.g., time allocations) is not sufficient—one must also articulate the quality parameters and priorities for each area of responsibility.

Our expectations for specialists and for generalists are constantly evolving. Some people develop expertise in an emerging area and end up performing a function that was never clearly intended to be, and certainly not officially documented as, "theirs." Several decades ago, specialization with business reference tools evolved in this manner. Currently Internet experts are making the transition from in-house hackers to posted positions. Often these people turn out to be those who are already overloaded with responsibilities. Middle managers are forced to find time for that person to begin training his or her colleagues. They must also negotiate the degree to which all professionals are expected to be competent and active, and determine the point at which referral to the experts is acceptable or desirable. Such ambiguity is particularly apparent in times when the kind of paradigm shifts are occurring in positions that straddle the fence between ownership and access and between technical and public services (e.g., interlibrary loan/document delivery staff). The sooner middle managers are able to articulate these tensions and take steps to define expectations for all, the better both users and staff will be served.

## VALUING THE ROUTINE

All librarians feel pulled in a number of directions. There is a tendency to get caught up in the latest hot project and relegate seemingly routine tasks to the back burner. The librarians who find themselves, for example, with more hours on the reference desk begin to feel taken advantage of and/or less important than their colleagues in more glamorous roles, such as those working on grants. Middle managers must find ways to acknowledge all professional contributions. They are responsible for ensuring that focus is on primary service initiatives. They are also in a position to decide who does the lion's share of less desirable tasks and who has a chance to "shine."

Some individuals do best with routine; others thrive on change and diversity. Some professionals are better at some activities; these activities may or may not be the ones they like to do most. We cannot continually take advantage of one person's good nature to pick up routine slack, for we might eventually end up stunting their career growth (King, 1987). We must guard against creating self-fulfilling prophesies in assessing individuals' capabilities. Those who are most flexible tend to be given chances more readily—a practice which only encourages recalcitrance/intransigence and ultimate deadwood among less flexible staff. It is the manager's responsibility to guard against obsolescence and burnout, and to work constructively with plateaued employees. We must continually reassess the degree to which senior and junior librarians should be treated differently in terms of tasks assigned and delegated. Providing rewards and incentives to try new responsibilities is part of that process.

## MAXIMIZING SUCCESS/MINIMIZING FAILURE IN WORK ASSIGNMENT AND DELEGATION

At its very essence, ethical practice is the process of trying not to cause harm; the potential to hurt others is a frequent management dilemma (Hosmer, 1991). We must place employees in a situation to succeed. Not to ensure that subordinates have the capacity and resources to see a task through would constitute ethical misconduct (Toffler, 1986). White's (1985) text on personnel work in libraries discusses four very basic requirements in work assignment to avoid creating stress and untenable pressures: (1) set attainable goals, (2) set identifiable limits and priorities, (3) be flexible, and (4) articulate expectations and rules.

When delegating responsibility fully, it is vital that several other components be added to this list to ensure success. The librarian must have sufficient credibility and legitimate authority to garner support and resources. A particularly tricky but essential resource is information. Walton (1986) calls for truth in management, claiming that everyone has a right to reliable communication on all matters that affect their welfare and the right to protection from dishonesty and deceit (p. 104). While we "have a duty to regulate the timing, manner, and amount of information provided, supervisors who withhold, distort, or delay communication for personal reasons, or with the intention of injuring or punishing individuals commit an ethical breach" (Rubin, 1991, pp. 11, 12). If you cannot provide the individual with everything she needs to feel empowered to take credit for accomplishment and responsibility for mistakes, it is best to assign work rather than to delegate.

How a supervisor deals with failure is also an ethical issue. Draconian punishment is obviously not only counterproductive, but violates the basic values of justice, honesty, and openness. "A trust relationship between leaders and followers will provide the framework within which new behaviors can be practiced, risk taking can occur, and failure will not be punished" (Webb, 1988, p. 4). Leaders who trust people create a cycle in which professionals come to recognize their own self worth and, therefore, are able to work more productively. Respecting oneself also implies the ability to accept accomplishments with its rewarding satisfaction and also to accept failure with its painful disappointments.... A personal injustice is done when an individual sinks into despair because of failure, or denies that failure has occurred, or tries to shift the reasons for failure to someone else, or becomes defensive in the face of failure. Success and failure are part of the learning process for all, but one can hope that those who live ethically might succeed more regularly.

When you jump from a high ledge,
It is a good idea to land upright, on all four legs.
This may require making adjustments in mid-flight.

It is Virtue that lets you make these adjustments,
Not just in jumping from ledges,
But also in the way you deal with others,
In your hopes and expectations,
In the goals you set for achievement,
And in the way you treat life.

If you can end up standing upright,
With all four legs on the ground,
In everything you undertake to do,
Then you know Virtue, and Virtue knows you.

If, on the other hand, you tend to get run over
By the steamroller of life,
You probably do not yet know everything

You need to learn.
(Japussy, 1990, p. 87)

## JOB ENRICHMENT OPPORTUNITIES AND
## PREPARING INDIVIDUALS FOR PROMOTION

In order to keep good people, a middle manager must challenge them. He must also acknowledge good performance with offers for enrichment. These are positive motivations—wise pragmatic actions as well as ethical imperatives. Most often, this reason for offering enrichment is mixed with sheer necessity. We need someone to take on something, and we need it to be someone we can trust. Be careful that you are not using a Machiavellian "means to an end" mentality in offering people what amounts to more work!

Obviously, affirmative action and other legal guidelines serve as minimum assurances of fairness in targeting individuals for enrichment and promotion. Every middle manager must also confront his or her less evident personal prejudices (against Southerners or obese employees, for example). Objective assessment is imperative (Rubin, 1991), and acts of favoritism and "personality clashes" must be minimized in making personnel decisions.

Depending upon one's notion of what is equitable and just, a middle manager can end up looking as if he or she is playing favorites or creating an "in-crowd" with promotion decisions. I have come to accept that a certain amount of this perception is an inevitable "occupational hazard" of middle management; there will always be "sour grape" responses from those who are not selected for enrichment opportunities. I agree with Herb White (1985), when he states that "Egalitarianism—a process in which everyone is treated exactly the same regardless of performance—is an ineffective management method because the noncompetitive environment this creates is one in which poor performers will thrive while strong performers will leave to find a place where their assets are appreciated" (p. 95).

## THE INCOMPETENT/UNPRODUCTIVE/
## COUNTERPRODUCTIVE PROFESSIONAL

"Discipline in the organization is an activity that is not only fraught with moral overtones but is increasingly taking on significant legal implications" (Coye and Belohlav, 1989, p. 159). In addition to potential legal costs if suits are filed, library management must consider the "insidious, hidden, and potentially more debilitating costs" of dysfunctional behavior (Coye and Belohlav, 1989, pp. 160-161). One of the most common ethical failings of middle managers is to display cowardice in giving negative feedback and dealing with unsatisfactory evaluations (Toffler, 1986).

Most non-administrative librarians display an ambivalent stance toward their less contributing or troublesome colleagues. On the one hand, they resent "carrying the weight for" and/or "having to deal with" these people. On the other hand, if they become aware that pressure is being applied to any individual, they not only empathize with that person, but often also at least subconsciously fear for their own jobs. A middle manager can expect widespread support for action only in the most egregious cases. However, if one is successful in removing "deadwood," constant irritants, or anyone or anything that constantly brings down the productivity or morale of the group, frontline staff are often grateful after the fact, in spite of their ambivalence at the time.

As budgets are squeezed and managers are asked to "do more with less" staff, we have far less leeway to juggle responsibilities and assign work— we can literally no longer afford those who cannot or will not keep pace. The trick, of course, is to figure out where the magic line is between a professional who needs extra support (coaching, in-house training, etc.) and one who is incapable of profiting or unwilling to profit from such efforts. Part of any professional's workload is to share expertise with colleagues. Thus, "carrying" an individual adds not only extra duties for every professional who must pick up the slack, but also the necessary time and energy to bring that person along. This burden must be factored into a middle manager's decision to take action.

Another point must be made here. Job descriptions are constructed vaguely enough to allow for a range of approaches. The spectrum of displayed interpretations in any organization is taken as a measure of the acceptable boundaries. What is considered a light, average, or heavy workload is in comparison with what one observes from others in the organization. "Unsatisfactory" and "exceptional" are in fact relative terms. If consistent standards are not upheld and too many mediocre performers are in an organization, expectations for all are lowered—over time only a few people may be operating at the professional level the director wants, and those individuals are considered "stars" rather than the norm.

## DROP EVERYTHING!: CRISIS MANAGEMENT

To this point we have been looking at relatively long-term workload assignment and delegation issues—ones that the middle manager has time to contemplate and gracefully rectify should plans begin to go astray. But "most of the time we are ad hoc problem solvers"(Cooper, 1990, p. 10). So what about those times when split-second judgment is called for, when something needs to be handled right away—what about crises? Middle managers reveal much about their underlying biases, priorities, and assumptions when faced with immediate decision making.

Let us take a sample scenario. An influential but cantankerous client storms into your office. You are on your way to an extremely important meeting which you *must* attend. Your client wants attention *now*. She feels she has received inadequate response to her inquiries, she has some gift items she is considering donating, and she has an idea to enhance service and promote the library. Who do you call? Your choices are: (1) your most diplomatic librarian, who is in the middle of a major project, (2) the librarian with the most relevant expertise but who lacks judgment skills about making promises, and who is on break in the staff room, and (3) the librarian who is sitting at his desk, with no known time pressures, but also no particular connection to the situation. There is no right answer. There are numerous overlapping ethical tightropes to be walked here. First, are you putting your client's needs above your staff's needs? Second, are you going to end up being perceived as dumping on someone or as looking to your "pet" librarians in a crunch? Third, will you allow a crisis to take precedence over longer-term and perhaps more important and broadly beneficial projects or tasks? Obviously, you cannot allow ethical concerns to paralyze you from taking action, but the more conscious we are of the messages we convey in such circumstances, the more we will temper our instinctive responses with reasoned ethical deliberation.

## THE PROCESS OF ETHICAL DECISION MAKING

Middle managers cannot expect to have all the morally and pragmatically "right" answers to our dilemmas. What we must do, however, is ask the right questions. Recognizing the ethical elements of the decisions we make is essential in improving our "ethical scorecards" as middle managers. In an ideal setting, a middle manager should go through the following rational ethical decision-making steps (culled from Guy, 1990; Cooper, 1990; Rion, 1990).

1. Define the problem or concern. State the goal in resolving the problem.
2. Look at the context in which the problem arose and identify all stakeholders. Recognize your boundaries of influence and responsibility.
3. Identify the values and principles that are at stake and those that are most important.
4. List all possible options and courses of action. Collect all resources and remove all blocks to generating ideas.
5. Evaluate solution alternatives. Note the pros and cons of the alternatives from a variety of perspectives. Identify the base values and assumptions inherent in each. Select alternatives that maximize the desired values but minimize negative results (side effects, drawbacks) both short term and long term.
6. Choose a preliminary course of action; find a solution that seems to fit. Check that the consequences will be ethical. Consult whoever you need to about your preliminary decision.
7. Make a commitment to your choice. Be sure you are ready to defend it.
8. Make the decision and implement it.

Such an analysis "leads to thoughtful resolution—not the right answer, but an ethically sensitive and well-considered judgment" (Rion, 1990, p. 13). Ethical pitfalls are to be found at every stage of this process. Unfortunately, for a variety of reasons managers rarely pursue the ideal process thoroughly. They are often under pressure to compromise their own ethical ideals to conform to those of the organization (Guy, 1990, p. 27); they do not have or take the time; they rationalize or otherwise limit their vision in considering options (Cooper, 1990, p. 26). Therefore, every middle manager must find safeguards in the ethical decision-making process.

## HOW TO AVOID UNETHICAL BEHAVIOR

There are two primary mechanisms by which you can check yourself for "doing the right thing." First, ask yourself the following questions:

- Do I have any nagging feelings of guilt, remorse, or uncertainty? Does anything about this decision not feel right in the pit of my stomach?
- Am I sure my motives are the best ones?
- If I were on a jury, hearing my case after the fact, how would I rule my behavior?
- Do I have the courage of my convictions to stand by my decision and act on it?
- Does my action solve the original problem in the best interests of the organization while also creating the greatest good for the most stakeholders?
- Am I being true to myself in this decision?

Second, don't make decisions alone. Seek out confidants with whom you can banter as you sort through options and weigh their consequences. Ideally one of the confidants would be your boss, and the others both like-minded and other-minded middle managers in your own library and elsewhere (i.e., some who know the situation and some who have a distance from it). As much as possible, establish a climate in which staff feel empowered to raise issues and suggest actions. More than one staff member has either purposely or inadvertently stopped me from making what would clearly have been a mistake. What is more important, they can point out situations you might not even have recognized as ethical delegation issues worthy of attention. If you can get your employees to help ensure ethical conduct in the workplace, then you have made their and your jobs easier and more enjoyable. You and they will be leading "the good life, the life worth living" (Hitt, 1990, p. 69).

## REFERENCES

American Library Association. 1970. *Library Education and Personnel Utilization: A Statement of Policy Adopted by the Council of the ALA*. Chicago: The Association.

American Library Association, Library Administration and Management Association, Task Force on the Library as a Humanistic Workplace. 1991. *The Library as a Humanistic Workplace: A Report to the LAMA Board.* Chicago: The Association.

Bechtel, J.M. 1993. "Leadership Lessons Learned from Managing and Being Managed." *Journal of Academic Librarianship* 18: 352-357.

Bullard, S. 1990. "Tribes and Tribulations: Ethical Snares in the Organization of Collection Management Units." In *Acquisitions '90: Conference on Acquisitions, Budgets, and Collections,* compiled and edited by D.C. Genaway. Canfield, OH: Genaway.

Burns, J.M. 1978. *Leadership.* New York: Harper.

Cooper, T.L. 1990. *The Responsible Administrator: An Approach to Ethics for the Administrative Role* (3rd ed.). San Francisco: Jossey-Bass.

Coye, R., and J. Belohlav. 1989. "Disciplining: A Question of Ethics?" *Employee Responsibilities and Rights Journal* 2: 155-162.

Guy, M.E. 1990. *Ethical Decision Making in Everyday Work Situations.* New York: Quorum.

Hitt, W.D. 1990. *Ethics and Leadership: Putting Theory into Practice.* Columbus, OH: Battelle.

Hosmer, L.T. 1991. *The Ethics of Management* (2nd ed.). Homewood, IL: Irwin.

Japussy, W. 1990. *The Tao of Meow.* Winchester, OH: Enthea.

King, P. 1987. *Never Work for a Jerk!* New York: Barnes and Noble.

Liedtka, J.M. 1989. "Value Congruence: The Interplay of Individual and Organizational Value Systems." *Journal of Business Ethics* 8: 805-815.

Myers, M. 1989. "Staffing Patterns." Pp. 40-63 in *Personnel Administration in Libraries,* edited by S. Creth and F. Duda. New York: Neal-Shuman.

Pastin, M. 1986. *The Hard Problems of Management: Gaining the Ethics Edge.* San Francisco: Jossey-Bass.

Peterson, K.G. 1983. "Ethics in Academic Librarianship: The Need for Values." *Journal of Academic Librarianship* 9:132-137.

Rion, M. 1990. *Responsible Manager: Practical Strategies for Ethical Decision Making.* New York: Harper & Row.

Rost, J.C. 1991. *Leadership for the Twenty-First Century.* New York: Praeger.

Rubin, R. 1991. "Ethical Issues in Library Personnel Management." *Journal of Library Administration* 14: 1-16.

Shapero, A. 1985. *Managing Professional People.* New York: Free Press.

Shaughnessy, T.W. 1990. "Ethics and Values in the Workplace." Pp. 129-132 in *Developing Leadership Skills: A Source Book for Librarians,* edited by R.L. Albritton and T.W. Shaughnessy. Englewood, CO: Libraries Unlimited.

Toffler, B.L. 1986. *Tough Choices: Managers Talk Ethics.* New York: Wiley.

Walton, C.C. 1986. *The Moral Manager.* Cambridge, MA: Ballinger.

Webb, G.M. 1988. *Changing Organizational Cultures in Libraries through Effective Leadership Communication.* (Eric Document #303 185).

White, H.S. 1985. *Library Personnel Management.* White Plains, NY: Knowledge Industry Publications.

Ziolkowski, D. 1993. "Common Sense, Integrity, and Expectations of Excellence: Practical Advice on Dealing with Employee Problems." *Library Administration and Management* 7: 24-30.

# PLANNING TOOLS AND STRATEGIES USED BY ACADEMIC LIBRARIANS IN FOUR SUN BELT STATES AND FOUR RUST BELT STATES

Mary Kathleen Geary

While conducting a review of the literature relative to the future of academic libraries, the researcher was struck by three recurrent themes, namely the decline in general populations and state revenues; the staffing and monetary demands placed on academic libraries to keep up with new and expensive electronic information technologies; and the number and diversity of planning tools and processes recommended by the authors to develop strategic plans to help deal with the effects of the aforementioned obstacles.

Current library literature stresses that economic factors and a general population decline are having an adverse effect upon public universities. That being the case, it was surmised that these factors should be more influential upon public academic libraries in the Rust

Advances in Library Administration and Organization, Volume 13, pages 129-161.
Copyright © 1995 by JAI Press Inc.
All rights of reproduction in any form reserved.
ISBN: 1-55938-931-1

Belt states, which are partially defined by both the loss of population and revenue. Conversely, these factors should be less influential in the Sun Belt states which are partially defined by increases in both population and revenue.

Extensive forecasting literature exhorts academic librarians to form planning committees, engage in resource sharing, develop budget responsive collection development plans, include the patrons through surveys and end user studies and to utilize a variety of staffing patterns. Academic library administrators are advised to stretch the library's dollar and assure the future of their facilities through aggressive inter-campus politicking, the utilization of competitive business tactics, the formation of intricate electronic networks, and the implementation of new and inventive fundraising techniques.

While a body of literature exists that forecasts the future of academic libraries and proposes solutions for their present and foreseeable problems, there appears to be little that documents the attempts of academic library administrators to utilize the recommended planning tools and strategies. Also, there is no literature that explores any differences in the strategizing between these two geographic regions that face the problems of diminishing revenues and declining populations to far different degrees.

## PURPOSE OF THE STUDY

The purpose of this study is to fill a gap in library forecasting literature by determining whether public academic library administrators are actually engaging in planning activities and, if so, whether public academic library administrators in the Sun Belt states are engaging in these activities to the same degree as their counterparts in the Rust Belt states.

The objectives of this research project are:

1.  to compare and contrast planning activities in both regions, considering different finances, demographics, and environments,
2.  to provide library administrators with an opportunity to evaluate the tools and processes they have used to facilitate strategic planning, and

3. to provide library administrators an opportunity to share any tools, strategies or influential literature, which were not included in the survey instrument, but which the administrators have personally found useful in planning the futures of their programs and facilities.

## DEFINITION OF TERMS

For the purposes of this study, the following seven terms must be defined. *Rust Belt* refers to those northern and midwestern states which encompassed the nation's steel industry and the manufacture of heavy goods, until the early 1970s. The *Sun Belt* is defined as those southern and southwestern states to which were transferred the manufacture of heavy goods and many other important industries, in the early 1970s. *Planning Strategies* are on-going processes conceived, developed, or implemented to maximize the library's resources. *Planning Tools* are devices used to facilitate planning for the library's needs. *Effectiveness*, as reported on the four-point Likert Scale, is defined as the power to bring about the intended results. *Influential Literature* refers to those pieces or bodies of literature the academic library administrator has consulted as part of the planning process. *Option* is defined as an aggregate term which may include any or all of the tools, strategies, and literature covered by the survey instrument.

## BACKGROUND OF THE STUDY

The concept of strategic planning is at the heart of this study. According to Nicholas Henry, "Strategic planning is the process of deciding the goals of the organization and on the broad strategies that are to be used in attempting them" (Henry, 1986). The process is based deeply within the organization's consciousness and goes well beyond simply setting long- and short-term goals. Successful strategic planning requires that administrators and those who work in the libraries they lead believe that they can overcome or at least ameliorate the obstacles to their survival and progress presented by their environments.

It [strategic planning] attempts to go beyond a simple surrender by the organization to environmental conditions, and in this sense it is by no means a way of eliminating risks. What a strategic plan does is place line decision makers in an active rather than a passive position about the future of their organization. It incorporates an outward looking, aggressive focus that is sensitive to environmental changes, but does not assume that the organization is necessarily a victim of changes in its environment (Anthony and Young, 1984).

Finally, the utilization of planning tools and strategies can be viewed as an outward sign of an administration's interest in addressing its problems and willingness to wrestle with the future rather than merely accepting what comes. Strategic planning is a journey of exploration, and to set out on such a journey is to admit, at the very least, that the destination is within reach and the journey is worth taking.

The results of this study will be of use to academic library administrators in the targeted survey group and throughout the country in that it illustrates, not only what strategies and tools are used to develop strategic plans, but what works. Authors and publishers of library literature, university administrators, and planners should be able to glean from it a clearer picture of the planning processes as they are, not merely as one would expect them to be.

## THE LITERATURE

Writers addressing the needs of academic libraries treat a wide array of topics that range from funding to collection development to personnel matters. But there is a consensus of opinion among these writers and researchers that there is an increasing need to analyze problems within their strategic context in order to help develop meaningful solutions to the problems confronting the library communities. Otherwise, they contend that library managers risk wasting the diminishing resources available to public academic libraries.

Academic libraries do not exist in vacuums. Instead, they operate within the same socioeconomic context that affects industries, grocery stores, and movie theaters. The following review of literature is meant to define this socioeconomic environment and the major problems facing public academic libraries in two distinctly different parts of the country—the Rust Belt and the Sun Belt. The articles encompassed by the following survey of literature were chosen not just because they advocated some form or level of strategic planning, but because each article recommends one or more planning tool or strategy to complete the process. These recommendations include, but are not limited to, resource sharing, networking, collection development strategies, fundraising efforts, and the use of census statistics and surveys.

William Miller discusses the continuing drain of jobs and population from the Rust Belt states to the Sun Belt states. The Rust Belt is defined as those northern and midwestern states whose wealth and population were founded on the steel industry and the manufacturing of heavy goods in the early twentieth century. In the early 1970s, a migration of industry left this region for the southern and southwestern states due both to the cheaper energy costs in the warmer climates and the cheaper, nonunion labor traditionally available in the south (Miller, 1993).

The 1990 census shows a population shift from Rust Belt states to Sun Belt states of approximately 18.5 percent since 1980. This represents a significant increase in taxable income for the Sun Belt states and an equal decline for the Rust Belt (U.S. Department of Commerce, 1992).

John Budd and David G. Robinson explain that, due to shifts in the general population caused by the maturation of the Baby Boomers, all American schools of higher education have suffered significant decreases in student population and a consequent loss of tuition revenue. These authors calculated a 8.3 percent decrease in enrollment in four year colleges from the period of 1984 to 1993. This includes a 14.3 percent decrease of full-time students and a 6.4 percent increase of part-time students.

No population trend is permanent. Budd and Robinson report a slight increase in the birth rate in the mid 1970s which should give a boost to college enrollment; however, the steady increases in the high school drop-out rate may negate the increase in general population. In any event, the authors stress that the importance of strategic planning cannot be overestimated and argue that library administrators must be able to use and interpret strategies and information on hand to determine courses of action that will ensure optimum use of resources in a time of change (Budd and Robinson, 1986).

Malcolm Getz draws upon the same demographics and revenue projections as those noted earlier. He offers several strategies for the academic library administrators to follow in hard times. Getz contends that library leaders should seek flexible commitments, such as programming that can be implemented or dropped as the budget dictates, and should avoid fixed commitments, such as branch building and the creation of new personnel positions. He also warns academic librarians that a failure to develop strategic planning skills during hard times will result in having to develop crisis management skills in harder times (Getz, 1990).

Nicholas Henry, in the context of public administration, has defined strategic planning by recognizing,

> ...that organizations have both localized, short term, bottom line demands and all-organization, long term and invested-strategies-for-the-future demands. They must live with the familiar today, yet also must be forever looking out for how to live in a very different tomorrow. Strategic planning is an attempt to recognize this reality (Henry, 1986).

James McGrane (1991) discusses the need to perceive the academic library as a business in a competing information market. He urges the use of strategic planning (which he defines as "...a process by which an organization seeks to discover a profitable fit between itself and its environment") in technologically outfitting the academic library to exist and prosper in the information hungry twenty-first century.

James Govan calls for rethinking the academic library in terms of staff, the coordination of print and electronic collections, and each facility's mission and goals. He contends that we have created in less than twenty years an information glut, making the academic library an unusable resource for many students and scholars. Govan addresses the need to strategize the implementation of future technologies that will answer the specific needs of individual users rather than those of some mythical "typical" patron. He reports that, to date, the costs of the new, electronic technologies have far exceeded expectations and that, in an era of budgetary rigidity, more thoughtful planning and coordination of resources will be necessary if academic libraries are to survive (Govan, 1991).

Planning can be useful for dealing with uncertainty at the department level as well as for the library as a whole. Susan Goldberg studies a newly opened development office at the University of Arizona Library. The success of this development office in fundraising has depended on its use of such strategies as needs assessments, interlibrary/community committees, a university-wide master plan, nationwide networking with other academic library development offices, and considerable intra-campus politicking (Goldberg, 1990).

Planning for the use of collections also is viewed as important. Robert F. Munn acknowledges that traditional collection development in academic libraries will shift to include varied information networks and resource sharing. At the same time, he warns that resource sharing, which may be an inevitable and valuable development for large research libraries, may not be in the best interest of medium- to small-sized colleges and universities, where research takes a back seat to curriculum support. The author calls for careful planning within each academic library before adopting a resource sharing system. He advocates the use of a decision-making process that includes the analysis of the requirements of each university participating in the network as well as feedback from faculty and all other library users on individual campuses (Munn, 1983).

Richard M. and Ann P. Dougherty asked members of the Board of Editors of the *Journal of Academic Librarianship* to discuss the greatest challenges facing academic libraries in the future. Changing technologies, leadership, changing needs and expectations of library users, access versus ownership, funding, and copyright issues were assessed by the authors to be major concerns. The authors suggested that it is of equal importance for an academic library to adopt a facility-wide strategy for dealing with its complex problems as it is to acknowledge the existence of the problems in the first place (Dougherty and Dougherty, 1993).

Patrick W. Leonard recommends an extraordinary strategy in the academic library's continuing struggle for self-justification. He advises academic librarians to make use of the "subtle linkages among libraries, faculty offices and classroom...to identify the connection between library usage and success, academically and in the work place." Leonard contends that only a library use/benefit system will provide the hard and fast evidence that administrators require before adjusting the library line item in the university budget (Leonard, 1991). (If his recommendation is to be taken seriously, it may be a negation of the patron's right to privacy.)

Stephen E. Atkins perceives the academic library as a cell in the political body of the university. He faults academic librarians for their isolationist thinking and their failure to develop political strategies that would enhance the library's image within the academic community. He states that this is why the budgets of academic libraries have dropped in these hard times, from the desirable six percent of their institutions' budgets to an unmanageable three percent in many instances.

Atkins makes the interesting observation that academic librarians only know those faculty members who are active, productive researchers who use the library. The vast majority of the faculty never go near the library and think of it as a sidecar on the great academic machine that could just as well be dumped. This author advocates that academic librarians develop and tend networks, committee meetings, and liaisonships throughout their academic communities. These efforts should serve to promote the library and to garner enough political clout to deal with harsh budgetary realities (Atkins, 1991).

In a sense, nearly all articles written about academic libraries address their futures and recommend planning strategies. Each recommendation, survey result or management theory that appears in the professional literature is meant to help optimize resources, streamline service delivery, broaden the range of information availability and improve the quality of the patron's library experience. These goals are not just long term, they are perpetual.

## THE STUDY

In order to study the utilization of planning tools, strategies, and literature in the planning processes of the targeted population, a two-section survey was developed (see Appendix A). Section A consists of five questions that address the facilities' environments. Section B is comprised of four parts that address the thirteen planning tools and strategies which are the subject of this survey.

Parts six through fifteen are accompanied by a four-part Likert Scale that allows the respondents to evaluate a planning tool or strategy for its effectiveness, as follows: 1 = low, 2 = medium to low, 3 = medium to high and 4 = high.

A cover letter explaining the nature of the project and general instructions was mailed out with each survey (see Appendix B). Also, key instructions were repeated at the top of the survey instrument itself.

The four year colleges and universities targeted for the survey were culled from *Peterson's Guide to Four Year Colleges* (Princeton University, 1994). The specific names of current library administrators were taken from the *Directory of American Libraries* (*American Library Directory*, 1993-1994). All together, 105 colleges and universities from four Rust Belt and four Sun Belt states were targeted. Fifty-one Rust Belt and fifty-four Sun Belt facilties received the survey instrument. The Sun Belt states represented are Florida, Georgia, New Mexico, and Texas. The Rust Belt states represented are Illinois, Michigan, Ohio, and Pennsylvania (*American Library Directory*, 1993-1994). These states were chosen to represent their regions because the subtotal of public academic libraries in these groupings were numerically close. All responses were limited to a time frame beginning with academic year 1988-1989 and ending in academic year 1993-1994.

Of the 105 surveys mailed out, 64 (61%) were returned. Thirty-one (61%) Rust Belt administrators responded, as did 33 (61%) of the Sun Belt administrators.

Tables analyzing the survey responses can be found here. All percentages reported here and in the tables have been rounded off to the nearest tenth.

The distribution of targeted states and respondents can be found in Table 1. Thirty-three, or 52 percent, of all the responses were submitted by Sun Belt administrators while 31 or 48 percent were submitted by Rust Belt administrators. Diverse responses were submitted regarding the budget, and these are noted in Table 2. A substantial 74 percent of responding Rust Belt facilities (RBs) receive three to five percent of the parent institution's budget, compared to only 49 percent of the Sun Belt facilities (SBs). While 24 percent of SBs are receiving more than five percent of the parent institution's budget, only seven percent of RBs fall into this enviable position. On the other hand, 27 percent of the SBs are receiving less than three percent of their parent institution's budget, compared to the RBs 16 percent in this category.

A look at the FTE growth in Table 4 reveals that 85 percent report enrollment growth and thus revenue growth. Of the RBs, only 45

**Table 1.**  Distribution of Libraries in Sun Belt States and
Rust Belt States, Surveyed and Responding

| STATES | #surveyed | #respondents | %surveyed/ responding |
|---|---|---|---|
| Rust Belt: | | | |
| Illinois | 12 | 5 | 42 |
| Ohio | 10 | 8 | 80 |
| Pennsylvania | 14 | 9 | 64 |
| Michigan | 15 | 9 | 53 |
| Subtotals: | 51 | 31 | 61 |
| Sun Belt: | | | |
| Florida | 10 | 5 | 50 |
| Georgia | 15 | 8 | 53 |
| New Mexico | 5 | 5 | 100 |
| Texas | 24 | 15 | 63 |
| Subtotals: | 54 | 33 | 61 |
| Totals: | 105 | 64 | 61 |

**Table 2.**  Library's Budget in Relation to the Parent Institution's Budget

| Relation to P.I.'s Budget | Sun Belt | | Rust Belt | | Total | |
|---|---|---|---|---|---|---|
| | f | % | f | % | f | % |
| Less than 3% | 9 | 27 | 5 | 16 | 14 | 22 |
| 3% to 5% | 16 | 49 | 23 | 74 | 39 | 61 |
| More than 5% | 8 | 24 | 2 | 7 | 10 | 15 |
| Fluctuating | 0 | 0 | 1 | 3 | 1 | 2 |
| Total | 33 | 100% | 31 | 100% | 64 | 100% |

percent report enrollment growth. The SBs are not only receiving a larger portion of their institutions' budgets, but they are functioning in institutions which are experiencing impressive increases in tuition revenues.

The greatest differences between SBs and RBs in the collection development section are reported in the number of both serial and periodical subscriptions held in reporting libraries. While the SBs are experiencing considerable growth in these areas (39%), RBs report a substantial reduction in the number of subscriptions received (58-61%) (Table 3).

Differences in full-time enrollment are illustrated in Table 4. The SBs report a growth in enrollment in 85 percent of the colleges surveyed, compared to the RBs reported growth in only 45 percent of the sample. Equally significant is the fact that RBs report a diminishment of FTE in 30 percent of the cases. This researcher finds these figures more dramatically divergent than would be expected from the 18.5 percent population shift from the Rust Belt to the Sun Belt reported by the 1990 census. Further research is needed to determine the nature of and rationale for this divergence.

Table 5 reports on changes in library staffing. The greatest disparity exists in the way in which growth in the number of full-time professional librarians in the SBs outstrips that in libraries in the RBs. SB libraries noted a growth in the number of librarians employed in 42 percent of its libraries and a decline in that number in only 18 percent. RBs noted a growth in the number of librarians in only 6 percent of its members, while a distressing 39 percent noted a decline in the number of librarians employed.

It is also interesting to note that 48 percent of SBs report growth in the area of student employment while only 29 percent of R Bs report growth in this area. Since student labor can be had cheaply, one would consider this to be a cost effective way to supplement a dwindling staff in certain areas. However, this does not seem to have happened in most of RB libraries. All in all, the Sun Belt states report a pattern of holding their own or thrusting ahead in all staffing areas. Conversely, Rust Belt libraries report far less growth and, in fact, showed an alarming pattern of diminished human resources available to support their programs.

The rise and fall of staffing in both regions appears to be linked directly to the rate of FTE growth/diminishment in the region. The indication is that, as FTE grows in the SB schools, so does the parent institutions' revenues, and that more money is then made available for additional staff to serve a growing student population. Conversely, the slower growth and, in many cases, reduction of FTE in RB institutions and the subsequent loss of tuition revenue can account for the loss of staff in the RB facilities. The growth/loss of staff could be a reasonable administrative maneuver by the library administrator to adjust to the changing student population in the represented institutions. On the other hand, 23 percent of the SB facilities and 13 percent of the RB facilities admit to having no personnel policy regarding staffing patterns (see Table 8).

To verify the linkage of FTE and growth/reduction of library staff it would be necessary to compare the reported staffing patterns with the actual student populations of the responding institutions. For example, if Institution SB1 had grown to the size of Institution RB1, it would account for the growth of library staff in Library SB1 but

**Table 3.** Collection Development - Status

| Total Collection areas: | Sun Belt Percent | | | | Rust Belt Percent | | | | Total Percent | | | |
|---|---|---|---|---|---|---|---|---|---|---|---|---|
| | Gr. | Dim. | SS. | NR. | Gr. | Dim. | SS. | NR. | Gr. | Dim. | SS. | NR. |
| Monographs | 72 | 21 | 6 | 1 | 68 | 29 | 3 | 0 | 70 | 25 | 5 | 0 |
| Serials | 39 | 39 | 18 | 4 | 23 | 58 | 16 | 3 | 31 | 48 | 17 | 4 |
| Periodicals | 39 | 45 | 15 | 1 | 20 | 61 | 16 | 3 | 30 | 53 | 16 | 1 |
| CD-ROMS and other electronics | 94 | 0 | 6 | 0 | 97 | 0 | 3 | 0 | 95 | 0 | 5 | 0 |

**Notes:** Gr. = grown
Dim = diminished
SS. = stayed the same
NR. = not reported

**Table 4.** Enrollment FTE - Status

| Population: | f | %Grown | f | %Diminished | f | % Stayed the Same | %Total |
|---|---|---|---|---|---|---|---|
| Sun Belt | 28 | 85 | 3 | 9 | 2 | 6 | 100 |
| Rust Belt | 14 | 45 | 10 | 32 | 7 | 23 | 100 |
| Total | 42 | 66 | 13 | 20 | 9 | 14 | 100 |

not for the reduction of staff in Library RB1. This could be the subject of an extension of the current study.

## PLANNING EFFORTS IN ACADEMIC LIBRARIES

The first section of the survey instrument was designed to provide a snapshot of the environments in which the targeted facilities exist. Responses for this section indicate that the Sun Belt academic libraries are faring better than their Rust Belt counterparts in the areas of budget share, collection development, personnel, and full-time enrollment.

Table 6 deals with the usage of planning tools, strategies, and literature. The scores represent the percentage of options utilized by the respondents from academic year 1988-1989 to academic year 1993-1994. Within this time frame, it is possible for a respondent to have utilized several, even opposing, options, such as both centralizing and decentralizing staff.

The respondents' preferences in format, for influential literature, can be found in Table 7. Both regions report an overwhelming preference for journal articles. This is interesting in light of the fact that so many of the pieces of influential literature recommended by the administrators in number seventeen are monographs.

The respondents were also given the opportunity to select no plan/no utilization for options 6-11. It is interesting to note that 26 percent of SBs and 13 percent of RBs report no changes to their personnel policies though, in the library staff section, all respondents reported changes in their staffing. It would appear that at the no plan/no utilization facilities, trends in staffing counts and patterns are occurring with no formal planning on the part of the academic library administrators. Equally noteworthy is the fundraising measures section wherein 21 percent of the SBs and 13 percent of the RBs report no fundraising plan at all. In an era of widespread budgetary

**Table 5.** Library Staff - Status

| Position: | Sun Belt Percent | | | | Rust Belt Percent | | | | Total Percent | | | |
|---|---|---|---|---|---|---|---|---|---|---|---|---|
| | Gr. | Dim. | SS. | NR. | Gr. | Dim. | SS. | NR. | Gr. | Dim. | SS. | NR. |
| Ft professional libr | 42 | 18 | 39 | 1 | 3 | 39 | 52 | 6 | 25 | 28 | 45 | 2 |
| Pt professional libr | 21 | 3 | 51 | 25 | 29 | 16 | 13 | 42 | 25 | 9 | 33 | 33 |
| Ft paraprofessional | 33 | 15 | 48 | 4 | 23 | 29 | 16 | 32 | 28 | 22 | 42 | 8 |
| Pt paraprofessional | 18 | 6 | 48 | 28 | 10 | 3 | 29 | 58 | 14 | 5 | 39 | 42 |
| Administrators | 18 | 15 | 67 | 0 | 16 | 35 | 45 | 4 | 16 | 25 | 56 | 3 |
| Technicians | 21 | 21 | 45 | 13 | 29 | 13 | 45 | 13 | 24 | 17 | 45 | 13 |
| Student Employees | 48 | 27 | 24 | 1 | 29 | 45 | 23 | 3 | 39 | 36 | 23 | 2 |

**Notes:** Gr. = grown
Dim = diminished
SS. = stayed the same
NR. = not reported

**Table 6.**   Utilization of Planning Tools, Strategies and Literature

| Options: | %Sun Belt | %Rust Belt | %Total |
|---|---|---|---|
| Planning tools: | | | |
| economic indices | 58 | 61 | 59 |
| census statistics | 42 | 59 | 41 |
| circulation statistics | 85 | 90 | 88 |
| head counts | 82 | 87 | 84 |
| surveys initiated by the library or parent inst. | 91 | 74 | 83 |
| other tools | 33 | 30 | 31 |
| Planning Committees/networks: | | | |
| intra library | 94 | 87 | 91 |
| intra institution | 35 | 90 | 88 |
| inter library/community | 67 | 74 | 70 |
| other committees or planning teams | 39 | 30 | 34 |
| Changes to personnel policies/practices: | | | |
| downsizing through attrition | 36 | 58 | 47 |
| centralizing staff | 32 | 42 | 38 |
| decentralizing staff | 24 | 26 | 25 |
| multiple assignment of staff | 54 | 22 | 63 |
| other changes | 24 | 23 | 23 |
| Changes to collection development policies/practicies: | | | |
| cut backs - monographs | 64 | 58 | 61 |
| cut backs - serials | 76 | 84 | 80 |
| cut backs - periodicals | 79 | 87 | 83 |
| a move toward interlibrary/ community information networks and linkages | 79 | 84 | 81 |
| a move away from ownership & toward access | 85 | 74 | 80 |
| a move to purchase more/newer hardware & software | 72 | 74 | 73 |
| other options | 9 | 6 | 8 |
| Fundraising Measures: | | | |
| a library fundraising plan | 39 | 45 | 42 |
| a library development office/liaison officer | 36 | 35 | 31 |
| user fees | 48 | 39 | 44 |
| use parent institution's development office | 60 | 25 | 70 |
| other efforts to generate revenue for library | 21 | 32 | 27 |
| Engagement in resource sharing: | | | |
| library planning interlibrary networks OPACs, ILL, linkages | 9 | 6 | 8 |
| library has initiated these efforts | 24 | 32 | 28 |

*(continued)*

***Table 6.*** (Continued)

| Options: | %Sun Belt | %Rust Belt | %Total |
|---|---|---|---|
| library has completed these efforts | 58 | 61 | 59 |
| Influential literature: | | | |
| publications of professional library assoc. | 91 | 97 | 94 |
| publication of professional non-libr assoc. | 48 | 81 | 64 |
| federal, state and local government publications | 58 | 55 | 57 |
| published survey results such as Murfin-Bunge or ALA surveys | 58 | 61 | 60 |

constraints, one is reminded of a high wire act with no net. This matter is illustrated in Table 8.

Within the limits of this study it is not known if the administrators of the no plan/no utilization facilities have lapsed into this status by neglecting to plan or if they have consciously adopted an "ad locism" position to only cross administrative bridges when forced to by impending doom. In either event, they have placed their programs at risk. While neglecting to plan for the future is reprehensible, choosing to ignore the future until it is the present limits options and reduces the administrative function to crisis management.

In Table 9, the ratings of the effectiveness of the options are presented in accordance with the values built into the four-part Likert Scale as laid out in pages 30-31. The two scores presenting the most highly rated (4) options are 59 percent for "intra library committees," and 50 percent for "library has completed resource sharing efforts." Those options most often rated low in effectiveness (1) are, "census statistics," at 31 percent and, "use of parent institution's development office" at 27 percent. The effectiveness ratings tend to be positive, with the greater percentage of responses appearing in the three to four range. Table 12 lists the ten highest rated options, in descending order.

Of the 29 planning options available on the survey, the RBs exceeded the SBs utilization of 18 options, 62 percent greater utilization of the surveyed options.

62% of Rust Belt utilization > Sun Belt utilization
38% of Rust Belt utilization < Sun Belt utilization
  0% of Rust Belt utilization = Sun Belt utilization
100%

**Table 7.**   Preference for Format of Influential Literature

| Population | Percent Monograph | Percent Journal | Percent No Preference | Percent Total |
|---|---|---|---|---|
| Sun Belt | 3 | 79 | 18 | 100 |
| Rust Belt | 0 | 77 | 23 | 100 |
| Total | 2 | 78 | 20 | 100 |

**Table 8.**   Nonutilization of Options

| Planning Options | %Sun Belt | %Rust Belt | %Total |
|---|---|---|---|
| No planning tools | 3 | 0 | 2 |
| No planning committees | 0 | 0 | 0 |
| No change in collection development p/p | 6 | 6 | 6 |
| No change in Personnel p/p | 27 | 13 | 20 |
| No fundraising plan | 21 | 13 | 17 |
| No resource sharing efforts | 3 | 0 | 2 |
| No consulting professional library publications | 6 | 0 | 3 |
| No professional non-library publications | 48 | 16 | 33 |
| No federal, state or local publications | 36 | 39 | 38 |
| No published surveys | 36 | 32 | 34 |

This matter is further illustrated in Table 10.

Table 11 addresses the ranking of the top ten options, by greatest usage. Four of these options also appear in Table 12, which ranks the top ten options by highest evaluations. These are: "intra-library planning committees," "surveys initiated by the library or parent institution," "a move away from ownership and toward access," and "a move toward interlibrary/community information networks." The preference for these last two options helps to explain the dramatic growth in the access of "CD ROMS and other electronics," collection development, as noted in Table 3.

This preference is worth further study. The library administrators may be opting for a library-without-walls concept by stocking up or plugging into more full text electronic databases. On the other hand, they may be purchasing/accessing more and more electronic indexes while reducing the number of indexed serials and monographs in their own collections. This second option leads to a user frustration recognized by all reference librarians—all indexed but nowhere to find.

**Table 9.**   Effectiveness of Utilized Planning Tools, Strategies and Literature

| Options: | % 1 Low | % 2 M to L | % 3 M to H | % 4 High |
|---|---|---|---|---|
| Planning tools: | | | | |
| economic indices | 9 | 16 | 14 | 17 |
| census statistics | 13 | 13 | 6 | 8 |
| circulation statistics | 11 | 13 | 23 | 27 |
| head counts | 6 | 23 | 23 | 27 |
| surveys initiated by the library or parent inst. | 5 | 16 | 28 | 31 |
| Planning Committees/networks: | | | | |
| intra library | 2 | 8 | 23 | 53 |
| intra institution | 3 | 23 | 39 | 19 |
| inter library/community | 3 | 22 | 25 | 19 |
| Changes to personnel policies/practices: | | | | |
| downsizing through attrition | 1 | 19 | 2 | 19 |
| centralizing staff | 3 | 23 | 39 | 19 |
| decentralizing staff | 5 | 15 | 6 | 2 |
| multiple assignment of staff | 2 | 19 | 27 | 14 |
| Changes to collection development policies/practicies: | | | | |
| cut backs - monographs | 11 | 16 | 13 | 22 |
| cut backs - serials | 6 | 22 | 19 | 31 |
| cut backs - periodicals | 5 | 17 | 30 | 28 |
| a move towards inter library/community information networks and linkages | 3 | 11 | 30 | 33 |
| a move away from ownership & toward access | 3 | 13 | 31 | 28 |
| a move to purchase more/newer hardware & software | 5 | 5 | 36 | 23 |
| Fundraising Measures: | | | | |
| a library fundraising plan | 3 | 13 | 13 | 9 |
| a library development office/liaison officer | 5 | 5 | 13 | 13 |
| user fees | 9 | 19 | 8 | 6 |
| use parent institution's development office | 19 | 9 | 27 | 14 |
| Influential literature: | | | | |
| publications of professional library assoc. | 6 | 11 | 23 | 23 |
| publication of professional non-libr. assoc. | 9 | 11 | 13 | 16 |
| federal, state and local government publications | 8 | 17 | 13 | 6 |
| published survey results such as Murfin-Bunge or ALA surveys | 6 | 17 | 13 | 6 |

It should be noted that two of the options appearing on the list of the ten least effective evaluation strategies, listed in Table 13, also appear on the list of the ten most effective evaluation strategies in Table 9. These are: "cut backs-monographs" and "downsizing through attrition." This listing as both the bottom and top strategies

**Table 10.** Tools Used More Often in Rust Belt Libraries
Than Sun Belt Libraries

| Option Usage: | % Sun Belt | % Rust Belt |
|---|---|---|
| Economic indices | 58 | 61 |
| Circulation statistics | 85 | 90 |
| Head counts | 82 | 87 |
| Intra institution committees | 85 | 90 |
| Inter library/community committees | 67 | 74 |
| Downsizing through attrition | 36 | 58 |
| Centralizing staff | 33 | 42 |
| Decentralizing staff | 24 | 26 |
| Cut backs - serials | 76 | 84 |
| Cut backs - periodicals | 79 | 87 |
| A move toward inter-library information networks and linkages | 79 | 84 |
| A move to purchase more/newer hardware and software | 72 | 74 |
| Library fundraising plan | 39 | 45 |
| Initiating resource sharing efforts | 24 | 32 |
| Completed resource sharing efforts | 58 | 61 |
| Consulting professional library publications | 91 | 97 |
| Consulting professional non-library publications | 48 | 81 |
| Consulting published surveys | 58 | 61 |

give credence to the old maxim that one man's meat is another man's poison. Equally interesting is the appearance of "user fees" on the list of least effective strategies (see Table 13). This option had an overall utilization rate of 44 percent of all respondents. However, it was rated as either medium low or low in effectiveness by 64 percent of the respondents. This evaluation rating is perhaps worthy of future study. The debate over ethical considerations in the application of users' fees may be irrelevant if it can be proved that the use of this option is not effective.

The "other" line on options 6-11 allowed respondents to complete each section with responses that were not printed on the survey instrument. (Their replies are listed in Appendix C). Because of the wide variety of these responses, and, in some instances, because of their length, these entries do not fit neatly into tables. They are reproduced verbatim. All entries are followed by an Arabic numeral representing the administrator's evaluation of the entry, according to the Likert Scale used throughout this study. All of the "other" responses are interesting, but the declaration of a Rust Belt

**Table 11.** Ten Most Often Used Options in Descending Order

| Options: | # Usage | % Usage |
|---|---|---|
| 1. Consulting publications of professional library assoc. | 60 | 94 |
| *2. Intra library planning committees | 58 | 91 |
| 3. Circulation statistics | 56 | 88 |
| 4. Intra institution planning committees | 56 | 88 |
| 5. Head counts | 54 | 84 |
| *6. Surveys initiated by the library or P.I. | 53 | 83 |
| 7. Cut backs - periodicals | 53 | 83 |
| *8. A move toward inter library/community information networks | 52 | 81 |
| *9. A move away from ownership and towards access | 51 | 80 |
| 10. Cut backs - serials | 51 | 80 |

**Note.**  *also on highest rated list

**Table 12.** Ten Most Effective Options in Descending Order

| Options: | % of 4 Evaluations |
|---|---|
| *1. Intra-library planning commitees | 59 |
| 2. Library has completed resource sharing efforts | 50 |
| @3. Downsizing through attrition | 40 |
| *4. A move towards inter library/community information networks | 40 |
| 5. Library is planning resource sharing efforts | 40 |
| 6. Cut backs - serials | 39 |
| *7. Surveys initiated by the library or P.I. | 38 |
| @8. Cut backs - monographs | 36 |
| *9. A move away from ownership and toward access | 35 |
| 10. A library development office/liaison officer | 35 |

**Notes:**  *also on greatests usage list
@also on bottom ten list

**Table 13.** Ranking Bottom Ten Options by Lowest Evaluation 1 Descending Order

| Options: | % of 1 Evaluation |
|---|---|
| 1. Census statistics | 31 |
| 2. Use parent institution's development office | 27 |
| 3. Centralizing staff | 25 |
| 4. User Fees | 21 |
| 5. Decentralizing staff | 19 |
| *6. Cut backs - monographs | 18 |
| 7. Economic indices | 16 |
| 8. Consulting publications of professional non-library association | 15 |
| 9. Consulting federal, state or local government publication | 14 |
| *10. Downsizing through attrition | 13 |

**Note:**  *also on top ten evaluation list

administrator that, "We are totally driven by the Institutional budget...." was particularly refreshing for its artless simplicity.

Questions #17 and #18 allowed the respondents to share any recomendations that they might have found useful regarding literature and planning options. The recommendations are reproduced here, verbatim (see Appendix D).

A wide range of influential literature was recommended. Several periodicals were mentioned more than once. These include: ARL publications, *The Chronicle for Higher Education* and *ACRL News*. Electronic resources are recommended, such as listservs on the Internet. Recommended monographs include: *Managing Libraries in Transition*, Cargill; *Strategic Planning for Libraries*, Riggs; *The Virtual Community*, Rheingold; *Teaching the Elephant to Dance*, Balasco; *Future Edge*, Baker; *Managing Professional People*, Shapiro and *The Prince*, Machiavelli (a recommendation made by a Rust Belt administrator).

Specific planning tools and strategies recommended include: survey feedback; Total Quality Management; strategic planning; relying on the strategic planning of other libraries; using the budget as a planning tool; using the mission statement of the parent institution; politicking on campus; outside consultants; the use of entry counts and circulation data, and marketing the library.

These recommendations emphasize public relations, professional networking, intra-institution lobbying and dialogue and other necessary but intangible efforts to market the university library. Strategic Planning and Total Quality Management received three recommendations each. Two respondents did indicate the importance of good food in the planning process. The recommendations are listed on pages 51 through 58.

## CONCLUSIONS

The survey revealed four major points relevant to this study. They are:

1. Academic library administrators in the Sun Belt states report a work environment improving more rapidly than that of their Rust Belt counterparts, in terms of FTE, personnel, collection development, and budget share.

2. Rust Belt administrators report that they engage more aggressively in strategic planning activities (62% utilization) than their Sun Belt counterparts (38% utilization).
3. The greater percentage of responses regarding effectiveness (83%), are in the 3-4 range, indicating the respondents are generally satisfied with their efforts.
4. The write-in responses revealed both an interest in and an optimism about the future of planning in academic libraries. The few darker comments made by the Rust Belt administrators could be an expression of personal disposition rather than professional angst. On the other hand, it could reflect the frustration of those who must work in institutions with declining resources.

The purpose of this study was to determine if there was an observable difference between the strategizing activities of public academic library administrators in the Rust Belt states and their counterparts in the Sun Belt states. Given the problems inherent in any survey model, that purpose has been fulfilled.

The utilization of planning tools and strategies in the Rust Belt facilities exceeds that of the Sun Belt libraries by 24 percent. The reporting of no plan/no utilization is only 13 percent for the Rust Belt facilities while it is 23 percent for their Sun Belt counterparts. It appears that pain and retrenchment encourage planning and that the efforts of the Rust Belt public academic library administrators are appropriate to their circumstances. If the Rust Belt administrators are treading water, they are at least paddling vigorously.

The respondents from both regions have revealed themselves to be active, thoughtful professionals ready to steer their libraries into the future, many admitting they do not know what the future holds. Lynch (1989) offers a view of an ever transforming planning process, "While one might wish that the library's program could be completed, by its nature, it never is. That is the future."

# APPENDIX A

School of Library and Information Science
(216) 672-2782
Fax 216-672-7965

P. O. Box 5190, Kent, Ohio 44242-0001

January 24, 1994

Re: Planning Tools and Strategies Used by Academic Librarians

Dear Academic Library Director:

I am a graduate student in the School of Library and Information Science at Kent State University. As part of the requirements of my master's degree I am conducting a study about the tools and strategies used by academic library administrators in conducting the strategic planning necessary for their facilities. The study includes a comparison of strategic planning tools and strategies used by public academic library administrators in northern states versus southern states, acknowledging the different economic environments of these two geographic regions.

The enclosed questionnaire elicits information that will help me to discern which planning tools and strategies are employed, if any, and if these tools and strategies are deemed effective. While library literature abound with suggestions for strategic planning and the tools which an administrator should utilize to optimally plan the use of available resources, there is a paucity of literature addressing the actual usage and efficiency of recommended tools and strategies.

Confidentiality and anonymity are guaranteed as you do not need to sign you name to the questionnaire. Of course, there is no penalty if you choose to not participate in the survey; your withdrawal is effected by simply refraining from submitting the questionnaire. Your cooperation, while highly valued, is strictly voluntary. Please remember to mark the box on the questionnaire if you would like to be apprised of the results of the study. If you have any further questions please contact met at (216) 672-2782 or Dr. Lois Buttlar, my research advisor, at the same number. If you have any further questions regarding research at Kent State University, you may contact Dr. Eugene Wenninger, Vice Provost and Dean for Research and Graduate Studies at (216) 672-2851.

Thank you for your kind attention to this matter.

Sincerely,

Mary Kathleen Geary
Graduate Student

# APPENDIX B

Planning Tools and Strategies Used by Academic Librarians

Introduction: Please check each tool, strategy of form of literature which you use in planning for your academic library. at the same time, indicate your estimation o the effectiveness of each item by circling the appropriate number on the scale provided. For the purposes of this study, effectiveness will be defined as the power to bring about the intended results.

Please note that the time frame for all responses is from academic year '88-'89 to the present, unless otherwise indicated.

Thank you for your attention to this matter and for your cooperation with this survey. If you would like to receive a copy of the analysis of the data provided by this survey, please check this box □.

**Section A:**
1.   Please check the state in which your facility is located.
____ Ohio, ____ Penn., ____Ill., ____ Florida, ____ Georgia, ____ Texas

2.   Since academic year '88-'89, how would you describe your library's budget in relation to your present institution's budget?
____ less than 3% of parent institution's budget,
____ 3% to 5%,
____ more than 5%,
____ flunctuating.

3.   Since academic year '88-'89, has your collection, in the following areas, Grown, Diminished, or Stayed the Same?

|                          | Grown | Diminished | Stayed the Same |
|--------------------------|-------|------------|-----------------|
| • monographs             | ____  | ____       | ____            |
| • serials                | ____  | ____       | ____            |
| • periodicals            | ____  | ____       | ____            |
| • c-d roms & other electronics | ____ | ____  | ____            |

4.   Since academic year '88-'89, has your library staff, in the following areas, Grown, Diminished, or Stayed the Same?

|                          | Grown | Diminished | Stayed the Same |
|--------------------------|-------|------------|-----------------|
| • ft professional librarians | ____ | ____    | ____            |
| • pt professional librarians | ____ | ____    | ____            |
| • ft paraprofessionals   | ____  | ____       | ____            |
| • pt paraprofessionals   | ____  | ____       | ____            |

- administrators      ____     ____     ____
- technicians         ____     ____     ____
- student employees   ____     ____     ____

5. Since academic year '88-'89, has your student enrollment (FTE) Grown, Diminished, or Stayed the Same?

|  Grown  |  Diminished  |  Stayed the Same  |
| --- | --- | --- |
| ____ | ____ | ____ |

**Section B:** **In this section please check the tools, strategies, and literature you may have used and rank their effectiveness on a scale of 1 to 4 (4 being the highest).**

PART I.   Planning tools: devices used to facilitate planning for the library's needs.

6. Planning tools:

| | | | | |
| --- | --- | --- | --- | --- |
| ____ economic indices | 1 | 2 | 3 | 4 |
| ____ census statistics | 1 | 2 | 3 | 4 |
| ____ circulation statistics | 1 | 2 | 3 | 4 |
| ____ head counts | 1 | 2 | 3 | 4 |
| ____ head counts | 1 | 2 | 3 | 4 |
| ____ surveys initiated by the library or parent institutions, e.g., tests, end user studies, etc. | 1 | 2 | 3 | 4 |
| ____ other tools (please indicate) | | | | |
| _____ | 1 | 2 | 3 | 4 |

____ no planning tools used

PART II.   Planning strategies: On-going processes conceived, developed or implemented to maximize the library's resourses.

7. Planning committees/networks:

| | | | | |
| --- | --- | --- | --- | --- |
| ____ intra library | 1 | 2 | 3 | 4 |
| ____ intra institution | 1 | 2 | 3 | 4 |
| ____ inter library/community | 1 | 2 | 3 | 4 |
| ____ other committees or planning teams | | | | |
| _____ | 1 | 2 | 3 | 4 |
| _____ | 1 | 2 | 3 | 4 |

____ no planning committees/networks

8. Changes to personnel policies/practices:

| | | | | |
| --- | --- | --- | --- | --- |
| ____ downsizing through attrition | 1 | 2 | 3 | 4 |
| ____ centralizing staff | 1 | 2 | 3 | 4 |
| ____ decentralizing staff | 1 | 2 | 3 | 4 |
| ____ multiple assignment of staff | 1 | 2 | 3 | 4 |

____ other changes

| | | | | |
|---|---|---|---|---|
| _____ | 1 | 2 | 3 | 4 |
| _____ | 1 | 2 | 3 | 4 |

____ no changes in personnel
policies/practices


9.  Changes to collection development policies/practices:

| | | | | |
|---|---|---|---|---|
| ____ cut backs-monographs | 1 | 2 | 3 | 4 |
| ____ cut backs-serials | 1 | 2 | 3 | 4 |
| ____ cut-backs periodicals | 1 | 2 | 3 | 4 |
| ____ a move towards inter library/ community information networks and linkages | 1 | 2 | 3 | 4 |
| ____ a move away from ownership and toward access | 1 | 2 | 3 | 4 |
| ____ a move to purchase more/ newer hardware and software | 1 | 2 | 3 | 4 |
| ____ other options _____ | 1 | 2 | 3 | 4 |

____ no changes in collection development
policies/practices


10.  Fundraising measures:

| | | | | |
|---|---|---|---|---|
| ____ a library fundraising plan | 1 | 2 | 3 | 4 |
| ____ a library development office/ liaison officer | 1 | 2 | 3 | 4 |
| ____ user fees | 1 | 2 | 3 | 4 |
| ____ use parent institution's development office | 1 | 2 | 3 | 4 |
| ____ other efforts to generate revenue for the library _____ | 1 | 2 | 3 | 4 |

____ no fundraising plan


11.  Engagement in resource sharing:

| | | | | |
|---|---|---|---|---|
| ____ library is planning inter library network such as opacs, ILL, linkages | 1 | 2 | 3 | 4 |
| ____ library has initiated these efforts | 1 | 2 | 3 | 4 |
| ____ library has completed these efforts | 1 | 2 | 3 | 4 |

____ library is not planning these efforts at this
time


PART III.    Influential Literature. Pieces or bodies of literature you have consulted as part of your planning and decision making process.

12.    Do you routinely consult the publications of professional library associations?
____YES,  ____NO

13. Do you routinely consult the publications of professional non-library associations?

\_\_\_\_YES, \_\_\_\_NO

14. Do you routinely consult federal, state and local government publications?

\_\_\_\_YES, \_\_\_\_NO

15. Do you routinely consult published survey results such as Murfin-Bunge or ALA surveys?

\_\_\_\_YES, \_\_\_\_NO

16. As a rule, do you find monographs or journal articles more useful as sources regarding library trends and planning strategies?

\_\_\_\_MONOGRAPHS, \_\_\_\_JOURNAL ARTICLES \_\_\_\_NO PREFERENCE

17. Please specify, by title or author, any piece or body of literature which you have found particularly useful in planning the future of your library.

_____

_____

18. Please indicate any planning tool or strategy which you have found particularly useful in dealing with the problems facing academic libraries at this time. Do not discount necromancy or astral projection.

_____

_____

This survey is a self mailer. Please fold the survey in three parts so that the stamped, addressed third is outstanding.

Please don't forget to staple the trifold closed before mailing.

Again, thank you for your cooperation with this survey.

Mary Kathleen Geary
3724 West 133rd Street
Cleveland, Ohio 44111

# APPENDIX C

## "OTHER" DESIGNATION

6. Planning Tools:
*Sun Belt*
    1. Serial/book prices, projection (3)

2. IPEDS Reports (4)
3. University produced reports and projections (3)
4. Comparisons with other libraries/analysis of institutional data from own university (3)
5. FTE statistics (3)
6. Peer comparisons (3)
7. College self study, '87 (3)
8. CACD CD ROM for collection analysis (4)
9. OPAC users searches in library ____ and ____ ILL data (1)
10. University master plan (4)
11. ALA standards, various accreditation standards (3)
12. *Library Issues* (4)

*Rust Belt*
1. Normed assessment tools i.e. Wisc-Ohio reference study (1)
2. Self study (4)
3. System (opac, etc.) statistics/management information (?)
4. We are totally driven by the Institutional budget.
5. Campus statistics/reference statistics (4)
6. Library literature (2)
7. University 5 yr. plan requiring specific information (4)
8. ARL Spec Kits, ARL statistics (4)

7. Planning committees/networks:
*Sun Belt*
1. State university system planning (2)
2. Regional Planning among librarians (3)
3. Increased staff involvement in planning, quality decisions (3)
4. Regional consortia (4)
5. This library is within a 9 member system (3)
6. New Mexico Consortium of Academic Libraries (4)
7. System-wide (3)
8. Institutional Automation Committee (3)
9. Library com... (3)
10. Florida Board of Regents (4)

*Rust Belt*
1. Director's advisory council (4)
2. Inter-campus (1)
3. Library of the Future (4)
4. Program review (3)
5. Academic Affairs Productivity, Quality, Priority—part of a state-wide program—(?)
6. Library Senate Committee
7. Grant Writers' coordinating committee (?)
8. University Program Review efforts (4)

8. Changes to personnel policies/practices:
*Sun Belt*
1. Keeping positions vacant at time (2)
2. Redistributed librarians' duties (3)

3. Reassignment (?)
4. Redistribution of assignments (3)
5. More flexibility in assignments (4)
*Rust Belt*
1. Reallocation (4)
2. Empower people to make appropriate decisions (?)
3. Team management approach (?)
4. Reorganization of departments (3)
5. Analysis of services - existing and proposed (4)
6. Combining positions (4)
7. Implemented clustering of units to share staff resources (3)

9. Changes to collection development policies/practices:
*Sun Belt*
1. Purchase full text CD ROMS (4)
*Rust Belt*
1. Reassignment of budget to reflect academic curriculum needs - New formula (4)
2. A move to ownership *and* access (3)

10. Fundraising measures:
*Sun Belt*
1. Grants (3)
2. Course fee (4)
3. Friends of library (2)
4. Legislative Education (3)
5. Grants (1)
6. Foundations-Establish (4)
7. We have combined user fees with membership in a Library Association group. We get a group of interested users, not merely benefactors. (4)
*Rust Belt*
1. Faculty, alumni (2)
2. Grants (4)
3. Endowment (4)
4. Friends organization (?)
5. Grants (2)
6. Grants (4)
7. Grants (3)
8. Asking for money from parents of graduating students to buy books honoring students (3)

---

*grants have been repeated to show the diversity of the evaluations of this funding measure

# APPENDIX D

## ADMINISTRATOR'S RECOMMENDATIONs

17. Please specify, by title or author, any piece or body of literature which you have found particularly useful in planning the future of your library.

*Sun Belt*

1. *Managing Libraries in Transition*, Cargill, Jennifer
2. Performance Measures
3. *Library Technology, Library Issues*, ACRL publications, James Williams' "Strategic Planning in Higher Education," 1991.
4. Riggs, *Strategic Planning for Libraries*
5. Internet literature
6. Literature and information on CD-ROM sources and networks
7. Stephen E. Atkins, *The Academic Library*
8. ARL Spec Kits
9. ARL Annual Statistics and other ARL publications
10. Ranganathan, Peter Druber (sic)
11. *The Chronicles'* "Information technology and academic libraries," *Current Issues Newsletter*
12. Buckland, Lancaster
13. "College and Research Libraries" and "ACRL NEWS"
14. Varies
15. Rheingold's *The Virtual Community*
16. Strategic plans of other universities. Purdue's is excellent.
17. I browse (in an unprofessional manner) through current journals when I can't stand it in my office. You also find things in the oddest places. Example: *Wayfinding, People, Signs and Architecture* by Paul Arthur, McGraw Hill '92. The book was requested by a faculty member in Architecture, but was great for revamping signage in the library.
18. Automation publications such as *Computers in Libraries*
19. Listservers: Collib and Libadim
20. *Rethinking Reference*

*Rust Belt*

21. ALA standards; internal planning documents
22. There are too many to list - "Trends in Higher Education," found in *The Chronicle of Higher Education*, etc.. etc.
23. Michael Buckland's *Redesigning Library Services: a Manifesto*. Chicago: ALA, 1992.
24. "Library Issues Newsletter"/other journal articles
25. An assessment of CODSWLI space needs (prepared for Illinois State University Library by info systems consultant)
26. Balasco, James, *Teaching the Elephant to Dance*; Baker, Joel, *Future Edge*; Shapiro, Albert, *Managing Professional People*

27. *University Libraries and Scholarly Communication; Metropolitan Universities; Managing Information Technology on Campus*
28. *University Libraries and Scholarly Communications*
29. ADA literature; collection development and management periodicals; management literature; ERIC literature
30. *Measuring Academic Library Performance - a Practical Approach* by Nancy A. Van House, Beth T. Weil and Charles R. M. McClure
31. "Library Issues"
32. Victor Baldridge; Kenneth Howard; Barbara Moran
33. *The Prince* by Machiavelli
34. Lots of good stuff out now!
35. Hodgepodge
36. Visions basic assumptions; work over Internet; Dougherty's work computing/library interaction and planning strategies
37. *Greenwood Library Management Collection* - monos
38. Multitudes of similar studies done by other libraries; CADA (Amigos) ACRL and other statistics

18. Please indicate any planning tool or strategy which you have found particularly useful in dealing with the problems facing academic libraries at this time. Do not discount necromancy or astral projection.
*Sun Belt*
1. Survey feedback and group participation
2. Networking at meetings, ALA
3. Full exploitation of electronic access to information
4. TQM
5. Common sense and kindness
6. Our major problem in planning the future is making sure the higher levels of university administration understand what is possible and what is not.
7. Budget is a planning tool - spread sheets, forecasts, scenarios, projections (or inner spirituality and intuition).
8. Try modified TQM
9. I have relied on the strategic plan of another, larger library for which I have great respect.
10. Total Quality Management has been considered along with strategic planning.
11. Basic management principles remain the same, but must be fit to a new paradigm.
12. Varies
13. Team management by need in a variety of services.
14. Tools: Counterparts in other libraries - ask for help and they will talk your arm off. Library staff - everyone knows more about what they do than you do. Strategies: Market yourself. Don't fall into the trap of thinking that libraries don't have to sell themselves. The faculty and administration can be very supportive if you take the time to explain the costs and benefits

to them. It's like writing a grant proposal. Too many library directors feel that everyone knows that libraries cost an unlimited amount of money and what libraries do with that money is too complicated to be understood by anyone else. Success that we have had with an on-line catalog, LAN for CD-ROM products, even a project to cancel underused journals has been due more to public relations and gathering support.

15. Meetings with other library directors
16. Prayer and lobbying state legislature
17. Dialogue with colleagues in librarianship and in higher education is probably the most helpful in looking at trends, funding, telecommunications and assessments, etc.

*Rust Belt*

18. Lots of talk sessions with all shareholders
19. Consultation with teaching faculty and academic administrators. Demos on access services.
20. ARL spec kits
21. Those appearing in *The Chronicle of Higher Education* plus library journals - however, most helpful was a library consultant brought in in 1990 to evaluate library personnel
22. The mission, vision and focus statements of the parent organization - the library must fit its vision, mission or focus into the parent organization.
23. Networking with other library directors and higher education administrators, community outreach and planning groups
24. Talking with faculty in each department; eating lunch with faculty from around campus; attending appropriate programs at ALA and Michigan Library Association; reading everything I can get my hands on; e-mail lists on various topics
25. Document need - present logical justification, show benefits or negatives - and always do in writing. Above all, get support of faculty. Present library favorably
26. We used outside consultants during our 5 yr. program review - most effective on our campus.
27. Common sense
28. Participated in strategic planning for university. Developed 5 yr. plan based on that and university mission.
29. Open exchange of ideas based on decision-making at lowest level. "Ad Locism" - try anything that sounds plausible and then fix it if it doesn't work.
30. Focused retreats with decent food seems to help.
31. We use a typical strategic planning process and self directed approach.
32. Internal self-study
33. Activity statistics, e.g., entry counts, reference, circulation and ILL data

# REFERENCES

*American Library Directory* (46th ed.). (1993-1994). Providence: R.R. Bowker.

Anthony, R.N., and D.W. Young. 1984. *Management Control in Non-profit Organizations* (3d ed.). Homewood, IL: Irwin.

Atkins, S.E. 1991. *The Academic Library in the American University.* Chicago: American Library Association.

Budd, J., and D.G. Robinson. 1986. "Enrollment and the Future of Academic libraries." *Library Journal* 111: 43-46.

Dougherty, R.M., and A.P. Dougherty. 1993. "The Academic Library: A Time of Crisis, Change and Opportunity." *Journal of Academic Librarianship* 8 (6): 342-6.

Getz, M. 1990. "Economics: Retrenchment." *The Bottom Line* 4: 43-6.

Goldberg, S. 1990. "Starting a Development Office: One Academic Library's Experience." *The Bottom Line* 4: 31-3.

Govan, J.P. 1991. "Ascent or Decline? Some Thoughts on the Future of Academic Libraries." Pp. 24-44 in *The Future of the Academic Library.* Urbana, IL: University of Illinois.

Henry, N. 1986. *Public Administration and Public Affairs* (3d ed.). Englewood Cliffs, NJ: Prentice Hall.

Leonard, P.W. 1991. "Beyond Metaphor." *Journal of Academic Librarianship* 17: 163-4.

Lynch, B.P. (ed.). 1989. *The Academic Library in Transition: Planning for the 1990s.* New York: Neal-Schuman.

McGrane, J. 1991. "Target 2000: Strategic Imperatives for Academic Libraries." In *The Future of the Academic Library.* Urbana, IL: University of Illinois.

Miller, W.H. 1993. "More Rust for the Rust Belt." *Industry Week*, 21: 46.

Munn, R.F. 1983. "Collection Development vs. Resource Sharing." *Journal of Academic Librarianship* 8: 352-3.

Princeton University. 1994. *Peterson's Guide to Four Year Colleges.* Princeton, NJ: Peterson's Guides.

U.S. Department of Commerce. 1992. *1990 Census of Population: General Characteristics.* Washington, DC: GPO.

# MANAGING QUALITY AT BOWLING GREEN:

## A CASE STUDY

Barbara A. Ford-Foster and Cliff Glaviano

## INTRODUCTION

Although Total Quality Management (TQM) or Continuous Quality Improvement (CQI) has begun to be discussed within the library profession, the discussions to date have been mostly informal, chiefly limited to non-refereed journal articles, and to papers given at regional and national professional meetings. There are few, if any, published case studies of academic library implementations. In lieu of substantive case studies, the problem becomes one of identifying the extent to which academic libraries are embracing elements of the total quality movement, how those elements have been conceptualized or implemented, and how librarians might assess the successes or failures of these implementations.

**Advances in Library Administration and Organization, Volume 13, pages 163-193.**
Copyright © 1995 by JAI Press Inc.
All rights of reproduction in any form reserved.
ISBN: 1-55938-931-1

Since academic libraries are most often subordinate organizations within our institutions of higher education, it can be expected that most incidences of library TQM initiatives will have been influenced strongly by similar initiatives within the parent institutions, with implementations perhaps even mandated by college or university administrations. Not surprisingly, independent academic library TQM implementations can be expected to be rare.

This study describes how elements of TQM might be successfully used in implementing quality programming in academic libraries. Chiefly this will involve description of an independent implementation of aspects of TQM in the College of Libraries and Learning Resources (LLR) at Bowling Green State University (BGSU). Though the implementation in LLR was independent, neither mandated by BGSU nor influenced by similar university-wide initiatives, the problem areas encountered in conceptualization and implementation of quality programming in the Bowling Green implementation could easily be generalized to other implementation scenarios.

## BACKGROUND

In 1988, a Strategic Task Force was convened at Bowling Green State University to develop logistics for the creation of a strategic plan for Libraries and Learning Resources (LLR). The Task Force began by reading and discussing books and articles about strategic planning and about the future of academic libraries. Subsequently, the Task Force was able to redefine its role, the breadth of its charge, and its goals and objectives in light of its new understanding of the planning process and the future of libraries as envisioned by experts. The definition of strategic planning used by the Task Force (1988) was:

> Strategic planning is a method of planning that matches an organization's strengths to its best opportunities. Best opportunities are areas of endeavor where it appears possible to achieve significant progress toward realizing aspirations stated in the mission (p. 2).

As the Task Force progressed it also read, analyzed, and discussed previous LLR planning and review documents, departmental annual reports, and LLR general planning documentation for the previous two years. It also reviewed the most recent annual report of BGSU Computer Services, the latest annual report of University President, Dr. Paul J. Olscamp, and both the LLR and the Bowling Green State University goal and mission statements. At the same time, the Task Force prepared an environmental analysis that described the Weaknesses, Opportunities, Threats, and Strengths (WOTS) affecting the operations of LLR units. The Ohio Board Of Regents (OBOR) report, *Progress Through Collaboration, Storage, and Technology*, was also read, reviewed, and discussed by the Task Force along with other OBOR documents related to planning for the Ohio Library Access Project (later known as OhioLINK).

The Report of the Task Force included a draft revision of the LLR mission statement and (WOTS) environmental analyses for various LLR divisions. At the suggestion of the Task Force, the LLR staff was surveyed and encouraged to express opinions regarding the report and its implications. The final report of the Task Force, *Libraries and Learning Resources Strategic Plan 1988-89* (1988) envisioned a five-year strategic plan including:

A.  Revised Mission Statement.
B.  LLR's Driving Force. Critical Issues and Strategic Areas.
C.  Strategic Areas and Goals Related to University Goals.
D.  Strategic Goals and Objectives with Specific Actions Required and Target Dates (p. 11).

The *Strategic Plan Update '90* (1990) was based on the earlier document but introduced the concept of each subsequent *Update* serving as the planning document for the next three succeeding fiscal years' LLR operations.

The revised Mission Statement of Libraries and Learning Resources stated that:

The divisions of Libraries and Learning Resources—University Libraries, Instructional Media Services, Center for Archival Collections, and Institute for Great Lakes Research—directly support teaching, research and service by developing and organizing relevant collections, providing access to information resources regardless of location or format, instructing patrons in the effective utilization of information resources, and designing and assisting with the effective use of instructional technologies for teaching and research (Annual Report 1990, p. 1).

The *Strategic Plan* and *Updates* soon became effective new tools for LLR management, serving as the basic documents for LLR operations using Management By Objectives (MBO) and allowing for the setting of department, unit and individual goals and objectives related to LLR goals and objectives enumerated in the plan. Strategic planning's impact on LLR's operations under MBO was positive. Each spring, the dean of Libraries and Learning Resources and LLR administration participated in a management retreat at which updating the *Strategic Plan* was a major order of business. Policy and procedural issues relating to staffing, library systems, office information systems, funding availability, and operating priorities were related to LLR goals, objectives, and mission found in the *Strategic Plan* through the update process.

Following the publication of *Progress Through Collaboration, Storage, and Technology*, the report of its Library Study Committee in 1987, the Ohio Board of Regents (OBOR) agreed to supply increasing support for its Ohio Library Access Project initiative. In the late 1980s and early 1990s educators, automation specialists, and librarians began to meet frequently to establish criteria for the OhioLINK system, and for the evaluation of available vendors and automated systems compatible with OBOR's vision for OhioLINK.

Simultaneously, an economic downturn began to severely adversely affect state funding for the Ohio state colleges and universities. In 1991, LLR units were required to assess their needs and adjust program priorities for the contingencies of small, medium, and large reductions in operating budgets. To assist LLR units in completing their contingency budgets and for evaluating priorities, products, and services across the units, LLR management developed a needs assessment process compatible with the *Strategic Plan* for analyzing LLR unit- and library-wide needs, with the aim of enabling units to make plans based on a variety of budget projections. Facing a "best case" scenario of a frozen operating budget, and with the realistic expectation of a moderate operating budget decrease, the surety of rising serial and book prices, and probabilities that personnel restrictions would be instituted by the university, LLR was looking at a bleak future indeed.

Fortunately, funding from the Ohio Board of Regents (OBOR) for OhioLINK's library network was secure. The selection of Innovative Interfaces, Inc. as the vendor for OhioLINK combined with BGSU libraries' early, voluntary placement in the OhioLINK installation queue indicated probable early replacement of BGSU's outdated automated catalog with an INNOPAC integrated system. Anticipation of the installation of the OhioLINK supplied system provided the dean with additional options for reappraising staffing in Libraries and Learning Resources (LLR). The new system architecture would necessitate some shifting of staff responsibilities, provide some OBOR incentives for new equipment and furniture, and potentially allow some shift in continuing operating expenditures. It was widely felt that efficient use of the INNOPAC system would allow for some downsizing within the organization without any loss in service to users.

The convergence of these assorted threats and opportunities led LLR management to consider reorganization with an overall downsizing of the organization. LLR management also considered enhancing operational management through the utilization of self-guided teams with an organizational operating philosophy enhanced with aspects of TQM. Management's plan pointed to downsizing with no loss in personnel excepting by attrition. The increased efficiencies and increased effectiveness of BG-Link, BGSU's OhioLINK/ INNOPAC node, were expected to enable the delivery of LLR products and services at a quality level at least as high as that experienced using the previous automated system.

Since there was no university-wide quality initiative yet in place, Libraries and Learning Resources, bolstered by a firm sense of its mission, role and priorities as iterated in its *Strategic Plan*, was free to contemplate an independent implementation of quality programming, including aspects of TQM, within its LLR reorganization.

## TQM IN PERSPECTIVE

The precursors to TQM are many. Some would insist that striving for quality is not a new concept at all and will find guidelines for quality management among the military tactics of Sun-Tzu, in Aesop's fables, or in Socratic philosophy. Although it is true that work and management are timeless human activities, the history of TQM is based primarily in the twentieth century, beginning with the introduction of statistical methodologies for quality control/quality assurance in the manufacturing environment. The history of the modern quality movement is undoubtedly familiar to practicing library administrators and will not be outlined in detail in this study.

For the purposes of this study, the working definition of total quality management is taken from the *Federal Total Quality Management Handbook* (1992):

> Total Quality Management (TQM) is a comprehensive, customer focused system that many organizations are adopting to improve the quality of their products and services. It is a way of managing at all levels, top management to frontline, to achieve customer satisfaction by involving all employees in continuously improving the work processes of the organization.

But, why consider TQM in higher education? Strong motivators identified in the higher education literature include financial crises and mounting pressures for educational accountability. Regarding higher education in general:

> Faced with soaring operating costs and persistent public demands for accountability, a growing number of colleges and universities are turning to TQM—and its principles of customer satisfaction, teamwork, and employee empowerment—as a tool to improve how institutions are managed and, in some cases, how classes themselves are run (Mangan, 1992).

or,

> Shrinking resources and increased pressures from the public and private sectors are causing more schools to look to business to provide proven strategies for both economic survival and quality customer service ("Total Quality" ... teleconference, 1992).

The magnitude of these problems in specific instances can be readily understood from a description of the North Dakota University System's plan for initiating system-wide TQM:

> The impetus ... is spelled out in the plan's executive summary: total revenues fell nearly $40 million short of inflation during the 1980s while serving an increasing number of students. The strategies for the 1980s included a tripling of the tuition, equipment and capital cutbacks, larger classes, and increase in part-time faculty, fewer student services, salary freezes, and 'other desperate measures.' The conclusion is blunt: 'Such strategies have reached their limits. Continuing them into the 1990s would decimate higher education' (Seymour, 1992, p. 35).

Higher education has a long history of adopting management concepts and adapting management practices from the world of business to the management of universities and colleges. According to Sherr and Lozier (1991, p. 3):

> Examples include the establishment of multiple levels of management (supervision) and a formal chain of command; the generation of many forms, reports, and data, many of which go unused; the implementation of multiple checks and approvals (inspections); the encouragement of competitive bidding that often results in inexpensive (not to say cheap) materials but frequently increases total costs; and the institution of elaborate planning systems that often do not work well in setting direction, allocating resources, or both. These practices have been largely unsuccessful in achieving their designed objectives...

Higher education is in serious trouble. Facing soaring operating costs, persistent demands for accountability, increasing distrust of the way public higher education resources are used, decreasing enrollments and increasing competition for students; institutions of higher education are looking again to business to remain competitive. Being competitive is becoming identified with being recognized as a quality institution of higher education and/or research in the eyes of legislators, the public at large, and prospective students. The system of choice for managing quality in higher education is quickly becoming TQM.

In discussing the concepts of the modern quality gurus, Deming, Crosby, and Juran, Daniel Seymour (1992), an explorer of quality in higher education notes that, "While each of the leading advocates has his own notions... there is still more agreement than disagreement among the three" (p. 13). For higher education, Seymour reduces the concepts to four philosophical principles, four critical management methods, and three tools for strategic quality management:

### Philosophical Principles

1.  Quality is meeting or exceeding customer needs.
2.  Quality is everyone's job.
3.  Quality is continuous improvement.
4.  Quality is leadership.

The leadership of an organization must, by word and deed, convey the message that, customer satisfaction, through a process of continually improving quality, is the responsibility of every member of the organization.

## Critical Management Methods

1. Quality is human resource development.
2. Quality is in the system.
3. Quality is fear reduction.
4. Quality is recognition and reward.

The management of an organization should make a conscious investment in helping people perform their jobs better by reducing their fears and rewarding their quality-causing efforts.

## Tools

1. Quality is teamwork.
2. Quality is measurement.
3. Quality is systematic problem-solving.

People need to work together to generate objective data concerning the processes in which they work and then apply that wisdom to a systematic methodology for improvement (pp. 13-20).

According to Seymour these eleven essentials taken together then provide, "a powerful set of means to respond to the motivation for change in organizations—including higher education (p. 21).

## WHY LIBRARIES?

Since academic libraries reflect the culture of academe, they too have adopted or adapted business methodologies to the running of the library. They too are the victims of rising costs, increased customer expectations, and demands for accountability. Like their parent institutions, they too have been subject over time to such business concepts as participative management, management by objectives (MBO), matrix organization, strategic and long-range planning, scientific management, and so forth. These particular business concepts, unfortunately, may or may not be consistent with TQM and an emerging focus on organizational quality.

Even if the parent academic institution is not yet working in the realm of quality improvement, TQM must naturally appeal to the library. In the words of Donald E. Riggs (1992), Dean of Libraries at the University of Michigan:

> Simply put, libraries are a natural environment for TQM. Is there any library not pursuing improvement in its service? To take this line of thinking a step further, most libraries are pursuing excellence in their products and services. We do not hear library staff saying, 'We are committed to mediocrity around here.' Libraries are essentially service organizations, and nearly all people working in academic libraries want to offer the very best service...(p. 481).

## CUSTOMER FOCUS

It is the focus on the "patron," the "user," the "researcher," in short, the customer, in academic libraries that makes TQM irresistible. As one author has written in the management literature:

> Total Quality Management (TQM) is nothing more nor less than focus on the customer. We begin with a focus on the external customer. The purpose of an organization is to serve a customer. Without such a focus, TQM, good management, and continued company existence are not only impossible, but may be viewed as antithetical to the continued improvement of society itself. Given that focus on the customer, we must ask what is the level of focus. The answer is 100 percent.
>
> The goal of TQM indeed of any company that has succeeded in the past, whether it knew the initials TQM or not, has been and must be customer 'delight.' Please note that we do not say customer satisfaction. Those organizations, those companies, and those corporations that focus on customer satisfaction will indeed have satisfied customers who will go elsewhere when someone else can satisfy them more. TQM is focused on building customer loyalty through providing a product and/or service of never-ending increasing quality. They're focused very much on the external customer, their wants and needs (Gilbert and Nelson, 1991, p. 52).

Academic libraries traditionally have found difficulty in identifying their clientele, in defining library services in relation to their clients' perceived needs, and in responding to or aggregating expressed needs of that clientele. In an exploration of TQM in academic libraries, the fact that the literature continues to call for further refinements in identifying patron information needs can be seen either as an asset or as a significant liability. Customer wants and needs are not yet well enough defined within librarianship to provide much direction for academic library TQM implementations.

In a thoughtful article in *Library Journal*, Richard M. Dougherty (1991) suggests to his readers that librarians might begin by working to dispel the "myth" that:

> Researchers and scholars are skilled users of research libraries. If library services to scholars were geared to the actual abilities of scholars to locate and retrieve library resources much more could be done to improve the effectiveness of libraries (p. 60).

This clearly indicates that current systems are ineffective and that academic libraries need to develop a much better customer and service focus. Present assumptions and methods are not working. Dougherty goes on to elaborate on what library service could be, and how potential customers are coping to fill their information needs:

> A campus-based library/information system should be designed to accommodate known library user information-seeking behavior. Users seek information from those sources they find most productive, convenient, and timely. This explains why personal collections and colleagues are so frequently consulted (pp. 61-62).

The conclusion that one might make concerning the "myth of the skilled researcher" is that academic libraries do not understand the needs of at least this particular group of customers, and also that these "library avoiders" are also comprised in large part of the teaching faculty, those professional colleagues for whom many library services are presumed to exist.

Another researcher, Kathleen M. Heim (1989), describes the problem as:

> Rather than interact with the library staff, faculty have deployed an intermediate army of graduate assistants to protect their delicate sensibilities from the harsh realities of information retrieval (p. 198).

If it can be conceded from this that academic libraries are also failing to identify and supply the presumed needs of their customers, perhaps a new focus on process management under TQM, predicated on the assumption that the organization as a whole, and each member of the organization needs to be fully involved in focusing on the needs and expectations of the customer, may lead to continuous improvements in library products and services. The approach to improving services and delivering better products suggested by TQM is in continuous, perhaps incremental, improvements in processes by which services and products are effected. It is in the broadening of the concept of "customer" under TQM to include both the traditional external customer (researcher, student, patron) and the internal customer (coworkers or other library operations receiving the outputs of one's work) and in examining those customers' needs with the aim of improving both the products (outputs) and the processes (operations) by which outputs are produced, that Total Quality Management becomes effective process management in the academic library.

Process management would effectively encompass management of virtually everything which is accomplished in a library. Traditional (materials acquisitions, cataloging, interlibrary loan, reference/ information services) and emerging processes (document delivery, full-text image processing and delivery, virtual information services) are processes amenable to improvement, and under TQM amenable to continuous improvement. If "process" can be defined as an action, or series of actions by which "inputs" (products, queries, services) may be modified to become "outputs" (answers, new products, enhanced services) desired or needed by library "customers," improving a "process" can easily be equated with improving services to "customers." In redefining "customer" for the purposes of TQM, it may be helpful for library practitioners to consider a broader, more general interpretation than what we consider for the end-users of library services. This may be paraphrased from Webster's *New World Dictionary* as, "one who regularly, customarily, or repeatedly has dealings with another person or establishment." In short, our customers are our patrons, but patrons now include our organizations, our coworkers and ourselves.

## TQM PROCESS MANAGEMENT

A glance at the following, adapted from an unpublished paper written by Susan Stass (n.d.) of Delaware County Community College, used in presentations on TQM will facilitate the point:

- Managing the process means understanding its boundaries, interfaces, and capabilities, its customers and suppliers—how it all works.
- Inputs: Materials, people, processes, machines...all contributions which affect the process.
- Process: A series of interrelated steps which result in an output, product, service, action. Processes can be seen to have defined starting and ending points.
- Outputs: Results of completed processes. These may be inputs to further processes. Those who receive outputs are customers.

Clearly, management of libraries has comprised the management of library processes and those personnel performing library processes. For libraries, the process management is not new. The newness under Total Quality Management is in how one looks at the process and those personnel supplying inputs and serving as customers of outputs as well as how one looks at personnel performing the process.

## BGSU CASE STUDY: QUALITY, TEAMS AND CUSTOMERS

Bowling Green State University Libraries (BGSU Libraries) have been fortunate to have had leadership sensitive to the needs of the customer, knowledgeable about emerging library, information, and communication technologies, and sensitive to the potential influences of technological change on organizations. While big business was beginning to downsize to enhance competitiveness in a weak economy, BGSU's College of Libraries and Learning Resources (LLR) management was able to consider, suggest, and implement "right-sizing" in LLR. This was accomplished by reassigning key personnel and reorganizing the organizational structures in place to meet the requirements of a new automated library system (BG-Link, Bowling Green's local implementation of an Innovative Interfaces, Inc. system as part of the OhioLINK project), and to meet the increasing demand for library services with fewer library personnel. While big business downsized to meet economic demands, the LLR considered restructuring to better meet perceived customer needs without having to resort to layoffs of LLR personnel.

The need for organizational change was based in the LLR administration's perception that budget restrictions, including

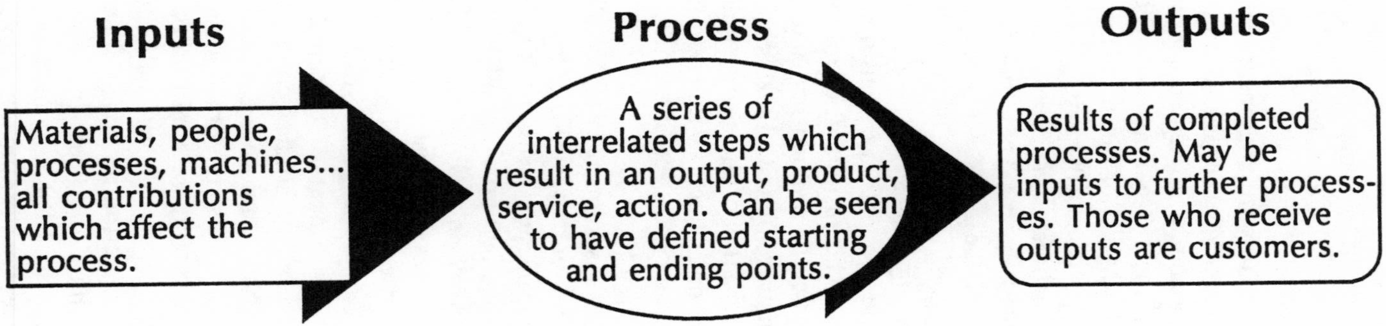

## Inputs

Materials, people, processes, machines... all contributions which affect the process.

## Process

A series of interrelated steps which result in an output, product, service, action. Can be seen to have defined starting and ending points.

## Outputs

Results of completed processes. May be inputs to further process- es. Those who receive outputs are customers.

*Figure 1.*

175

projected constraints on hiring replacements for personnel leaving LLR due to resignation or retirement, would certainly have a negative impact on the delivery of library services, but that the customer service potential provided by the imminent installation of the new automated system would allow for restructuring to maintain library services while simultaneously implementing BG-Link. The LLR reorganization envisioned breaking down the organizational compartmentalization which can occur in any organization, and which was in evidence particularly in BGSU Libraries. Essentially, separate "library" functions were combined to offer broader, customer service oriented services. These redefined service definitions were more consistent with the tenets of TQM. For example, the initial definition of the reorganization included collapsing the separate functions of the cataloging, acquisitions, and serials departments into a single unit with the broader more customer-descriptive name bibliographic services. The proposed operation of bibliographic services would be focused to respond better to customer needs for bibliographic information on BG-Link. Similar changes were involved in the reorganization of the nearly twenty BGSU Libraries departments into three departments with customer oriented charges to provide information services, access services, and the aforementioned bibliographic services.

LLR administration's vision for TQM implementation was bolstered by the realization that BGSU Libraries goals, objectives, and operations were consistent with LLR's *Strategic Plan*. The strategic planning process had provided a forum for staff input and reaction, while the *Strategic Plan* itself, reviewed and updated annually, provided the basis for division and departmental planning and a strong general sense of LLR goals and objectives for a three-year planning cycle. Additionally, BGSU Libraries had a strong tradition of periodic assessment of customer needs and library capabilities from independent studies conducted by library and university personnel. These studies were made available to staff as they were published and when interim updates were issued. The strategic planning process and the tradition of surveying external customers contributed to a good general staff knowledge of the role, mission, and expected direction for BGSU Libraries, as well as of the customers for which most library services existed. Such knowledge was thought by LLR administration to be essential to successful staff empowerment throughout implementation of TQM under the proposed reorganization as well as for continuing LLR operations under TQM. At the same time that local implementation of BG-Link was forcing functional changes in staff assignments and responsibilities envisioned by the LLR reorganization plan, separate training for LLR staff was provided in team building to encourage staff to embrace the team operating structure envisioned as driving the total quality implementation and for continuing LLR operations under TQM.

To facilitate staff understanding of the reorganization, the dean of Libraries and Learning Resources identified the initial cross-functional team structure envisioned. Following input from LLR staff, the dean and the LLR management team identified the nine initial teams for the TQM implementation as: Access Team, Collection Development Team, Human Relations Team, Library Technology Team, Physical Facilities and Environment Team, Preservation Team, Professional Development/Training Team, Research Services Team, and Technical Services Team. Voluntary team membership and participation was envisioned as an individual commitment based on interest in expected team activities. The LLR management team encouraged broad staff participation and encouraged team membership for all levels of LLR staff. Team appointments were made by the LLR management team from LLR volunteers, and structured to ensure broad representation of staff classifications and functional areas. The broad structuring ensured a "cross-pollination" on each team which would offer opportunities for staff interaction and communication across all classifications and levels. Within the broadest possible guidelines suggested by LLR management, the teams were charged with adopting agendas, developing methods of operation, self-government, and team self-development. Team building was championed as the primary methodology for investigating current LLR products and services and for developing or modifying operations and services from the viewpoint of the internal and external LLR customer. In essence, the teams were empowered!

Considerable creativity was expended by the LLR management team to identify local experts in TQM and team building so that arrangements could be made for low-cost, high-quality training for the LLR staff during a time of constrained finances. Eventually, LLR management gave priority to providing all LLR staff training in small group communications and team building. While team members met to discuss leadership among themselves, and teams selected their team facilitators, a local expert from the BGSU faculty began a series of team building seminars. Beyond the seminars, very little direction was given in how teams would conduct their operations. For example, some teams rotated facilitators monthly, others quarterly, and some, two years after the reorganization, have retained their original facilitators. It should be understood that teams were established by the administration to meet ongoing operations in LLR and BGSU Libraries during the period of TQM implementation. LLR management clearly envisioned that operating in a total quality environment would eventually require realignment, dissolution of, or the establishment of new teams as the needs of LLR customers changed or services evolved.

Following initial training, teams began to develop into teams and began to establish and work on projects appropriate to their areas of library operations. While the LLR administration remains informed of team operations and deliberations, its continuing support for and leadership of the BGSU Libraries TQM implementation is generally conveyed to the teams as part of the dean's monthly all-staff meetings. Dean Rush Miller's awareness of the tenets of TQM are evidenced in the patience he displays in allowing the teams to develop, his subtle direction of the change in organizational culture that TQM requires, and his understanding of the considerable investment in training and staff time expended developing the team-centered approach to organizational operation and assessment that TQM requires. Fine tuning of the process has caused LLR administration to develop mechanisms by which team proposals may be approved for consideration by either Libraries and Learning Resources Council (LLRC), the larger administrative group of LLR, or by the LLR management team. LLRC and the LLR management team are empowered to form any task forces which might be required to implement team suggestions.

Current practice is for team facilitators to meet monthly with the assistant dean to communicate with and to update other teams on their various activities, and to receive an assessment from the assistant dean concerning proper channels for implementing team suggestions. The monthly meetings also provide the opportunity for the assistant dean (as a representative of the LLR management team) to update team facilitators on management's interest in and concern for promoting new team projects perceived to be needed by LLR management. The role of facilitators' meetings has been in part to ensure that individual team proposals to be presented to Libraries and Learning Resources Council (LLRC) or the LLR management team for consideration should have the administrative support for implementation if approved by those bodies.

## TEAM INITIATIVES/RESULTS

Approximately one and one half years after initial training, LLR teams had achieved the following:

The Physical Facilities Team had investigated ergonomic furniture and its impact on staff physical well-being. The team evaluated glare-screens for computer users as part of its investigation.

The Preservation Team proposed the methodology for implementing a library-wide disaster plan. The implementation plan included recommendations for recovery equipment and supplies and suggestions for selecting key personnel to be responsible for disaster recovery operations. The team surveyed each collection area and had each area librarian/specialist set recovery priorities for their collections based on collection value and ease of replacement.

The Human Relations Team scheduled several workshops including one developed with BGSU personnel services on "Grievance Procedures." The team has recently recommended surveying LLR staff on the effects of LLR's change to TQM and team operation on LLR services. The team is consulting with faculty in Applied Psychology to develop the survey.

The Library Technology Team surveyed LLR computer hardware and software applications and continues to explore fax/modems to determine whether that technology would be useful within LLR. The team recently began to establish a timetable for equipment modernization in LLR.

The Collection Development Team evaluated approval plan vendors according to relative cost, service, and reliability. Their recommendation included the rationale which resulted in a change in approval plan vendor.

The Professional Development/Training Team recommended centralizing LLR student assistant training and assisted in Systems Training Task Force planning for staff training on BG-Link and OhioLINK.

The Research Services Team proposed the indexing of the MARC 780 and 785 (Continues...and Continued by...) fields in BG-Link to provide more complete access to serials titles. The team was also given the charge to develop procedures for selection of CD-ROM products for locally networked index databases.

The Technical Services Team recommended additional location information be added to the BG-Link locations and undertook a study of Dewey bibliographies with call number anomalies. Their recommendations resulted in the weeding or reclassification of the retained bibliographies for better patron access in BG-Link.

## ASSESSMENT

The reader may find this listing of team suggestions to be rather mundane. In fact, the observation that these achievements result in adjustments to normal library operations or procedures is quite appropriate. The continuous improvement seen to be essential to quality management in organizations can be envisioned as a series of incremental improvements like these achieved by the teams. Some of the incremental improvements are quantifiable and over time may be measured and compared with historic data as an indication of progress. More important are similar incremental improvements in process (the flow of how work is done, the organization of conditions and interactions which repeatedly interact in accomplishing some task) known collectively as the continuous-improvement process (CIP). Quality gurus Deming and Juran both estimate that eighty to eighty-five percent of quality problems are process problems, problems with the system itself, which might be eliminated incrementally as organizational processes are investigated and continuously improved.

Continuous improvement ideally is customer driven:

> The outcome of a process is a product or service which falls short of, meets or exceeds the requirements of the 'customer.' The customer in an internal process is the next step in that process, all the way to the final end-user customer. Customers determine the quality of a product; management determines the quality of a process (Conway, 1989, p. 9).

Since library patron needs and wants are constantly changing, and since technology, library resources and information products and services are also changing, there is always need for continuous improvement in library process to anticipate and discern the needs, and to satisfy library customers.

Implementing TQM at BGSU Libraries did not involve a total shift from the provision of library products and services, nor did it involve a totally different approach to offering library services, at least to this point in its evolution. The "newness" of TQM is not in a radical departure from traditional library processes and services. The "newness" is rather how one looks at library processes and services and how one looks at and manages library personnel.

As an example of what the writers mean by this, consider the following team recommendation which was not reported earlier. Approximately six months after team formation, the Physical Facilities Team recommended the installation of emergency lighting in the Ogg Science and Health Library. It is of note that this recommendation and subsequent installation came from a team empowered to explore aspects of building operations, in a comparatively short time after the team was formed. Consider also that previous management systems used in BGSU Libraries neither perceived the problem inherent in an emergency situation nor took effective steps to remedy the lighting problem. The installation of emergency lighting in the science library seems also to have stimulated the installation of other emergency lighting within LLR. In essence, traditional management, over a period of more than twenty years, was unable to solve the problem that a TQM team noticed, evaluated, and solved in six months.

The preliminary, informal assessment of the implementation of aspects of TQM as part of a reorganization of Libraries and Learning Resources must be that TQM is a success. The "bottom line" in terms of delivery of information products and services is that BGSU Libraries has succeeded in either maintaining or improving its level of services while maintaining or improving the quality of its information products. LLR products and services are being delivered at the same or higher rate as that prior to reorganization, with fewer LLR staff. LLR now affords improved access to information resources, local and remote (dial or Internet access) to users of BG-LINK. Indeed, LLR is even offering new services such as OhioLINK document delivery, and end-user access to full-text periodical databases, after its downsizing through attrition.

## CAUTIONS

Although an early assessment would indicate that BGSU's implementation of aspects of TQM in the operation of Libraries and Learning Resources (LLR) is a success, the realization that the BGSU implementation is not a "complete" TQM implementation may serve to caution potential practitioners in academic libraries. Determining that the mission of academic libraries is consistent with TQM philosophy, knowing the essentials of the systems of the quality masters from their works, having seen derivative works and case studies of organizations similar to ones own, speaks little to assessing the probability of success of the library CEO's implementation of TQM in the local organization. As prelude to describing aspects of TQM which need to be addressed in order to complete LLR's evolution as a TQM organization, the following is offered as a set of absolute requirements for successfully implementing full-blown TQM. There are bits and pieces of knowledge and potential applications of TQM theory to be gleaned from each TQM theorist's approach to implementation, but the three key concepts consistently evident in successful TQM implementations seem to involve:

1. The absolute need for total involvement and active, continuing commitment from top management to build and sustain an organizational culture committed to continuous improvement.
2. Involvement of each individual of the organization in focusing on internal and external customers' needs and expectations.
3. Recognition of people as the organization's most important resource and teamwork as the most important aspect of working toward process improvement.

These seem deceptively simple, apparently are self-evident, and, by all reports, are extraordinarily difficult to sustain for long periods of time in a given organization. TQM theorists continue to remind themselves and TQM practitioners that success in TQM implies a total change in organizational culture. The extent of that cultural change, and its relationship to successful implementation of quality management is aptly summarized by the Federal Quality Institute (1992) as:

> If the culture emphasizes quantity, power, inspection, blame, win-lose competition, and conformity, the culture itself is an obstacle to quality. The

culture sought through TQM emphasizes a commitment to excellence, mutual respect among employees and managers, encouragement of risk-taking and change; a commitment to customers, and continuous improvement (p. 5).

Managerial and supervisory commitment extends to supplying resources for education, facilitating team-training, and providing time for group problem-solving. The cultural change for the organization, even if aided by a history of commitment to continuing employee education, is much larger than may be initially estimated in TQM implementation planning. This caution is offered by Robert S. Winter (1991):

> Most training workshops dealing with TQM in the United States focus on increased employee participation in decision making and on techniques to identify and analyze problems and to develop and implement solutions. Unfortunately, training programs can overlook the most significant requirement for program success: the need to change the culture of an organization so that it can take full advantage of the experience and skills of its human resources. Lacking attention to culture, organizations may use problem-solving processes and techniques such as employee teams and quality circles as a cure-all. The true foundation for a cure is an organizational philosophy and commitment that ensure a continued, consistent effort toward the improvement of quality (pp. 53-54).

These points on changing organizational culture are further emphasized by the Federal Quality Institute (1991) as:

> TQM is not simply a set of specific management techniques and tools. It is a way of managing that is embedded in the culture and environment of the organization. The culture of an organization reflects the prevailing norms, values, beliefs, and assumptions that determine how workers relate to one another and to their jobs... Experience shows that it takes years to create a new culture that places a premium on excellence; to build structures that will sustain and manage change; and to provide training to support the effort (p. 3).

Certainly library administrators are as well aware of the tenets of TQM as they are of current trends in higher education. In tough financial times, however, administrators may not see significant advantage in implementing TQM. Even those most committed to the concept must balk at the allocation of resources necessary to provide adequate training to effect necessary change in the library's organizational culture. Moreover, the past few years have generally forced administrators to concentrate on maintaining essential services during times of retrenchment. Clearly, implementation will be easier to consider if it is accompanied by additional support, perhaps if implementation is part of an institution-wide initiative; or conversely, if library TQM implementation may serve as a test case for the parent institution's implementation, with the additional support for the library's TQM effort implied.

The librarian's TQM dilemma is summarized by Donald E. Riggs (1992) as:

> TQM is not an entirely new management technique for libraries. It does, however, offer a more formal, systematic approach to focusing on continuous improvement. The customer/user is TQM's centerpiece. One should not expect TQM to solve all problems nor should it be viewed as a quick fix. Organizations that have failed in their TQM endeavor have tried to implement it too quickly without proper staff training. An effective TQM process is gradually implemented in a library over a two- to three-year period. And it will require a commitment of resources, especially for the intensive training (p. 481).

It cannot be emphasized enough how much staff indoctrination in the precepts of TQM will be necessary to give quality management programs reasonable odds of successful implementation and ongoing functionality. Academic libraries and their parent institutions have traditionally made much less of their budgets available for training and staff development than have business organizations. Where the costs of in-house TQM awareness training run at about an average of $200 per employee in American businesses implementing TQM, it is expected that expenditures in higher education are much less. Even though recent initiatives have shown that TQM teaching and TQM implementations are at work in American higher education, quality consultants from the business world feel that a lack of university level courses in quality remains a major stumbling block to U.S. competitiveness in the global market. (Haavind, 1992)

In a successful application of TQM at Fox Valley Community College in Wisconsin, voluntary in-house training courses offered for new teaching faculty comprise thirty-six hours of formal instruction. For other FVCC staff, some fifty-six hours of mandatory formal instruction is provided for new hires. These are significant allocations of resources in training for a system in which, unlike in industry, improvements in quality cannot always be shown to contribute to "bottom-line" profits.

It also is possible to seriously underestimate the amount of time implementing TQM may take. Riggs has estimated two to three years for libraries. Ebel (1991), on the other hand, estimates between three and seven years for achievement of a "Total Quality culture" in industry.

## RESOURCE ALLOCATION

Riggs' (1992) estimate of time to effect TQM's change in the organization may also be overly optimistic since academic libraries are in considerable flux at the present time. While information delivery is increasingly positively influenced by technological advances in electronic and optical systems, libraries are increasingly negatively impacted by the costs of acquiring and maintaining new technologies (CD-interactive databases, advanced workstations to provide access to remote databases or other library catalogs by way of the Internet, etc.) as well as by the increasing cost of acquiring traditional resources (enormous increases in the costs of journal subscriptions, similar price increases for scientific materials, increased costs of material preparation and supplies, etc.). New technologies for academic libraries are sometimes funded through savings in personnel. New technologies providing access to information (with the costs of such access passed through to the end-user) are sometimes funded by savings from canceling traditional agreements (often periodical subscriptions) which libraries employed to provide the information "free" to the end-user. Ironically, new personnel to oversee new technologies sometimes now are being funded by canceling subscriptions and passing the costs of access to journal articles on to library patrons.

Difficult choices are constantly being made between personnel and technology, and as a result, change in academic libraries is becoming nearly constant. Under such circumstances, it may prove to be very difficult for even the most charismatic library CEO to keep the library staff focused on TQM for the length of time required for its implementation. Time spent implementing TQM has its own set of costs that will need to be considered. An example used by Robert

S. Winter (1991) indicates that costs of forming problem-solving teams could raise concerns based on:

- *Productivity*. Recurring weekly or biweekly meetings may be considered a drain on resources because they draw employees away from a "productive" use of their time.
- *Training Costs*. Training for team members on problem-solving techniques normally provided by outside firms and consultants, requires an investment of time and financial resources.
- *Solutions*. The impact of solutions is underrated when they do not translate to the "bottom line," as in the private sector.
- *Time Involved*. Solutions may take longer to develop. Management may not have the patience to wait (p. 60).

## NEW DIRECTIONS

Although the preliminary assessment would indicate successful implementation of TQM at BGSU Libraries and Learning Resources, the authors wish to point out limitations to the BGSU implementation in order to suggest future directions for refinements in BGSU quality programming. This critique is intended both to give the reader conversant with the TQM literature a stronger sense of LLR's location on the total quality "road map," and to suggest potential elements or strategies for implementing aspects of TQM in other library settings.

## CURRENT PROCESS

Individuals have been empowered to serve as team members, and teams have been empowered to deliberate and make recommendations. Although teams work to resolve problems they perceive and propose well-documented solutions to those problems, it has not always been clearly understood how these recommendations and proposed solutions are to be implemented. Nominally, team proposals are reviewed by the assistant dean for Library Services and introduced by either representatives of the team or by the assistant dean to the Libraries and Learning Resources Council (LLRC), which is expected to make determinations as to implementation priority, level and method of support required, and to determine of how proposals might best be implemented (Task Force, existing LLR Team, existing LLR Department, etc.) within LLR.

The ideal, as early identified in the program by LLR management, is a situation in which team recommendations and proposals reaching LLRC would have the full backing of the LLR management team, would certainly be supported by LLRC, and would be implemented as resources allowed. It must be admitted that this ideal has not always been achieved. It is also unclear whether breakdowns in the process can be attributed more to incomplete staff understanding of the roles and responsibilities LLR management envisioned for teams and LLRC, or more to BGSU Libraries relative inexperience in implementing team suggestions during the first two years the program was in effect. Some of this naturally is involved with LLR's "growing" into its TQM method of operation, but it is clear that at times, implementation expectations are not being met. Teams seem to have met nearly as many frustrations by seeing the TQM operation "short circuited" by implementations or purchases which seemingly were initiated and considered outside of the team process, or to have team recommendations adopted in LLR prior to their having been aired at Libraries and Learning Resources Council (LLRC). There have been times that teams perceived that team efforts were belittled by others seen as not "playing by the rules." Clearly, expectations could be met if the LLR management would issue more detailed plans for implementations of team recommendations and if that group would insist that everything merits due process within the organization by being processed by teams whenever possible.

Management, though supportive and encouraging of team operations, has yet to integrate its leadership with the TQM implementation. The best example of this appears to be that of the annual review and revision of the LLR *Strategic Plan* and the *Plan*'s relationship to team operations. The expressed purpose of the annual management retreat in recent years has been to review and update the *Strategic Plan*. Generally, this can be described as management (LLR Management Team and Libraries and Learning Resources Council (LLRC), augmented as appropriate by team facilitators and other LLR staff) getting together to evaluate progress, identify problems, document shifts in organizational structure, or propose new structures in light of the *Strategic Plan*. The *Plan* is discussed and revised according to management's assessments of past initiatives, the focus for future LLR products and services, needs of, threats to, and directions for the various LLR units. Prior to reorganization, LLR units under MBO were encouraged to set goals and objectives for their operations based on the *Strategic Plan*. In effect, the broad goals and objectives set by management in revising the *Strategic Plan* were operationalized into specific operational goals or continuing and special projects designed to fulfill the management goals and objectives iterated in the *Plan*.

Since LLR's TQM restructuring in which functional operations (e.g. circulation, reserve, cataloging, etc.) were augmented with the addition of teams, there seem to be no mechanisms defined for management to translate the *Strategic Plan* into team goals, team objectives, or team projects. Goals and directions seem not to yet be definable at the team level. Clearly, time well spent in allowing teams to explore their group dynamics and explore their abilities to discover proper tasks for deliberations has passed and the LLR management team will soon need to develop the channels with which they feel most comfortable to translate their *Strategic Plan* goals and objectives into team concerns and projects.

## TRAINING ISSUES

As mentioned earlier, initial training as teams and in TQM concepts was done on a very limited budget and with considerable creativity, chiefly through the use of expert faculty members at Bowling Green State University. Budgetary constraints continue to severely limit formal training opportunities within LLR. Aside from supporting liberal amounts of release time from job responsibilities for those involved in the various teams, the LLR management team has found it impossible to support initiatives to provide ongoing coaching of team facilitators, or coaching, evaluating, or updating of group relations skills of team members. Though the tenets of TQM would indicate that continuing quality improvement goes hand-in-hand with continuing education, LLR management has had to make the conscious decision to upgrade staff technical skills through formal training centered on access to information through BG-Link and the Internet at the expense of continued training in TQM or in group relations. In essence, LLR management's priority became upgrading LLR staff's functional ability with information access systems, but with no concurrent emphasis on continued training to improve team processes.

Potential implementors should be cautioned that even within more supportive environments for their initiatives, that some difficult choices will need to be made. There may not be sufficient resources available to enable management to make good their commitment to TQM training without external support.

## TOOLS, CUSTOMERS, BENCHMARKING

Closely related to training issues at BGSU and as a partial result of the local need to provide creative, inexpensive initial training, is the fact that there appears to be less understanding across the organization of the tenets of Total Quality Management than was expected or needed to implement quality programming effectively. As circumstances dictated, initial training chiefly comprised group relations training, and more specifically, training in small group communications oriented to team building and team decision making. Though members of the LLR management team were afforded the opportunity of formal instruction in TQM, the limited training budget made it impossible for all LLR staff to receive formal training from experts in quality program implementation. Teams have generally not yet been introduced formally to TQM philosophy nor to quality management tools such as Ishikawa (cause and effect) diagrams, Pareto analysis, Gantt charts, or PERT charts. At least in part this is because the emphasis in the early stages of BGSU's implementation on team building that was designed to facilitate reorganization. Similarly, flowcharting library operations has been uncommon and statistical analyses of processes and simulation or modeling quite rare in the LLR. As quality programming and team management evolve in Libraries and Learning Resources (LLR), administration must look closely at finding means for additional staff training and reinforcement in quality theory and for introducing LLR staff to these concepts and for effective training in the use of the tools of TQM.

Although the predominant missions of Libraries and Learning Resources (LLR) and its constituent units involve customer service, there have been no attempts by teams and very few attempts by functional (output creating) units to identify LLR's internal and external customers since the LLR reorganization. This appears again to have some relationship to the difficulties in obtaining funding for ongoing training and on the need to focus initial training on team building. Since customer identification and customer satisfaction provide the measures for organizational success in TQM, the absence of customer (internal or external) satisfaction initiatives underscores the selective nature of the BGSU implementation and indicates an area for future management attention. For example, several modifications in library forms and procedures for ordering and tracking in-process items recently were instituted in acquisitions. It can be assumed that internal customer identification and indoctrination in customer satisfaction for acquisitions staff would have obviated confusion in cataloging since copy catalogers downstream from acquisitions found the revised forms confusing and/or redundant. Similar isolated instances would indicate that the TQM implementation at BGSU would benefit greatly from further instruction in the customer identification aspects of TQM.

Additionally, identification and surveying the various categories of external customers for LLR products and services is the proper adjunct to the LLR Strategic Plan to ensure that LLR resources are indeed being used most efficiently to meet the needs of LLR's external customers. It is well understood that formal customer surveys are expensive, but they must be considered (where resources exist) to augment librarians' perceptions with additional data from the user's perspective. But until the resources needed for customer surveys become available, LLR will undoubtedly have to rely on informal methods to assess customer needs to include brief one-on-one interviews with reference desk clientele; discussions of curriculum support needs with library liaisons; anonymous inputs from the BG-Link suggestion box; and brief, less-formal surveys, perhaps including focus group interviews.

The final area for consideration for improvement in current processes, or charting new directions for Bowling Green's TQM implementation relates to benchmarking. Although some data is becoming available from BG-Link and OhioLINK, deeper historic data is scarce. It is not yet clear how the LLR management team will provide leadership in identifying data types, standards for measurements of data, or in establishing the periodicity of data collection required to support this effort. Likewise, the LLR Management Team will need to take the initiative in identifying proper comparative aspects of external benchmarking such as the identification of peer institutions or collections which might be used to identify strengths, weaknesses, or potential directions for LLR collections and services, and to identify the measurements by which comparisons and incremental increases in quality might be determined. Thomas Shaughnessy (1993) captures the essence of benchmarking for library management as:

> Libraries need to begin collecting data on the patron/library interface so that internal progress toward improvement might be measured. Those libraries that are able both to collect reliable data and demonstrate high-quality service based on the data collected may, at some point, serve as true benchmarks for the library profession (p. 11).

Measurement of progress is necessary under TQM. Benchmarking will allow the measurement of even incremental increases in quality or process efficiency.

## CONCLUSION

Introduction of selected aspects of Total Quality Management in the College of Libraries and Learning Resources (LLR) at Bowling Green State University indicates that academic library administrators can be successful in their TQM initiatives even if there are no corresponding TQM initiatives within their parent institutions. Though considerable resources must be made available for initial and ongoing training for a full-scale TQM implementation, it is possible to implement selected aspects of TQM using limited resources and to achieve significant results. Indeed, the BGSU experience resulted in considerable change in organizational climate and organizational processes without a great deal of staff indoctrination in the statistical tools of TQM and without much emphasis on internal and external customer identification and without surveys of customer satisfaction. Since libraries are already heavily involved in customer service, customer identification, and other aspects of TQM can be emphasized after quality programming is initiated and as resources become more available for continuing TQM education. At the same time that enthusiasm and support for TQM is evidenced by library administration, care should be taken not to raise staff expectations for the process too high. Similarly, implementors should be prepared to expect the changes in organizational culture required by TQM to take effect gradually over a period of many months. Proponents of TQM must learn to deal with any expectation that TQM will effect quick changes in quality or quantity of library products and services or a quick change in the work environment. Total Quality or Continuous Quality Improvement programming implies incremental improvements in products, in services, and in the organization. To the set of absolutes proposed earlier (total management commitment to continuous improvement; focus on the customer; human resources and teamwork) add the patience to expect, recognize, and assess incremental improvement as the final attribute of leadership in successful TQM implementation.

## REFERENCES

*Annual Report Summary 1990-91*. 1991. Bowling Green, OH: Libraries and Learning Resources, Bowling Green State University.

Conway, E.C. 1989. *Total Quality*. Cincinnati: Corporate Quality Improvement, Proctor & Gamble.

Dougherty, R.M. 1991. "Needed: User-Responsive Research Libraries." *Library Journal* 116 (1): 60.

Ebel, K.E. 1991. *Achieving Excellence in Business: A Practical Guide to the Total Quality Transformation Process*. Milwaukee, WI: ASQC Quality Press; New York: Marcel Dekker.

Federal Quality Institute. 1992. "Education and Training for Total Quality Management in the Federal Government." *Federal Total Quality Handbook, 3*. Washington, DC: Federal Quality Institute.

Gilbert, G.R., and A.E. Nelson. 1991. *Beyond Participative Management: Toward Total Employee Empowerment for Quality*. New York: Quorum Books.

Haavind, R. 1992. *The Road to the Baldridge Award: Quest for Total Quality*. Boston: Butterworth-Heinemann.

Heim, K.M. 1989. "The New Prime Directive: User Convenience." *Journal of Academic Librarianship* 15 (4): 198.

*Libraries and Learning Resources Strategic Plan 1988-89*. 1988. Bowling Green, OH: Libraries and Learning Resources, Bowling Green State University.

Mangan, K.S. 1992. "TQM: Colleges embrace the concept of 'Total Quality Management'." *Chronicle of Higher Education* (August 12): A25-26.

Riggs, D.E. 1992. "TQM: Quality Improvement in New Clothes." *College & Research Libraries* 53 (6): 481.

Seymour, D.T. 1992. *On Q: Causing Quality in Higher Education*. New York: Macmillan.

Sherr, L.A., and G.G. Lozier. 1991. "Total Quality Management in Higher Education." P. 3 in *Total Quality Management in Higher Education*, edited by L.A. Sherr and D.J. Teeter. San Francisco: Jossey-Bass.

Stass, S. "How Did the Japanese Succeed?" (photocopy). Media, PA: Delaware County Community College.

*Strategic Plan Update '90.* 1990. Bowling Green, OH: Libraries and Learning Resources, Bowling Green State University.

"Total Quality Management in Colleges and Universities: How To Make It Happen." 1992. Notes from a teleconference, October 20.

Winter, R.S. 1991. "Overcoming Barriers to Total Quality Management in Colleges and Universities." Pp. 53-54 in *Total Quality Management in Higher Education*, edited by L.A. Sherr and D.J. Teeter. San Francisco: Jossey-Bass.

Shaughnessy, T.W. 1993. "Benchmarking, Total Quality Management, and Libraries." *Library Administration & Management* 7 (1): 11.

# TWELVE YEARS LATER:
## THE ORGANIZATIONAL MODEL IN PLACE AT THE UNIVERSITY OF QUEBEC AT CHICOUTIMI (UQAC) LIBRARY

Gilles Caron

## INTRODUCTION

Librarianship is confronted with an identity problem following the emergence of the postindustrial or service society characterized by, among other things, the proliferation of data or information and the rapid expansion of communications. Librarians and libraries are seeing themselves being bypassed by organizations and people identifying themselves as "information providers" of all kinds, because they have access to a terminal and control the communication infrastructure or the equipment that supports it. More and more people in the library community are predicting an apocalyptic situation where librarians will become guardians of stocks of ever more obsolete publications, isolated in a kind of "no man's land"

Advances in Library Administration and Organization, Volume 13, pages 195-219.
Copyright © 1995 by JAI Press Inc.
All rights of reproduction in any form reserved.
ISBN: 1-55938-931-1

between the archivist and these new providers of information who eventually will benefit from a heightened level of prestige and consideration from their own clients and from society in general. This anguish is a constant presence in professional publications, some of which are desperately trying to "shoot everything that moves" in an almost panic to make a claim on all new situations or information products. On the other hand, others are sticking to the position that the book must be seen as the cornerstone of human knowledge, impervious to time or any changes whatsoever.

This debate is omnipresent in libraries. More over, it is exacerbated by the organizational model used in most libraries, a model that can by itself serve as an illustration of these antagonisms. Public services see themselves as defenders of the access to information for the client, while technical services defend the document as the prime focus of the library. Librarians' ambivalence is the exact result of the structural context imposed by the library, as an organization, to the profession. In fact, it will be very hard to resolve this dichotomy without a reflection on the organization itself and, more profoundly, on the goals of our profession in that organization called "the library."

During the last ten years many authors have expressed their views about the challenges confronting librarians and the library. Some have proposed new organizational models for libraries and new ways to use our personnel. Martell (1983), Jennings (1992), and others (Altman, 1988; Howard, 1985; Johnson, 1990), have proposed their own analysis of the situation and their own recipe to control the shift that will permit the library and librarians to reconcile themselves with their future and maintain their position as the main providers of information to their clients. The number of publications relating to "the library of the year 199?... and up" is astonishing (Drabenstott, 1994). Unfortunately, as some authors have said "the literature on innovation is a call for its exercise and/ or a list of possible areas of need or application" (Reynolds and Whitlatch, 1985, p. 409), more than an illustration of concrete realizations of the capacity of the profession to deal with change. At the University of Quebec at Chicoutimi, we have put forward our solution and made it operational. For more than 12 years now, this university library has been operating on the basis of a coherent vision of what should be the final "raison d'être" of our library. Inspired by that vision, we have developed programs and implemented an organizational model that has permitted us to deliver some value-added services that are appreciated by the client, to reconciliate the library with itself, and to create for library employees an opportunity and an environment that can enable them to exploit their true potential as intellectual workers and individuals. This article is a description of this model.

## THE UNIVERSITY OF QUEBEC AT CHICOUTIMI AND ITS LIBRARY

The University of Quebec at Chicoutimi (UQAC) was created in 1969. UQAC is one of 11 members of the University of Quebec, a network covering most of the territory of the Province of Quebec (Canada). The main campus is located at Chicoutimi, a city of 65,000 residents located about 200 kilometers (130 miles) north of Quebec City. UQAC serves a population of about 400,000 people, including 300,000 in the immediate neighborhood of the main campus, the Saguenay-Lac-Saint-Jean region of Quebec.

UQAC has an enrolment of 7,500 students (4,300 FTE) in programs leading to bachelor's, masters' and doctoral degrees. One of the main characteristics of UQAC is the breadth of its curriculum which includes no less than 105 active programs covering most of the disciplines present in large universities with the exception of medicine and law. Even in these disciplines, related programs like nursing and business law are offered. This dispersion, necessarily, creates a problem for the library.

The University library employs 39.4 people, including 10.4 professionals (including 2 in management positions), 12 library technicians, and 17 clerical employees. The library collections include nearly 850,000 items, including about 350,000 printed volumes. The library offers most of the services available in modern academic libraries including access to an on-line public access catalogue (OPAC) which has been in place since 1975 (SIGIRD).[1]

One of the main characteristics of the library is the extreme importance it places on the information literacy of its clients. This program served about 70 percent of new undergraduates in 1993-1994, including nearly 45 percent who receive academic credit for this training.

## THE NECESSITY OF STRATEGIC CHOICES

In 1979, we had the opportunity to build a new library on campus and, as a result, we initiated a global reflection on what was required to realize our mission to support research, teaching, and the development of the region. This strategic planning initiative began with certain assumptions that were important in the development of the library program.

The assumptions can be summarized in this way:

1.  Considering the level of resources generated by UQAC, the library will never be able to make available locally the documentation it needs to support the span of research and teaching programs offered by the university.
2.  Nevertheless, our students and researchers have to function in an essentially competitive environment where access to accurate and quality information is a must. Without access to the same pool of information available to other scholars it is an illusion to think that UQAC could develop advanced studies and research programs that could in any way be significant.

It might not be possible to have all pertinent documents at hand, but, considering the importance of information for the competitiveness of our clientele, the realization of the university mission was viewed as impossible unless at least the tools and expertise necessary to locate the needed information were available and the library was prepared to obtain documents located elsewhere rapidly. The library had to put forward a strategy which could permit its clientele to bypass the problems associated with geographical isolation and its status as a small university. Otherwise the survival of UQAC as a quality institution could be jeopardized.

Up to now, nothing in this rationale is very original. Most of the university libraries in North America could make the same diagnosis of their own situation. Nevertheless, these assumptions were for us extremely important. Initiatives based on them should have tremendous implications for our library. Logically, if our appraisal was correct, it imposed for the library one great priority: to do everything we could to *optimize the capacity of information within the library system to serve its clients in a setting essentially and totally dedicated to the satisfaction of user's information needs.* This statement, the expression of our vision, became our new goal.

We could discourse at length on the scope and consequences of this statement and its impact on the organizational revolution that took place in our library. We have had the occasion to briefly discuss these matters in other publications and refer the reader to those (Caron, 1975; Caron and Boivin, 1980; Caron, 1977).

## THE ORIENTATIONS OF UQAC LIBRARY

The conclusions of our reflections should find a response in "the orientations" whose text is included in Appendix A. For more than twelve years now, this general statement has been used as a guide and a grid of interpretation for all our actions.

Let's comment briefly on its main parameters:

First, priority has been given to the development of the means and tools required to optimize our capacity to provide information. This implies the presence of competent personnel having at their disposal the appropriate technical facilities and working in a physical and organizational environment suitable for the development of high-level subject expertise. The necessary complement to this strategic choice implies that we have had to take measures to make this capacity known and shared with our clientele. Thus the importance we grant at UQAC to provide training for information literacy to our clients. If it is true that access to quality information is a must for the competitiveness of individuals and organizations, our clients should be able to use efficiently and effectively the tools that we make available to them. Consequently, it is imperative that teaching our clients to use information be seen as a necessary component of their basic education particularly in the case of our students.

Secondly, the library had to develop and make available to its clients collections identified for three main purpose: to meet the needs of our undergraduate students; to provide the instruments needed to access information and to develop some relatively exhaustive collections in what we identify as the research priorities of the Institution. All of these objectives had to be supported by an efficient interlibrary loan (ILL) system.

Third, the library had to make its services available to the regional community.

Once we assume that the library shall find its first justification in its capacity to make available to its clients information, not documents, everything was open to question and a lot of new questions emerged. For example we asked, is the traditional organizational model which is oriented toward the availability to clients of documents instead of information optimal, considering our orientations? Are the people we hire, trained in traditional library techniques, suited to meet the new expectations associated not to the processing of documents or managing of an organization, but to the development of high-level disciplinary expertise in information? Is our own management, grounded on a Taylorist model, efficient for the pursuit of objectives more associated to the management of intelligence rather than the handling of inanimate objects (documents) or quasi-robotized humans? In short, the implications of the strategic choices we made early on were tremendous and few guides could be found in existing organizations that could help comfort us in our choices. We tried to answer these questions by developing the new organizational model whose description follows.

## CONCEPTUAL FOUNDATIONS TO THE ORGANIZATIONAL MODEL IN PLACE AT UQAC LIBRARY

Structurally, our library is organized around two main divisions, one the "Division des services de gestion documentaire" (Division of documents management services), the other the "Division des services d'information documentaire" (Division of documentary information services). But, there ends the similarity of UQAC to the traditional model that is in place in most academic libraries. Considering that our first priority is the availability of information to our clients and not documentation, the fact that information is by definition subject related (tied to a given field) and considering that information imposes to ourselves its own rules and constraints (as an example: most information is getting old rapidly, information has a tendency considering its abundance to be diverse and specialized, is of a very variable quality, etc.), we developed a model which could take care of the various constraints associated to our object, an object (registered information) that is not essentially a physical entity (the book) or a building (the library), but rather an entity that can be either tangible and intangible. This change in goal had to be reflected in the structural model proposed. We had to migrate from a highly efficient model designed to make available books or documents to

**Figure 1.** Matrix Chart of the University of Quebec at Chicoutimi Library

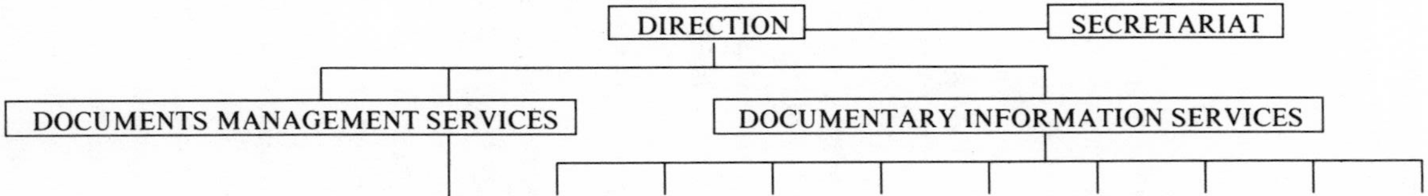

Organizational structure:

DIRECTION — SECRETARIAT

DOCUMENTS MANAGEMENT SERVICES

DOCUMENTARY INFORMATION SERVICES

| FUNCTIONS | Documents Management Services | Zone I A-B: U-Z | Zone II C-F | Zone III G: Cartoth | Zone IV Reg. stad. | Zone V Gov. pub. | Zone VI H-K | Zone VII L-P | Zone VIII Q-T | Zone IX Audiovid. |
|---|---|---|---|---|---|---|---|---|---|---|
| 1. Acquisition | E | - | - | m | m | - | - | - | - | - |
| 2. SIGIRD | Pd | P | P | P | P | Pd | P | P | P | m |
| 3. CD-ROM | P | P | P | P | P | E | P | P | P | P |
| 4. Selection | - | Ed | E | E | E | E | Ed | E | E | E |
| 5. Documents accounts | E | - | - | - | - | - | - | - | - | m |
| 6. Gifts & exchanges | - | Ed | E | E | E | E | E | E | E | E |
| 7. User information instruction | P | P | P | P | P | P | P | Pd | P | P |
| 8. Rare documents | - | Ed | E | E | E | E | E | E | E | E |
| 9. Interlibrary loan | Pd | P | P | P | P | P | P | P | P | P |
| 10. Processing of documents | E | - | - | - | - | - | - | - | - | m |
| 11. Circulation | E | - | - | - | - | - | - | - | - | m |
| 12. Shelving/Document maintenance | E | - | - | m | - | - | - | Pd | - | m |
| 13. Information/communication | P | P | P | P | P | P | P | P | P | P |
| 14. Référence (r) | P | P | P | P | P | P | E | P | P | P |
| 15. Online searching | - | E | E | E | E | E | E | E | E | E |
| 15.1 Bibliographic data bases | - | E | E | E | E | E | E | E | Ed | E |
| 15.2 Numeric data bases | - | E | E | E | E | Ed | E | E | E | E |
| 15.3 Others (INTERNET, etc) | - | E | E | Ed | E | E | E | E | E | E |
| 16. Document processing | - | E | Ed | E | E | E | E | E | E | E |
| 16.1 Indexing-classifying | - | E | Ed | E | E | E | E | E | E | E |
| 16.2 Cataloguing | P | E | Ed | E | E | E | E | E | E | E |
| 16.3 Inventory | - | P | Pd | P | P | P | P | P | P | P |
| 16.4 Pre-cataloguing | - | - | Ed | - | - | - | - | - | - | - |
| 17. Pre-acquisition checking | - | Ed | E | E | E | E | E | E | E | E |

r = Function animation assumed by the head of the division.
E = Function exclusive to one or the other division
P = Function assume by both divisions.
Xd = Physical location of the person in charge of a given function.
m = Marginal implication

201

clients to one which could base its justification and efficiency in meeting the information needs of these same clients, whether the information came from local collections, other libraries, electronic files or other sources.

The model we proposed used a matrix structure designed to deliver on these promises (see Figure 1).

## THE NEW LIBRARY ORGANIZATION

In practice, our library still has two (2) divisions. The division of documentary information services regroups all those peoples who identify themselves with the subject sectors or fields represented in the curriculum at UQAC. These people are expected, as their main duty, to execute a number of tasks that should contribute to the optimization of their expertise in information in their field, and by so doing to satisfy the information needs of their clients. As an example, this division handles the selection of materials, reference, user training, on-line searching, documentary analysis, classification, and cataloguing. The division of documents management services handles all those tasks that require no subject expertise. This includes acquisitions, physical processing, shelving and circulation, and the like.

All professionals and most of the library technicians are part of the documentary information services. The other division includes mostly clerical employees and three library technicians. Professionals and library technicians of the division of documentary information services work together in small teams (one professional and one technician), each team identified to one or more subjects (the whole called "secteur") and to a physical and precise location in the library called a "zone."

Except for the essentially technical operations (i.e., circulation, ILL), there are no line supervisors whose titles are identified with a functional responsibility (head of acquisition, reference services, technical services, etc.). Rather different staffers are charged, in the setting of a matrix structure centered on subject, with developing and implementing a given function. These functional responsibilities generally fall in the hands of one or another of the professionals of the documentary information services. As an example, the professional librarian in charge of the "Education-Psychology" secteur and identified with the "Education-Literature" zone (zone VII) also has the responsibility for the development of the "formation documentaire" (user training for information) function. He is the one who serves as support for his colleagues for all matters pertaining to the pedagogical models used. He is constantly aware of the developments in this area, and he supervises the development of new tools and provides counsel to the head of the division on all matters pertaining to policies and programs related to this function. The same pattern is adopted for all the functions traditionally present in the library, including on-line searching, the exploitation of CD-ROM, document analysis and cataloguing, reference, marketing, and so forth.

## IMPACTS OF THE ORIENTATIONS AND ORGANIZATIONAL MODEL ON THE "DAILY LIFE" OF THE LIBRARY

### Impact of the Orientations and Organizational Model on Physical Design of the Library[2]

The first thing glaringly obvious to people visiting our library is the physical dispersion of our employees. The operation and organization by zone which, follows the Library of Congress classification scheme dictates that our personnel be present at various places throughout the library. There are staff members every-where . . . and this has, at times, created some "image problems." There is no longer any specific area allocated to documentary processing (classification, indexing, and cataloguing) since everything is being done in the zones.

It was expected that this model would optimize the number of employees with a direct and daily contact with our clients. At UQAC, except for the four members of the administration, (the director, one assistant, and two secretaries), only six members of our staff are not in permanent and direct contact with the users. For most of them, the client is no longer an abstraction. He is a real person with concrete needs who, only by his presence, puts a considerable pressure on our people. This fact by itself should have a tremendous impact on the client-oriented vision that we wanted as our trademark.

Another major accomplishment of our system is that there is no longer any friction between the two divisions. This kind of friction is permanent in the traditional model because each division (technical services, public services) has its own culture and often has conflicting visions of service to client. At UQAC, employees of both divisions live with the same kind of permanent contact with the client, and this shared context contributes more than anything else to unify the perspective of the library.

## Impact of the Orientations and Organizational Model on the Current Operations of the Library

A number of elements could draw our attention here. Let's note two of them.

### The Operation in a Matrix Structure

Those who have had the experience of operating in the context of a matrix structure will probably agree that one of the main challenges associated with this type of organization lies in maintaining a balance between, on the one hand, how employees or teams compare to each other, and, on the other, how they balance responsibilities related to subjects versus functional ones. This last point is of primary importance. As an example, the individual who plays a role both as a subject specialist and function animator will be permanently confronted with some painful choices associated with the use of his or her time. Management of time imposes on these people a rigorous discipline, particularly since the level of intervention on their two mandates are quite different. In his or her status as disciplinary respondent, this person is confronted with an external client (student or teacher) who will ask for an immediate satisfaction of his or her needs. In his or her status as function animator and coordinator, that same person is offering a service to his or her own organization (his or her clients being his or her colleagues) in a context most often associated with the development of the function, consequently referring to matters whose incidences will have a middle- or long-term effect. Considering our expectation that everything should be focused on the needs and interests of our external client and considering the permanent pressure that one places on our personnel, there is a constant risk that the functional role of our people will be neglected and that this situation will damage the middle- and long-term interest of that same client and of the organization as a whole.

There lies the heart of the mandate of the head of the documentary information services. That person, serving as both animator-coordinator and line supervisor, has to permanently juggle the short-, middle- and long-term interests of our clientele. This implies that he or she must have a coherent and global vision of the organization. On the strict management side, he or she has to maintain if not impose on his or her troops the necessary balance between all their mandates, making sure that the quality of services to clients can be of the highest level both today and tomorrow. This kind of intervention by the head of the division generally occurs on the occasion of an annual planning exercise during which each sector team has to make known its annual projects concerning both mandates. All this has to be accompanied by respect for both the real autonomy of each sector in the definition of their own priorities and the necessary obligation of library managers to insure a coherent and smooth development of the whole library.

## The Organization of Work Chains

The technical aspect of the organization of work chains, particularly those pertaining to processing function, on the whole has not created enormous problems. As correctly noted by Martell (1983), technological tools now available have made it possible to alleviate obstacles that traditionally imposed centralization as the only way to operate within the library, particularly in technical services. Incidentally, document manipulations have been increased. On the other side, different ways to operate have created some new opportunities. For example, new documents may be made available in each zone as soon as they are received in the library. This new and value-added service largely compensates in itself for the requirement for additional handling of documents.

In truth, the most important adaptations had to come from the managerial level. Administrators had to modify both their managerial philosophy and the way they live with that philosophy on a day-to-day basis. These aspects will be considered later.

## Impact of the Orientations and Organizational Model on our Personnel

*The professionals.* Our organizational model has been in place since June 1982. It was not, as some might assume, a spontaneous birth. Gestation started a long time before. As a matter of fact, our professionals, in the context of the traditional organization were participating as subject specialists both in the reference activities and document classification and indexing as early as 1975. At that time, the question was omnipresent as to how we might develop recruiting and hiring policies necessary to position ourselves for the move that followed. In 1979, we specified the minimal qualifications required for professionals likely to work at our library. Very soon, consensus was obtained on the idea that at any time, subject expertise should be seen as essential and that this expertise should be of the highest level available. Concretely, that meant that we should try to hire professionals with both the highest subject qualifications and with an MLS. That also meant, as corollary, that if it was not possible to identify candidates with both formations, subject education was privileged.

Today, the documentary information services numbers eight professionals. Four of them do not have a degree in library science. Two of them are engineers (masters in chemical engineering and geology), one is a graduate in mathematics and the last has a PhD in literature. All are perfectly integrated into our system.

*The library technicians.* For most of our library technicians, the new structure represented a total change. Not surprisingly, reactions from this group to the new structure were strong and for good reason. Suddenly, we asked a person who had ten years of experience as cataloguer to now act as partner to a professional in a given subject sector, where the span of the new job included reference, cataloguing, participation in the activities of information training in the subject fields, and so forth, a span of action equivalent to that of the professional one although at a different level. As a result, implementation was quite tedious. But today it would be difficult to find one of our technicians who would be willing to go back to the old model.

*The library clerks.* The situation of our clerical employees was not noticeably changed by our new structure. But if job enrichment was not one of the objectives associated with the implementation of the new structure, it was effectively one of the by-products of the model. At the first stage, our clerical employees felt protected from the throes of change imposed on their colleagues, but they now see themselves as forgotten in the process. This situation has caused concern for us and will have to be addressed in the near future.

## Impact of the Orientations and Organizational Model on Management

The management model in place at UQAC is, not surprisingly, extremely decentralized at the operational level. The staff that is directly involved with the client assumes total responsibility for their day to day operations in their area.

Management plays two roles in operations: First, it assumes responsibility for the support, animation, and coordination of the whole organization. Second, it plays the role of watchdog for collective interests, particularly at the resources allocation level and in developing minimal rules to coordinate the operation of the library. Let us talk about two aspects of our management philosophy.

*The management of priorities.* Those in charge of sectors set their own priorities, the library sets its own, and the University does the same. The role of management is to harmonize the whole with the objective of producing a coherent annual plan that can be a source of motivation and mobilization for all the staff. Inside the "zone," it is the responsibility of those in charge to understand the needs of their clients and to define what they will do, when and how to meet those needs. One of the main consequences of this way of operating is that it produces large fluctuations of outputs of specific tasks according to the time of the year, the objectives of the zone, and so forth. As an example, the beginning of each year is largely monopolized by the need to serve incoming students and to train them to use information in their field. During that time, the number of documents processed will fall. Conversely, the end of semesters will see a reversal of these priorities. This presents a challenge to those in charge as they had to rethink their role as managers and develop new ways to appraise and do their job.

*Evaluation and control mechanisms.* Output control mechanisms had to be adapted to our "reality." At UQAC, production statistics only mean something when considered on a quarterly basis. It is not useful to consult daily, weekly, or even monthly statistics to determine the total yearly output. This situation imposes a price, this price being our quite limited capacity to react to situations in the short term. But the insecurity this can create is largely reduced by the importance we put on an extremely liberal way of managing information in our organization. To cope, we have put in place mechanisms of information transfer, in both directions, that can at any time permit an "appraisal" of the actual workload and output of the library.

The whole qualitative evaluation of our services is right now the object of our attention. As noted, we operate in a very decentralized way. Our staff is given much freedom in their day to day operations, but, per contra, administrators can not neglect their responsibilities as managers. We had to develop mechanisms to evaluate the global output of our organization, quantitatively and especially qualitatively. Beyond statistics and annual reports, this evaluation at UQAC is centered mainly around the clients, and that is done through the Library Committee (Comité de la bibliothèque) and eventually, the annual survey of clienteles.

Our Library Committee has been active for more than 15 years now. It includes one teaching/research member for each of our eight departments, two undergraduate students, one from the Humanities and Social Sciences sector and the other from the Pure and Applied Sciences sector, plus one graduate student, and the deans of undergraduate and advanced studies and research. Our committee meets officially three times a year and is consulted on all matters of interest to our clients. For three years now, we have created subcommittees acting as task forces on specific problem areas. These subcommittees propose recommendations to the full committee and the director. The feedback we receive from our committee is highly significant and most appreciated. Concurrently, we are now studying means to implement an annual mechanism of direct surveys of our clientele. This project is now in progress[3] and we plan to function that way in about two years.

## THE STANDARD SUBJECT ZONE

### Physical Aspect

Appendix B presents an example of a subject zone at UQAC. Each zone includes, in a specific physical location of the library, the totality of resources useful to the client in his quest for information in a given field. Around the professional and technician are grouped reference documents in the subject field, equipment permitting access to the different electronic databases (including the OPAC); tables; booths; rooms for group meetings; and one or more stacks regrouping the latest periodicals in the field and books that are not yet being catalogued. As possible, we try to identify the client with both "his" or "her" staff and physical location in the library. The staff of each of our nine zones is urged to accentuate the personalization of his or her zone, to make the zone, both in its physical aspect and in the type of services offered, a reflection of the "culture" of the subject field being served.

## Current Operations

Day to day priorities are totally in the hands of zone personnel who, in permanent and direct contact with clients, are the only ones able to manage them. Each staff member, professional and technician alike, execute one or the other of the tasks associated with service to their client freely inside the parameters of their job description. Interactions between professionals and technicians do not generally create any problems.

Interactions between zones are permanent. Grounded on the horizontal axis of our matrix operation, they take different forms. Usually, they consist of an exchange of ad hoc expertise or interrogations about current matters (on-line searching, cataloguing/ indexing, formation to information, etc.), or in the setting of more formal work groups joining together people from different areas to discuss and implement actions relevant to a specific problem or task (the local SIGIRD committee, the program of information/ communication to clientele, the staff development program, etc.).

Generally, even if some persons or groups assume the responsibilities of given tasks, we try to encourage collective solidarity as a value to be actively sought in our organization. Problems of one kind or another in any zone or division eventually affect everybody in the service. Everyone has to contribute to their resolution. All our personnel are familiar with our annual "blitzes" in which everyone from the director to the shelving staff regroup to address a major problem and/or reshape one aspect or the other in the organization.

To summarize, if by analogy we had to compare our model of functioning by zone to any other, the appropriate model would be that of the small- and medium-sized business enterprise (SME). The UQAC library is a cluster of SMEs, each of which operates inside a larger ensemble capable of providing common support, and each of which pursues objectives associated with the dispensation of quality information services to specific clienteles.

## LIMITATIONS OF THE MODEL

At the management level, the adaptation to the reality of a true decentralization of power and responsibilities and, more precisely, because of this reality, the model imposes some unavoidable constraints. As noted earlier, there is a clear need for a coherent set of external indicators to evaluate the quality of our services. This necessity is complicated by the fact that our product is no longer a physical element (document or something else), but a quasi immaterial product, information to client, whose evaluation is, by nature, highly subjective. We now invest resources and time in developing indicators that could reflect the goal we pursue, a task whose complexity has been recognized by others in this profession (Schlichter and Pemberton, 1992). Meanwhile, we give much attention to our Library Committee, whose recommendations and suggestions are of tremendous help to us.

Another major constraint of our model relates to the limited mobility afforded to our zone staff. The obsession we place on optimal subject competence has resulted in a loss of polyvalence for most of the personnel of the "Division des services d'information documentaire." This loss of polyvalence is important among our professionals and more and more present in the case of our zone technicians who, with time, feel incompetent outside the borders of their own respective fields. This situation is a source of preoccupation for us, and no solution is presently in sight.

## RESULTS ACHIEVED

We cannot actually count on any scientific data or evaluation which could permit a definitive judgment about the performance of the model we put in place at UQAC. At most, some indicators are available which could sustain the assertion that this model is delivering its promise, that is, it optimizes the capacity of information provided by the organization to benefit the client. Let's signal some of these. The "image" or service reputation of the library on campus is generally excellent as noted by either internal surveys[4] or external ones.[5] The performance of UQAC researchers is among the best in the University of Quebec network and among researchers all around Quebec Province. There is also still no departmental libraries or documentation centers on campus and the credibility of the library is good among both the administration of the university and its clientele. The University of Quebec at Chicoutimi library, with a very limited staff, has been able to develop original services which positions it as avant-garde among academic libraries in Quebec.

## HOW MUCH DOES IT COST?

Our orientation and the structure that supports it are neutral in terms of costs. The UQAC model library costs no more to operate than a traditional one. As illustration of this fact, let's note that the library budget for 1993-1994 will represent about 5.5 percent of the institutional budget. We are actually making representations to push this ratio to 6 percent and, on that basis, to reserve 28 percent of the budget for documentary acquisition. These two ratios will position our library inside the provincial mean. Our organizational model has as its main goal the optimization of the information capacity of the library system. It is essentially a qualitative model, a model whose intention is to offer better service to clients in a context liable to give a new sense to the daily work of everybody in the library. Consequently, it doesn't imply or impose any shift of resources from documentation to information or vice-versa. This point is of tremendous importance to keep in mind when discussing with administrators or our clientele who, when confronted with the growing paucity of our collections, could perceive in this reorientation of priorities another plot by "the library people" to exacerbate the absence of a documentation whose necessity and local availability is even now so crucial.

# DEVELOPMENTS TO COME

## Intra-library Developments

Three elements will retain our attention for the coming years.

First, we have to finalize the integration at the subject level of some collections still functionally separated. We refer particularly to the audiovisual collection and the government publications collection. Both these collections remain, at UQAC, physically separated entities. For a lot of reasons, they will probably maintain this status. Nevertheless, the integration of their contents to the subject zone will have to go beyond the simple identification of these resources on the same OPAC, a strictly minimal measure. The same as for other documents of the library, the contents of these collections or documents should be included in the "stock of knowledge" of our zone personnel. We have proposed some measures to reach this objective.

Second, the implication of our zone personnel in the development and support to functional responsibilities will have to be reinforced. The balance, as we mentioned before, between functional and disciplinary responsibilities is still fragile. Rigorous actions will have to be implemented to blend these two level of responsibilities in each staff position.

Third, we have to put in place a coherent training and continuing education program under the umbrella of the library. Up to now, most of the training activities of our employees were left to their own initiative and financed by one or the other of the union-management committees of the Institution. We think, considering the challenges associated with the implementation of new technologies, among other things, that we have to move beyond this view.

## Intra-institutional Developments

Every effort of the library is oriented toward meeting the needs and preoccupations of research and teaching at UQAC. This effort will concentrate on two aspects.

### On the Operational Level

The training for information literacy of our users has been given the highest priority at UQAC for more than 15 years now. These activities, more and more oriented toward the credited course, were up to now left to the initiative of individuals, directors of programs or teachers, who were convinced of its necessity for their students. These interventions, let's remember, were given to more than 70 percent of the incoming students at UQAC in 1993-1994. It is our conviction that it is time to go ahead with a new step in the expansion of this program. In the winter of 1993, the Office of Undergraduate Studies and the library have officially implemented a team effort whose mandate is to propose a conceptual and functional model to institutionalize the presence of a mandatory and credited activity of training on "information appropriation" in every undergraduate program at UQAC. The team is scheduled to complete its preliminary report in October 1995.

## On the Formal Level

We have initiated some interventions with the administration of the University with the intention of accentuating the presence of the library in the governing academic bodies of our institution. As an example, we encourage the participation of our professionals in the Academic Program Committees of their fields of competence. We have proposed the presence of library representatives on the Undergraduate Studies Subcommittee and the Graduate Studies and Research Subcommittee. In other respects, the deans of undergraduate and graduate studies and research are "ex-officio" members of our Library Committee. All these measures, we believe, are by their nature liable to optimize the harmonization and integration of the library to meet the needs and preoccupation of research and teaching at UQAC.

## Regional Developments

It is our goal to make available the expertise and resources of the library to the regional community we serve. We have produced in the spring of 1992 our strategic plan for an accentuated intervention to support the region, including the creation of an information service specially dedicated to the support of small- and medium-size business. We are now in the process of evaluating potential external resources to support the start of such a service.

## IS THE UQAC LIBRARY MODEL "EXPORTABLE"?

Our library is and will remain a small academic library. Most of the visitors we receive in Chicoutimi (library professionals in particular) inevitably ask us about the practical operationalization of a model like this one in the environment of a much larger academic library. Is a model like this possible and desirable in a large academic library and, if so, is it capable of the same outputs? At UQAC, we are convinced that this model is suitable for any organization whose mandate is to process and make available recorded information products to specific clienteles. This naturally includes documentary organizations (libraries, documentation centers, etc.), but also organizations whose object is specifically the handling or processing of recorded information (i.e., computer services, etc.) for the benefit of specialized groups.

Moreover, we are also convinced that the benefits associated with this model will proportionally grow with the quantitative importance of the staff in place. A much larger staff will permit the multiplication of subject teams, so that a more accurate level of specialization can occur and, consequently, if goals are well understood, better service can be provided to clients.

## AND WHAT ABOUT TECHNOLOGY?

Technology for us is a means, not an end. You may say this is common sense. However, we too often get the impression that means in this profession have taken the place of ends and goals. This fixation toward means (be they administrative or technological) probably has been one of the most important obstacles to a redefinition of our documentary systems. The coming of computerization, as an example, with the productivity increase it has procured, has made possible the perpetuation of practices and ways of doing things in this profession whose pertinence should have been questioned a long time ago. For some, technology was seen and used as a safeguard against change.

This being said, UQAC library, within the limits of its resources, puts great attention on the integration of modern technological tools in support of its regular functions. Nevertheless, we are convinced that the most important issues in this profession are not associated with technology or managerial modes. They relate instead to the ends and goals of this profession, a considerably more profound reflection whose treatment is still largely deficient in current library literature.

## CONCLUSION

Our management philosophy, our orientation as a library and the organizational model we have put in place, all demonstrate that they are feasible for use in an academic library. They have made possible the dispensation of some value-added services to our clients that are attainable only through the best information services. UQAC library now has the capacity and the specific expertise that advantageously positions this service to confront the challenges associated with the advent of the "virtual library" or the "information society." Considering these attainments, the whole vision of our role on the campus is evolving. We want to assume more than the traditional role associated with the library as a support service to research and teaching. Our wish is to position our library as a necessary partner in the development of research and teaching at UQAC and of our region.

## APPENDIX A

The Orientations of UQAC Library

Approved by the CAD (Board of governors of UQAC) in 82/06/30.

Considering:

A) *The mission of the library*
   - Support to teaching and research
   - Support to the collectivity

B) *The problematic associated with the development of our library, including*
   1. objective conditions imposed to its development
      - limited financing
      - geographical isolation
      - weakness of local documentary collection
      - growing importance of advanced studies and research
      - Extreme variety of disciplinary programs.

2.  present and foreseeable evolution of the information/documentation sector:
    -   continuous expansion of the volume of documentary publication
    -   growing multiplicity and complexity of access and support to information
    -   telematic revolution.

3.  means and possibilities that are those of UQAC library (developed expertise):
    -   in exploitation of on-line systems
    -   in documentary training of users
    -   in internal computerization (BADADUQ).

UQAC library proposes the following orientations as guidelines to its development:

A)  *At the access to information level*
    1.  UQAC library will make available to its users, particularly its researchers and graduate students, the adequate mechanisms permitting those to satisfy all their information needs.
    2.  UQAC library has to give to its users minimal training in information literacy which will permit those:
        a)  as professionals, to acquire the basics of an autonomous functioning relatively to the satisfaction of their information needs in their field.;
        b)  as students, to exploit the information resources that the library makes available to them.

B)  *At the access to documentation level:*
    1.  UQAC library will make available to its users:
        a)  a pertinent collection associated to the "axis of development" of the Institution, mainly Middle-North and regional studies and intervention.;
        b)  A large span of tools (reference books, manuals, etc.) needed to locate information.;
        c)  a functional collection of documents relevant to all the programs offered at UQAC.

    2.  UQAC library will make available to its users the most efficient mechanisms permitting the acquiring of documents not in the library (ex. ILL).

C)  *At the regional implication level*
    UQAC library, as far as its capacities permit, will make available to the regional population its resources and expertise.

# APPENDIX B

## Typical Disciplinary Zone

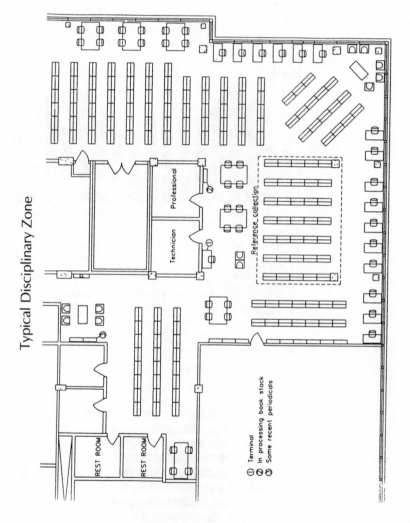

⊖ Terminal
① In processing book stock
②③ Some recent periodicals

# APPENDIX C

## User's Perception as Illustrated by Surveys

### 1. Institutional survey

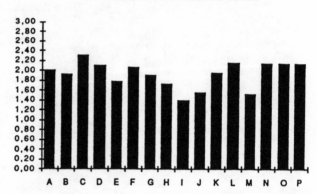

User's Satisfaction about Institutional Services

| a - | Salle de cours | i - | placement étudiant |
|---|---|---|---|
| b - | laboratoires | j - | bourses et aide financière |
| c - | bibliothèque (library) | k - | pastorale |
| d - | audio-visuel | l - | services de santé |
| e - | informatique | m - | orientation professionelle |
| f - | vente et livraison de notes de cours | n - | instalations et équip. de sport |
| g - | cafétéria | o - | activités sportives |
| h - | logement hors-campus | p - | activités socio-culturelles |

### 2. External survey

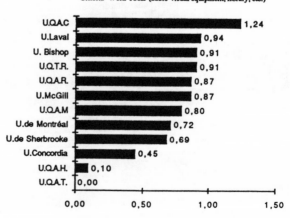

Criteria "Work Tools" (audio-visual equipment, library, etc.)

# NOTES

1. Created first as BADADUQ, redesign and expand by UQAM as SIGIRD and commercially known as Multilist.
2. See in Appendix B a croquis of the typical physical design.
3. A master student from our business department is actually working on the definition of indicators pertinent to the evaluation of the quality of our services. Her report is due for December 1995.
4. User satisfaction survey of UQAC graduate students (promotion 1987). University du Quebec a Chicoutimi. *Enquete-sondage sur le niveau de satisfaction des etudiants de l'UQAC, projet RELANCE 1987, Satisfaction a l'egard des services.* Chicoutimi: UQAC-Service des communications institutionnelles, 1987 (see graph in Appendix C).
5. CAMPUS-COORS survey of 2,400 undergraduate students from Quebec universities. The only place where UQAC was ahead concerned appreciation of "work tools" (Les outils de travail-Audio-visual equipment, library, etc.). Groupe Everest Inc./SEROM. *L'emploi a court terme et l'education.* Montreal, May 1987 (see graph in annex 3).

# REFERENCES

Altmann, A.E. 1988. "The Academic Library of Tomorrow: Who will do What?" *Canadian Library Journal* 45: 147-152.

Caron, G. 1975. "Vers une philosophie de la bibliotheconomie." *Documentation et bibliotheques* 21: 187-196.

———. 1977. "Bibliothecaire ou administrateur: un choix a faire?" *Argus* 6: 78-82.

Caron, G., and R. Boivin. 1980. "Le bibliothecaire, la bibliotheque et le changement." *Argus* 9: 53-56.

Drabenstott, K.M. 1994. *Analytical Review of the Library of the Future.* Washington, DC: Council on Library Resources.

Howard, H.A. 1985. "Improving Services through the Redesign of Organizational Structures" Pp. 11-18 in *Nos ressources humaines: la cle d'un bon service/ Personnel: Key to successful public service.* Montreal: Corporation des bibliothecaires du Quebec, 16e congres.

Jennings, L. 1992. "Regrowing Staff: Managerial Priority for the Future of University Libraries." *Public-Access Computer Systems Review* 3: 4-15.

Johnson, P. 1990. "Matrix Management: An Organizational Alternative for Libraries." *Journal of Academic Librarianship* 16: 222-229.

Martell, C. 1983. *The Client-Centered Academic Library*, Westport, CT: Greenwood Press.

Reynolds, J., and J.B. Whitlatch. 1985. "Academic Library Services: The Literature of Innovation." *College & Research Libraries* 46: 409.

Schlichter, D.J. and J.M. Pemberton. 1992. "The Emperor's new clothes? Problems of the user survey as a planning tool in academic libraries." *College & Research Libraries* 53: 257-265.

# CONTINUOUS ASSESSMENT OF THE ACADEMIC LIBRARY:

## A MODEL AND CASE STUDY

Donna K. Fitch

The academic library is enjoying a rebirth, a renewal of purpose, thanks in part to the burgeoning of electronic information sources. Distressed at the potential danger of being left without an on-ramp to the information superhighway, librarians are exploring ways to ensure that their patrons gain the access to which they are entitled. Evidence of renewal and self-examination are available in the form of advertisements for conferences on "rethinking reference," and even an article in *Forbes* magazine discussing the library in the electronic age (Churbuck, 1993). An editorial in *Library Journal* (Berry, 1994) asserts an optimism for the library's future amid prophecies of doom and gloom.

Accompanying this renewal and reexamination of purpose are budgetary restrictions. Opportunities to access electronic information are expensive, and must be balanced with older, more familiar types

Advances in Library Administration and Organization, Volume 13, pages 221-244.
Copyright © 1995 by JAI Press Inc.
All rights of reproduction in any form reserved.
ISBN: 1-55938-931-1

of access. This need for balance cannot be solved by "throwing money at the problem," because additional funding is not readily available. In common with the business world, libraries must make the best use of available resources. The old ways of doing things must be replaced with newer, more effective ways.

A traditional avenue to examination of an academic library's purpose and effectiveness is available at regular intervals in the form of accreditation. But the interval between accreditation visits is too widely spaced for continuous evaluation. Williams (1983) warns, "[e]valuation is not or should not be an isolated event that takes place within the library every so often." Instead, he suggests that "it should be part of an integrated and continuing planning process carried out within the organization" (p. 168). Echoing this warning is Seymour's (1992) statement that fostering improvement simply to meet accreditation requirements creates a "'good enough' mindset" that causes us to "rely much too heavily on occasional, externally-derived devices to convey the appearance of quality" (p. 81). Strategic planning is useful as an overarching concept in libraries, as discussed in an article by Birdsall and Hensley (1994). What is needed at a basic level, however, is a more detailed mechanism for a continuing examination of the library's purpose and for constant improvement of its processes, something that helps librarians explore the questions of "Who are we?" and "Where does the library fit on campus?"

The library's niche in higher education, to use a marketing buzzword, is the provision of well-organized information through personal, knowledgeable service. This niche is the foundation for our soul-searching, but, in our quest to improve what we do, documenting the contribution made through library service is not an easy task. Although user surveys abound in the literature, by themselves they fail to accurately answer the question, "How well are we doing what we are doing?" They also fail to answer other questions like "Why are we doing what we are doing?" and "Should we continue to do what we are doing?" that we dare not ask. What is needed is a strategy that includes an assessment of the present and a scheme for proceeding into the future.

Assessment is not new to libraries. In a 1990 article, Shaughnessy challenged librarians to improve the service quality of libraries by assessing the effectiveness of their processes and of themselves. Using the emphasis on assessment in the 1980s as a springboard, Shaughnessy says that "the assessment phenomenon presents library managers with an opportunity to focus staff attention on service quality and library effectiveness.... [I]f assessment of quality were to become one of several themes characterizing our organizations, the overall quality of our libraries would improve" (p. 2). Leonard (1992) expresses the need for improvement of the way we view ourselves and our patrons in much stronger terms. After recommending ongoing assessment, he warns, "Until we make our aspirations a credible reflection of our constituents' needs and wants, our optimism about the future is severely misplaced and we are, in fact, in danger of incrementally passing into extinction" (p. 305).

Assessment is being mandated by accrediting agencies. The Southern Association of Colleges and Schools (1992) now decrees that "an institution must engage in continuous study, analysis, and appraisal of its purposes, policies, procedures, and programs. An institution has an obligation to all its constituents to evaluate effectiveness and to use the results in a broad-based, continuous planning and evaluation process" (p. 15). Libraries, as a part of the larger university community, are not immune to the need for continuous study. Indeed, this emphasis should be welcomed by librarians as an opportunity to make improvements that will affirm the importance and usefulness of the library on campus.

Meaningful assessment must possess five key characteristics. Two of these are in the criteria mentioned earlier for institutional effectiveness: assessment must be a continuous process (not an isolated event) and it must involve analysis (not merely data collection for its own sake). A third characteristic is that it must be multifaceted. Statistics generated as tasks are completed and as people are served provide a one-dimensional view, and this view should be supplemented by qualitative data and interpretive information to provide a more accurate picture of the process or service. Fourth, meaningful assessment should be based on some clearly-understood standard. In the example presented here the mission-to-vision statement documents one library's statement of purpose and provides such a standard for that organization. Fifth and finally, meaningful assessment should result in a product, a tangible and recognizable improvement. A survey showing that student satisfaction with the library rose 15 percent is an example of a product of assessment. This is a concrete indication that changes made as a result of the assessment are effective.

This paper presents a continuous assessment model that meets this set of criteria for meaningful assessment. The model uses Total Quality Management (TQM) principles to help a library continuously improve its service quality and effectiveness. "Service" refers here not only to the departments which deal directly with patrons, but to any department that provides services to someone else, in the library or out. It includes everything from cataloging a videotape to explaining the intricacies of the National Trade Data Bank. Setting in motion this cycle of continuous improvement provides a framework in which the library staff clarifies its collective vision of what the library is and what it can become. The cycle is based on the premise that regular, incremental improvements provide greater benefit than irregular, sweeping changes. The cumulative result is mightier than the individual achievements indicate. Initial knowledge of TQM is not necessary to accomplish this. For those unfamiliar with its concepts, many good introductions are available. For general information on the quality movement, Schmidt and Finnigan (1992) provide an excellent overview, and D.T. Seymour's 1992 book *On Q* is excellent for an academic view. The library-specific perspective is given in a book edited by Jurow and Barnard (1993).

The framework for the TQM Management Cycle as discussed here (Hull, 1993a) was developed at Samford University under the leadership of President Thomas E. Corts and was instituted in 1991 as part of the university's ongoing "Student First Quality Quest." The cycle was then adapted for use in the Davis Library, where it is still undergoing revision. Following the presentation of the model in this paper is a case study of the use of the cycle in the Davis Library. The discussions and opinions of the author on the use of the cycle do not necessarily reflect those of the university administration. The cycle can be adapted to the unit or departmental level as well; it is in use in some form in the special collection and reference units of the Davis Library.

## THE MCPVV

The foundation for the assessment cycle model is MCPVV, or Mission, Customers, Processes, Values, and Vision Statement (often referred to as the mission-to-vision statement). This document provides the standard by which all library activities are measured, both during formal assessment and at other times when planning takes place. It is the statement that outlines the fundamental direction the organization expects to follow. This document is more inclusive than the traditional mission statement, in that it includes aspects of Block's definition of a vision. As Block (1987) expresses it, "a vision is really a dream created in our waking hours of how we would like the organization to be" (p. 107). Samford Provost W.E. Hull (1993a) summarized the MCPVV in the context of strategic planning when he wrote, "... [W]e design a strategy that will accomplish our enduring purpose (mission) for those whom we are best equipped to serve (customers) through a set of integrated activities (critical processes) that are controlled by norms rooted in our deepest beliefs (values) so that we will achieve our intended improvements within the current planning period (vision)" (p. 2). The MCPVV is a flexible document, evolving as the staff members better understand their roles and the role of the library on campus.

From the beginning, the library's MCPVV should reflect the sense of the entire library staff. Writing and editing by committee is unwieldy at best, but at each stage the document should include the ambitions and aspirations of everyone. No one will support a mission in which he or she does not believe. Compiling an MCPVV should be a uniting experience, not a divisive one. While the end result is important, the journey is just as important.

## Mission

The first section of the MCPVV is *Mission*. Most, if not all, organizations already have a mission statement. Block (1987) contrasts this with the organizational vision, referring to it as "a statement of what business we are in" (p. 107). This statement should answer this question, "... [C]ompared to all others in the world who do what our group does for a living, what is the unique thing we bring to our clients?" (1993, p. 69). The usefulness of such a niche statement is obvious in Folger and Harris' comment that "[t]he difficulty of trying to be all things to everybody becomes quite apparent when general aspirations are translated into specific targets" (1989, p. 39). A usable mission statement is one that uniquely defines the purpose of the particular library for which the MCPVV is written. In business terms, the mission statement "considers the scope,

essence, and growth direction of the business. It provides identity..."
(Aaker, 1984, p. 52). It is "a declaration of organizational purpose"
that is "usually short" and "also should be inspiring" (Bryson, 1988,
p. 104).

In a library, the mission statement should reflect the mission of
the university, and should place the library program within the
broader context provided by its parent organization. The mission
statement should be clear, concise, and succinct. It can serve as a
capsule of the MCPVV for the library to be used in promotional
material, such as brochures, staff bulletin boards, or even
introductory on-line catalog screens, to explain the library's purpose
to outsiders.

## Customers

The "C" stands for *Customers*, a term usually associated with
business enterprises, not libraries. Faculty members often object to
the term customer because of its commercial overtones, but it is used
in this context for a reason. According to Thomas E. Corts, President
of Samford University, a customer is someone who is served, who
is involved in an exchange, whether for goods or services. He admits
that "some other term, such as 'client' or 'constituent' may be
substituted, though neither carries quite the connotation of
responsiveness and service that could be desired" (1992, p. 2).
Seymour encourages universities to embrace the idea of the customer
as "a partner in the process of developing and delivering a product
or service," warning against allowing "administrative convenience"
to take "precedence over customer orientation" (1992, pp. 46-47).
Customer is a term that helps us remember who we serve.

Customers can be classified as either primary or secondary.
Primary customers are the people "who get 80% of your attention
and resources" ("Assessment Guidelines", 1994, p. 1). Secondary
customers comprise the other twenty percent. The list of primary
customers should include approximate numbers in each group, and
serves as a focus for organizational energies. Unquestionably students
will head the list in any academic institution, followed closely by that
institution's faculty and staff. Public colleges and universities would
probably include community users and perhaps high school students.
Those who control the purse strings, such as donors or trustees, are

not included as customers. They function as suppliers, contributing to the process.

A further classification of customers is by their relation to the library's processes, external or internal. External customers are those customers outside the library, frequently referred to as patrons. Internal customers are those who work in the library or the university. For example, catalogers are customers of the workers in acquisitions who send newly-received books to them.

Listing primary customers is more than an academic exercise; it may encourage philosophical discussions that reveal fundamental attitudes toward customer groups. The concept of the student as customer can be unsettling. It means that librarians must be responsive to their expressed or actual needs, and not to our perception of their needs. But professional judgment and creativity still have an important role to play in the interchange between librarian and customer. As Deming (1993) noted, customers did not ask for innovations such as photography, the telephone, or automobiles (p. 7). Professionals have an obligation to be creative with an eye toward meeting, not only the customers' immediate needs, but also anticipating what they might need in the future. The balance must also be struck between constituencies. What proportion of service do students receive? They outnumber faculty, but often receive poorer service than faculty. The library might decide to devote more resources to faculty, who touch a large number of students. All resource allocations should be made deliberately, after considering the reasons for preferring one over another.

Considering a patron as a customer is not difficult to grasp. But the concept of a coworker or colleague as an internal customer will profoundly influence an organization. Implicit in the term "customer," as mentioned earlier, is the concept of service. Members of the library staff, whether professional or support staff, have an obligation to serve their internal customers with the same spirit of continuous improvement they display toward external customers. For professionals, this means acknowledging the worth and value of the work of support staff, treating them with respect, and, above all, empowering them to perform their jobs as they know best. In practical terms, service to support staff customers includes soliciting and using their ideas for improvement, training them in quality improvement tools and techniques, treating them as co-laborers in the academic endeavor, and communicating with them the goals and mission of the library. Block (1993) stresses that "[e]ach member needs to believe the organization is theirs to create if any shift is to take place in how customers are served, students are taught, patients are healed" (p. 21). Empowerment in name only will merely serve to further alienate support staff. They will remain skeptical, and rightly so, until librarians prove that they mean what they say. This concept of librarians and support staff as each others' customers begins the process of breaking down the university class system that inhibits smooth working relationships and interferes with successful customer service. Researchers in a study of the campus climate at the University of Rhode Island concluded that the manner in which the institution collectively recognizes, respects, and values people— their contributions, their skills, and their human dignity—may offer the greatest contribution to enhanced quality. Improving interpersonal relationships among members of the university community is key to improvements in service and in the quality of life at the university (Carothers and Sevigny, 1993, p. 15).

Empowerment of all library staff is the key to this enhanced quality of life.

## Processes

The critical *Processes* are dealt with in the "P" of the acronym. As the word "critical" implies, these are the important activities within the library without which nothing is accomplished. Note that the word is "process", not task. A process is defined, according to *The Team Handbook for Educators*, "by grouping in sequence all the tasks and activities directed at accomplishing one particular outcome" (Scholtes, 1994, p. 2). The processes should explain the most important tasks in which the library engages, in a way that distinguishes it from, say, the campus bookstore or the English department. Seymour (1992) emphasizes that "solving problems is not the answer to causing quality. The solution is understanding and continuously improving the processes that give rise to problems" (p. 75).

## Values

The first of the two "V"s in MCPVV stands for "*Values.*" These are the library's nonnegotiable underlying beliefs, such as equal access to materials for all library users or maintaining a working environment that challenges the growth of library personnel. Statements of values tend to be vague, but Hull (1993b) cautioned against this tendency in a Samford memorandum. He suggested that units struggling with the concept "begin negatively by asking what it would take to corrupt and subvert the integrity with which you carry out the mission of your unit, then ask what values, actively practiced, would guard against such compromises" (p. 2). The values statement provides a philosophical and ethical foundation for library operations.

### Vision

The last letter of the acronym stands for "*Vision*." Despite the terminology, this should not be confused with the mission statement or the concept of the overarching vision for the organization discussed earlier. The Vision statement should include concrete goals that the library wishes to reach in the next five years. These goals should be attainable in keeping with the rest of the MCPVV so that the staff can achieve a feeling of accomplishment and progress. They should also represent the combined vision of a staff working in concert to avoid a sense that these goals were imposed "from above." If units or departments within the library craft separate vision statements, these can contribute to the library's vision, as appropriate.

The creation of the MCPVV is a major milestone in the life of the organization. The initial effort in drafting the document is important and worthwhile, for it becomes a point of reference for all assessment activities.

## THE ASSESSMENT CYCLE

The assessment cycle model consists of four steps, adapted from the Deming/Shewhart Plan-Do-Study (or Check)-Act cycle (Deming, 1993, p. 135). The steps of the cycle are as follows:

*Plan* - write an assessment plan based on the MCPVV.
*Do* - carry out the plan, gathering data for decision making.
*Study* - analyze the results, pinpointing needed changes.
*Act* - decide how to respond to the results and carry out suggested changes.

Dates should be established for the completion of each step in the cycle to ensure that it becomes a part of the library's routine.

Improvement is truly continuous when it is routinized. If the dates are set to coincide with the library's budgetary cycle, desired changes that require money may be planned in advance of the completion of the budget process. Linking assessment results to the budget in this way signals staff that the assessment process has meaning. This kind of signal is critical to the success of any assessment program.

## Plan

The first step in the cycle is "*Plan.*" It involves writing an assessment plan based on the MCPVV. Essential components of the plan are feedback from primary customers and evaluation of the library's processes, providing information from external and internal sectors each year.

Any of several approaches may be chosen to begin the planning phase: start with the goal in the Vision statement with the soonest target completion date, determine what is hindering achievement of any part of the Vision statement, or choose a process which has been causing trouble or is obviously overstressed. But, regardless of the approach chosen, various instruments should be employed to generate data to support the study with attention paid to maintaining a balance between quantitative and qualitative measures. Most libraries routinely collect statistics on library services that can provide quantitative data, to include the number of books checked out, interlibrary loan requests filled, informational reference questions answered. Van House, Weil, and McClure (1990) in *Measuring Academic Library Performance: A Practical Approach* provide examples, procedures, and forms for quantitative measures such as the materials availability survey, general satisfaction survey, and building use survey.

Qualitative approaches to assessment, such as one-on-one interviews and focus groups (Sapp and Temares, 1993) are common techniques used to flesh out the bare statistics. Using a variety of tools provides more depth to the study. Important issues exposed in a focus group can become questions on the next user survey. Puzzling or unexpected answers on a user survey are fleshed out in focus group or one-on-one interviews. Marshall, Lincoln, and Austin (1991), in their case study of faculty quality-of-life issues at Vanderbilt University, argue for the integration of qualitative and quantitative data. Although quantitative data is often easier to obtain, and numbers tend to persuade administrators, qualitative data must be collected for a well-rounded view of the issues. The researchers used focus groups in a town meeting format to ensure that all sides were represented. A content analysis of the qualitative data gathered in this way was used to construct a questionnaire to provide quantitative data.

Attention during the planning phase should not focus entirely on external customers, however. Ideally and eventually, each unit within the library should be continuously assessing service to its customers, in and out of the library, as well as the efficacy and efficiency of its processes. Scholtes' *The Team Handbook for Educators* (1994) provides an excellent resource for the analysis of processes. Teams composed of librarians and support staff involved in the process should meet to flowchart each activity to provide insight into the program, identify needs, and eliminate steps which do not add value. Participants in the process may be surprised at the redundant or convoluted nature of what they considered a straightforward series of tasks. Especially suspect are portions of a process that are performed only because "we have always done it that way."

The importance of this step cannot be overemphasized. Deming (1993) contends that people have a weakness to short-circuit planning and suggests that this tendency can prove painful. He also suggests that the choice of the approach taken in planning should be based on the question of "which one appears to be most promising in terms of new knowledge or profit?" (p. 135). In other words, which process, if improved, will help us effectively serve the most customers? This can reinforce the idea in the minds of staff that the library program is customer based.

Finally, unit teams should make decisions regarding the administrative and logistical aspects of the study. Mundane decisions about who will hand out the surveys, when will the focus groups meet, when the forms are to be turned in, and the like may seem unimportant. But assignments made at this stage will ensure smooth action throughout the planning process.

## Do

"*Do*" is the next step in the assessment cycle and involves carrying out the plans made in the first step. The surveys are mailed, the focus groups are assembled, the pertinent statistical data is gathered. It is important at this stage that the library be as unobtrusive as possible to avoid influencing the results. Interviewers and recorders from outside the library help eliminate the perception of bias in focus groups. Statistics students can undertake a user survey using library-determined parameters as a class project. This provides them with real-life examples while integrating the library into the academic program of the university. At the same time, the library gains access to expertise not otherwise available.

Creativity can also help make surveys more effective. Multiple distribution points for surveys can help produce a larger return rate: leave surveys in student mailboxes as well as handing them out at the door or providing a stack in the student lounge. Advertising the purpose of the survey in the campus newspaper may improve response.

## Study

"*Study*" is a vital and often neglected third step. To be useful, raw data must be converted to information. Assessment results should be analyzed and applied to planning, not filed away to gather dust. The results of the measures should be shared with the entire staff, and everyone involved in the study should be given an opportunity to comment on them. A report should be compiled explaining the measures used, detailing the results, and summarizing the data. This summary should indicate the staff's understanding of the department or the library's strengths and weaknesses as revealed through the assessment and outline areas that might require further study.

## Act

The preceding steps are pointless unless the library is prepared to "*Act*." The data analysis of feedback from external customers will suggest changes. When appropriate and possible, these changes should be made. When they are not made, a rationale for not making them should be offered. In either case customers should be apprised of the results of the study. This part of the feedback loop allows customers to feel that their opinions are valued and will reinforce their participation in the next cycle of assessment and planning.

The same considerations that apply to external customers apply to internal customers. Empowerment is a crucial and essential element for teams analyzing internal processes. If a team is used only for performing the analysis and its suggestions are not acted upon, the members will quickly lose interest in participation. Seymour (1992) phrases the need for empowerment bluntly: "Empower the people, all of the people, or suffer the consequences." A few of the consequences he enumerates for failing to do this are the loss of both customers and employees, the encouragement and reward of slothfulness, an inundation of bureaucratic thinking and policy manuals, and an organization that becomes a collection of underachievers (pp. 98-101).

## A CASE STUDY

This case study provides an example of the workings of the TQM Management Cycle described earlier in a private university.

Organized assessment using the TQM Management Cycle began in the Harwell G. Davis Library of Samford University in 1991. Davis has a collection of almost half a million volumes, and serves as the undergraduate library for the 4,400-student campus. The staff is composed of nineteen support staff and nine professionals, and was reorganized in 1990 using Total Quality Management principles. The hierarchical organizational structure, which evolved over more than twenty-five years, was replaced by a circular, team-based structure. All positions were redesigned and declared open, except the director's. Staff members, both librarians and support staff, requested new positions. The success of the reorganization and the accompanying boost to employee morale and quality of work life contributed to gains in respect for a library previously discredited by the university community (Fitch, Thomason, and Wells, 1993).

In the fall of 1991, the president of the university, Thomas E. Corts, acting through the vice-president for quality assessment, John W. Harris, directed each of the eighty-three budget units within the university, as part of an assessment of the entire university's programs, to submit an MCPVV to the Assessment, Planning, and Budgeting Panel (APB). This panel included seventeen faculty and staff from throughout the university, none of whom were themselves managers of a budget unit. They represented instructional and noninstructional areas of the campus. The author of this article was a member of this panel. The APB Panel reviewed all of the documents that were prepared by the units, commenting on sections that were well-done and suggesting improvements in others that would bring unit statements into closer alignment with the university-wide MCPVV.

The MCPVV's were also read by the Quality Council, a team comprised of the president, provost, and vice-presidents of the university. Their comments and the comments of the APB Panel were then returned to the budget units, with instructions that the members of these units were free to adopt or ignore the suggestions. Some units made superficial changes in wording, while others completely revised their MCPVV's. The final Davis Library MCPVV appears in the Appendix.

## Plan

The first iteration of the cycle began in 1992 after the MCPVV documents had been completed. Each budget unit was directed to "develop a plan to assess itself within the context of its MCPVV." The plan was expected to include "feedback from primary Customers" and a study of "at least one of its primary Processes" (Assessment Planning Guidelines, 1992?, pp. 2-3). In a flurry of activity, the staff of the library planned a materials availability survey, faculty and student focus groups, and a team to study the processes in the acquisitions unit.

One of the often-repeated complaints about the library was that it did not have the resources students and faculty needed. Informal opinion among staff suggested that the library did have resources, but customers had difficulty finding the materials they needed. To assess the validity of this opinion, the materials availability survey (MAS) was chosen from Van House, Weil, and McClure's *Measuring Academic Library Performance* (1990), and modified slightly to include patron classes applicable to the Samford campus. The MAS consists of five individual performance measures, assessing probability the library owns an item, user effectiveness in using the on-line catalog, multiple patron demand for an item, user ability to locate an item that is on the shelf, and procedures which keep materials out of the hands of the patrons, such as rebinding, slow reshelving, and security problems. Plans were made for its distribution during the month of October 1992, with a goal of eight hundred searches. This goal was derived from a table in the Van

House, Weil, and McClure book. Support and professional staff volunteers were assigned to hand the surveys to entering patrons, while others were asked to follow up the patron searches. The associate director and other volunteers were asked to tabulate the results as the searches were completed.

Focus groups were also set up to provide data for the assessment. Three groups of fifteen students each were planned, the first consisting of freshmen and sophomores, the second of juniors and seniors, and the third of library student workers. Each group was to be randomly chosen from a list of students in each category with both non-library faculty or staff serving as group leaders. Two library staff members were selected to act as recorders for these groups. Open-ended questions were designed to elicit responses on a wide range of topics. Each group was asked the following questions:

- What do you like best about the Davis Library? What do you like least about the Davis Library?
- If you could change one thing about the Davis Library, what would it be?
- What is the biggest challenge you face in getting the information you need from the library?
- What improvements would make you more likely to use the Davis Library?
- Have you attended any library instruction sessions as part of a class? Was it helpful?
- What would have made it more helpful?
- What could the library do to help you in research, study, and recreational reading?

Two randomly-chosen focus groups of fifteen faculty each were also planned, again with non-library faculty or staff serving as leaders and library staff members as recorders. Faculty were asked:

- How could the staff of the Davis Library help you more with your classroom teaching?
- Are there barriers that you perceive in your library use? In your students' use?
- Are there services that you've used at other libraries that you'd like to see at Samford?

- Would you be interested in sessions by the librarians to update your knowledge of new tools, such as databases?
- Do you use our library instruction sessions for your students? Do they help? What could we do to improve them?
- Do you use the library for your research? If not, why not? Does the library not meet your resource needs?

One of the requirements of the assessment of noninstructional units mandated by the Quality Council was the study of a process. A team was already studying the library's inefficient acquisitions process when this assignment was made, so it was included in the planning cycle. This team was studying the length of time required to place a book order with a vendor, and was led by the associate director. Coached by a School of Music faculty member, the team included all three members of the acquisitions unit and the collection development coordinator.

## Do

Plans that work well on paper must eventually meet the cold light of reality. Problems were encountered early in the data collection process. The number of completed materials availability surveys was disappointingly low, with a ten percent return rate, far short of the number desired. Fewer volunteers were needed to follow up on the search reports, and tabulation required little time.

Another disappointment occurred with the focus groups. Out of approximately two hundred students called, only fifteen agreed to attend the sessions; only four actually attended. Twenty faculty members agreed to participate, and these were grouped into one session instead of two. But despite the low level of participation, the responses were lively and indicated an interest and willingness to help the library improve itself.

Improvement was definitely needed in the area of acquisitions. Members of that team were alarmed to find that it took the library between one and 120 days merely to place an order (not including receiving or processing the order), with an average of about 70 days. An examination of similar processes with other subject areas showed distressingly similar results. Here was a process ripe for change.

## Study

Teams were formed to analyze information gathered as a result of the "Plan" and "Do" phases of the assessment cycle. Both professional and support staff were included, and some teams consisted entirely of support staff. One team dealt with the results of the materials availability survey. Analysis of the study was difficult, and the results were suspect because of the low response rate. The survey data indicated that users had a 69.3 percent chance of finding the desired materials. Almost 31 percent of the searches failed because the desired items were missing from the shelves and not checked out. This high percentage of missing items was not unexpected. Much of the apparent loss was attributed to unresolved problems following the library's recent retrospective conversion project. In many cases, books still lacked barcodes, or had "dumb" barcodes which indicated a book was available when it was checked out. Errors also occurred during retrospective conversion, such as titles being withdrawn without being removed from the OCLC record, and call numbers on the on-line system differing from the actual item. The circulation and cataloging units were already working together to clear up these problems when the MAS was done. Solutions suggested by the team dealing with the survey included adjustments to the cataloging workflow in updating on-line records, an investigation of the bindery process, and improvement in the shelf-reading process to find misshelved materials.

The team dealing with the student focus group assessment was concerned with the low response rate and suggested that professors be asked to allow students release time to attend future focus group sessions. But even though student participation was limited, the team analyzing the results produced a lengthy report that suggested solutions to many of the students' concerns. The student group pointed out the need for better signage and longer weekend hours. More CD-ROM database terminals and quiet areas for study were requested, as well as a way to renew books. One area they particularly wanted improved was the government documents floor. Because of the old design of the building, documents stacks were closed to browsers by a wire "cage," and often no staff members were available at night to assist patrons.

The faculty focus group responses were discussed by another team. One area of faculty concern was the unavailability of items sent to the bindery, a problem already identified in the materials availability survey. They wanted periodicals holdings listed in the on-line catalog, as well as an increased periodicals budget. Other suggestions for improvement made in the faculty focus group included improved signage, direct access to other libraries' on-line catalogs, availability of money for making change in the microfilm area, and the ability to view the publication date on interim on-line catalog screens.

Possibilities for improvement were also abundant in the acquisitions process. The team studying this process noted many steps which involved checks and rechecks, but added no value. These checks were intended to reduce errors, but wasted more time than was justified by the number of errors found. The team recommended that acquisitions staff order from vendors every week instead of batching and ordering monthly. They also asked that non-value-added steps, the checks and double-checks, be removed from the process. A schedule was developed for the workflow, and student assistants were used more efficiently for routine tasks such as filing order slips. These recommendations would greatly reduce the time required to place an order, consequently reducing the time in which new materials can be made available to customers.

## Act

As a result of information gleaned from the materials availability survey and the faculty focus group, a change was made in the bindery process. In this process, which had been in place for many years, a periodical volume was bound as soon as the last issue was received. Staff had assumed that the process increased efficiency, minimized loss, and, as a result, served patrons well. Unfortunately, the process removed periodicals from the shelves at precisely the time when they were most needed. Customers placed more value on having issues available when they needed them, while the library staff preferred a system that was more efficient and easier to administer. A study team was then formed, composed of staff members involved in the bindery process. They recommended and instituted a procedure for binding during breaks and between semesters, with staff from other parts of the library assisting in the effort. While this concentrated work in short time frames, the customers were better served.

Requests made by the student and faculty focus groups were varied, but many related to services already provided by the library.

This conclusion pointed out the continuing necessity for marketing the library's services and educating patrons about what the library could do for them. But other problems that could be remedied easily were identified. Among the actions taken as a result of the assessment were extending weekend hours, the provision of a suggestion box, and the improvement of on-line catalog signage.

During the time the acquisitions team was meeting, the coordinator of the acquisitions unit moved to another job in the library. The newly-streamlined process, incorporating the recommendations made by the study team, would theoretically ease the workload on the two remaining support staff members, but before this could occur a backlog of existing orders, some of which were four years old, had to be cleared. At the staff members' request, the associate director empowered them to work on the problems before hiring a new coordinator. As a result, the backlog was eliminated within six weeks, and, with the streamlined workflow, no one saw any reason to hire another person in the unit. One of the two staff members was designated the coordinator for the unit, although both of them share in coordinator responsibilities. The turnaround of this unit was perhaps the most important initial success of the assessment process and the one of which the library staff is proudest.

## The Second Year

The cycle began again in 1993. The Quality Council had asked that customer surveys that year deal with how well budget units were fulfilling their mission. Some of the librarians felt that the mission portion of the MCPVV, written two years before, no longer reflected the goals of the library and that it needed to be revised. A team was formed to draft a new mission statement, and the draft was then circulated to elicit comments from the entire staff. Changes were made, and a new mission statement was ready in time to survey customers. The remainder of the MCPVV will be reviewed for any needed changes in the next cycle.

One-on-one interviews by library staff of randomly-selected faculty, staff, and students were conducted in late 1993. The list of questions were designed by the staff to determine areas in which the library was fulfilling and failing to meet its mission. Comments from the interviewees indicated that the library was moderately successful in meeting its mission. Constantly stressed was the need for more adequate materials, particularly journals, in many subject areas. The highest marks were given for the responsiveness of library staff to the customers' needs.

Surveys were also mailed to all faculty, staff, and students on campus to determine whether additional library hours were needed, which were most desired, and for what purpose. As a result, library hours were extended to midnight in the 1994 fall semester.

The receipt, acknowledgment, and processing of gift materials was a major focus in this iteration of the cycle. Gift materials were received in at least three different units (special collection, acquisitions, and circulation), and this led to significant inefficiencies. The university's vice-president for quality assessment served as the leader for this study. Staff from all of the areas in which gifts were received joined the study team.

The team discovered that two different forms were being used for the same process, and that donors were being given extensive lists of their gifts whether they needed (or wanted) them. Some donors were thanked by the library for their gifts, while other gifts were acknowledged by the university's development office; some were thanked by both, and some were thanked by neither. The team proposed that a single form be developed, that the process be streamlined, and that one person in the acquisitions unit be designated to write all acknowledgment letters. They also suggested that a list of gift items would be provided only when the donor requested one.

The process of assessment continues, with new opportunities for improvement throughout the year. A positive reinforcement to persevere was received in the form of the results of a survey given every year to graduating seniors. It showed that the percentage satisfied with the library in 1993/1994 was up to 72.9 percent, a 14.9 percent increase. While some of that increase may be due to the completion of the new addition to the library, this positive indicator helps spur the staff toward continuing to improve service to their customers. This is a further indication that making small changes in many areas has a powerful cumulative effect on the efficiency and morale of the library that cannot be matched by one-time sweeping changes.

## SUMMARY

The TQM Management Cycle presented in this article provides a model for the assessment and continuous improvement of a library's processes. As shown in the Samford case study, change is possible when customers are asked for their opinions, and when library staff members at all levels work together to satisfy customer needs. For this process to succeed, the contributions of every staff member must be appreciated and respected. The library owes this level of respect to them and to their customers, the patrons who rely on them for their resources. Little changes in how things are done can produce big results. In a time of library change and growth, the challenge for librarians is to critically examine old ways of doing things, and to continuously improve the service attitudes that will carry the profession into the "plugged-in, electronic, highly individualized society" of the future (Berry, 1994, p. 6) in which librarians' expertise will be needed as never before.

## APPENDIX

### Davis Library MCPVV, 2nd 1994 Revision

The *mission* of the Davis Library is:

To support the curriculum of the university by acquiring, organizing, and preserving a broad, well-balanced spectrum of information and by providing access to that information through personal and technological services, to the fullest extent of our abilities and resources.

To improve the processes and services of the library on a continuous basis, in an effort to contribute to the furthering of the mission of Samford University.

The library recognizes the following primary *customers*:

Students    (4,443 in 1993/1994)
Faculty     (223 in 1993/1994)
Staff       (483 in 1993/1994)

The library's operation encompasses these critical *processes*:

Acquiring the tools and resources that will assist our patrons in gathering meaningful information, in accordance with written collection development guidelines focusing on curricular needs.
Organizing tools and resources in a clear and logical manner.
Providing access to information by means of manual and electronic avenues.

Preserving for future generations the information represented by the collection, by maintaining materials of artifactual value and by exploring options for retaining the intellectual content of other materials in less valuable formats.

Instructing patrons in the discovery, use, and critical evaluation of materials.

Assessing the strengths and weaknesses of materials and services on a continuous basis, in order to identify emerging needs and to eliminate that which is no longer needed.

Planning strategically for optimal delivery of tools and resources.

## The library affirms the following underlying *values*:

To serve our patrons in a way that demonstrates we value them as human beings.

To offer library and information services to patrons without regard to their sex, race, ethnic identity, age, or religion, in accordance with the American Library Association's Library Bill of Rights.

To develop balanced library collections containing diverse opinions and beliefs, which may or may not coincide with the personal or corporate convictions of library personnel.

To seek creative, innovative solutions to the complexities of practicing academic librarianship in an information age.

To maintain a working environment that encourages and challenges the growth of library personnel, affirming job performance and the need for continuing education.

## The library's *vision* of what we will accomplish over the next five years includes:

Evaluating the current collections and selection practices against the collection development policy to determine how well we are meeting curricular needs.

Investigating how adequately we are serving our student customers' needs in terms of scholarship.

Examining the materials budget to determine whether to continue allocation by format.

Providing more electronic indexes to a larger number of simultaneous users.

Completing the study of interlibrary loan processes and determining what response is necessary to continue to provide timely and efficient service, in light of access-versus-ownership issues.

Working with faculty to assess the usefulness of library instruction to their students and to find ways to improve it.

Developing and teaching Internet classes for students to familiarize them with this important information resource.

Developing a disaster preparedness plan for the library.

Assessing the efficacy of the library's current organizational structure in light of changing library and university needs.

# REFERENCES

Aaker, D.A. 1984. *Developing Business Strategies*. New York: John Wiley & Sons.

"Assessment Guidelines: 1993-94: Non-Instructional Unit." 1994. Unpublished manuscript, Samford University, Birmingham, AL.

"Assessment Planning Guidelines: 1992-93." 1992? Unpublished manuscript, Samford University, Birmingham, AL.

Berry, J.N., III. 1994. "Faith in a Library Future." *Library Journal* 119: 6.

Birdsall, D.G., and O.D. Hensley. 1994. "A New Strategic Planning Model for Academic Libraries." *College & Research Libraries* 55: 149-159.

Block, P. 1987. *The Empowered Manager: Positive Political Skills at Work*. San Francisco: Jossey-Bass.

_____. 1993. *Stewardship: Choosing Service Over Self-interest*. San Francisco: Berrett-Koehler.

Bryson, J.M. 1988. *Strategic Planning for Public and Nonprofit Organizations: A Guide to Strengthening and Sustaining Organizational Achievement*. San Francisco: Jossey-Bass.

Carothers, R.L., and M.L. Sevigny. 1993. "Classism and Quality." *New Directions for Institutional Research* 78: 13-15.

Churbuck, D.C. 1993. "Good-bye, Dewey Decimals." *Forbes* 152: 204-205.

Corts, T.E. 1992. "Customers: You Can't Do Without Them." Pp. 1-6 in *Quality Quest in the Academic Process*, edited by J.W. Harris & J.M. Baggett. Birmingham, AL: Samford University.

Deming, W.E. 1993. *The New Economics for Industry, Government, Education*. Cambridge, MA: Massachusetts Institute of Technology, Center for Advanced Engineering Study.

Fitch, D.K., J. Thomason, and E.C. Wells. 1993. "Turning the Library Upside Down: Reorganization Using Total Quality Management Principles." *Journal of Academic Librarianship* 19(5): 294-299.

Folger, J.K., and J.W. Harris. 1989. *Assessment in Accreditation*.

Hull, W.E. 1993a. *The TQM Management Cycle: A Proposal*. Unpublished manuscript, Samford University, Birmingham, AL.

_____. 1993b. *Inter-office Correspondence on Analysis of M-C-P-V-Vs by the Academic Support Units*. Unpublished manuscript, Samford University, Birmingham, AL.

Jurow, S., and S.B. Barnard. 1993. *Integrating Total Quality Management in a Library Setting*. New York: Haworth Press.

Leonard, W.P. 1992. "This too Shall Pass, or we Will." *Journal of Academic Librarianship* 18 (5): 304-305.

Marshall, C., Y.S. Lincoln, and A.E. Austin. 1991. "Integrating a Qualitative and Quantitative Assessment of Quality of Academic Life: Political and Logistical Issues." *New Directions for Institutional Research* 72: 65-80.

Sapp, M.M., and M.L. Temares. 1993. "Using Focus Groups to Clarify Customer Needs." *New Directions for Institutional Research* 78: 79-82.

Schmidt, W.H., and J.P. Finnigan. 1992. *The Race Without a Finish Line: America's Quest for Total Quality*. San Francisco: Jossey-Bass.

Scholtes, P.R. with D.L. Bayless, G.A. Massaro, and N.K. Roche. 1994. *The Team Handbook for Educators: How to Use Teams to Improve Quality*. Madison, WI: Joiner Associates.

Seymour, D.T. 1992. *On Q: Causing Quality in Higher Education*. New York: American Council of Education, Macmillan.

Shaughnessy, T.W. 1990. "Assessing Library Effectiveness." *Journal of Library Administration* 12 (1): 1-8.

Southern Association of Colleges and Schools, Commission on Colleges 1992. *Criteria for Accreditation, 1992-1993*. Atlanta, GA: Author.

Van House, N.A., B.T. Weil, and C.R. McClure. 1990. *Measuring Academic Library Performance: A Practical Approach*. Chicago: ALA.

Williams, D.E. 1983. "Evaluation and the Process of Change in Academic Libraries." *Advances in Library Administration and Management* 2: 151-174.

# ABOUT THE CONTRIBUTORS

**Rosie L. Albritton** is an Assistant Professor in the Wayne State University Library and Information Science Program. She holds the PhD in Library and Information Science from the University of Illinois; the MA degree in Library Science and a CLR Fellowship Certificate in Research Librarianship from the University of Michigan; and the MA degree in Educational Psychology from the University of Chicago. Dr. Albritton has published extensively on leadership and management development, including the book, *Developing Leadership Skills: A Source Book for Librarians*, (Albritton and Shaughnessy, 1990). She received two national awards for her research on the "transformational leadership" model: the ACRL/ISI Doctoral Dissertation Fellowship Award in June 1992, and the ALISE Doctoral Dissertation Competition Award in February 1994. This paper is based on research done in support of her dissertation, "Transformational vs. Transactional Leadership in University Libraries: A Test of the Model and Its Relationship to Perceived Organizational Effectiveness," completed in May 1993.

**Gilles Caron** has been Director of the Library at the University of Quebec at Chicoutimi since September 1990. Previously, he has been assistant to the rector in charge of institutional strategic planning

(1989-1990), assistant to the vice-rector research and teaching (1984-1989), and head of the division of information services at the UQAC library from 1977-1984. Caron is a graduate from Laval University (Political Sciences, 1970) and McGill University (MLS, 1975).

**Donna K. Fitch** is the Reference Unit Coordinator at the Harwell G. Davis Library of Samford University in Birmingham, Alabama. Her professional interests include facilitative management, integrating critical thinking skills and active learning techniques into bibliographic instruction, and support staff job satisfaction through participation in self-directed work teams.

**Barbara Ford-Foster** is the Head Librarian of the Ogg Science and Health Library at Bowling Green State University in Ohio. She is a graduate of the School of Library and Information Studies at the State University of New York in Buffalo and is interested in reengineering the way work is accomplished in libraries and what effect teams have on workers and work flow.

**Tara Lynn Fulton** is Assistant Director of Library and Information Services at the Bertrand Library at Bucknell University. She holds an MLS from Indiana University and an MA in education from The University of Texas at Austin. She has published widely on topics relating to public services and leadership, serves as an associate editor for *Teaching Education*, and is active in the College Libraries Section of ACRL.

**Mary Kathleen Geary** completed undergraduate and graduate work in Social Work at Bowling Green State University and North Texas State University, respectively. In August of 1994, she received the MLS degree from Kent State University. Since September, 1994, she has been employed at Lake Erie College in Painesville, Ohio, as the Reference/Acquisitions/Collection Development/ILL librarian.

**Cliff Glaviano** is Coordinator of Cataloging at Bowling Green State University in Ohio. He holds an MSLS from Syracuse University and the MBA from Bowling Green. Cliff served in Cataloging at Colgate University from 1974-1984 and has been at BGSU since mid-1984 working under a variety of job titles.

**E. Ruth Harder** is a Technical Information Specialist and manager of the Engineering Information Center at the University of California, Lawrence Livermore National Laboratory in Livermore, California. She received her MLS from San Jose State University.

**Ralph E. Russell** has been the University Librarian at Georgia State University since 1975. He holds an MLS and a PhD in Library Science from Florida State and an MA in English from New York University. Russell has taken a leading role among librarians both in the Southeast and nationally, publishing and speaking widely on topics relating to library administration and the special problems faced by an urban university library. He also has served as both the Chair of the Board of Directors of SOLINET and as the President of the OCLC Users' Council.

# Index

# J A I   P R E S S

## Advances in Library Administration and Organization

Edited by **Delmus E. Williams,**
*Director, Brice Library, University of Akron*

**REVIEWS:** "Special librarians and library managers in academic institutions should be aware of this volume and the series it initiates. Library schools and University libraries should purchase it."

*— Special Libraries*

"... library schools and large academic libraries should include this volume in their collection because the articles draw upon practical situations to illustrate administrative principles."

*— Journal of Academic Librarianship*

**Volume 12,** 1994, 282 pp.                    $73.25
ISBN 1-55938-846-3

Also Available:
**Volumes 1-11** (1982-1993)                    $73.25 each